Organizing for Sex Workers' Rights in Montréal

Organizing for Sex Workers' Rights in Montréal

Resistance and Advocacy

Francine Tremblay

ROWMAN & LITTLEFIELD
Lanham • Boulder • New York • London

Published by Lexington Books
An imprint of The Rowman & Littlefield Publishing Group, Inc.
4501 Forbes Boulevard, Suite 200, Lanham, Maryland 20706
www.rowman.com

6 Tinworth Street, London SE11 5AL

British Library Cataloguing in Publication Information Available

Library of Congress Cataloging-in-Publication Data

ISBN 9781498593892 (cloth)
ISBN 9781498593915 (pbk)
ISBN 9781498593908 (electronic)

This book is dedicated to Suzanne Saint-Georges and to sex workers who inspired me, supported me, the ones who I cried with, danced with, and who in many ways made me who I am today.

Contents

Acknowledgments

This was not an easy book to write; stuck between my academic and activist self, I often walked a difficult and painful line. At times I wondered why I continued to press on, especially after a few refusals. The book is based on my dissertation, which was contested and remains so both by some who never read it and by some who worked on it with me. Writing about sex work and community organizations is like walking through a mine field—sooner or later people get hurt. Some have been hurt by my analysis and the questions I asked; often, prohibitionists were waiting for me to give an interview in order to take my words out of context and distort their meaning. Nevertheless, I have persisted with the help of those mentioned below and those who cannot be named; yet, even with their invaluable advice, any errors that remain in this text are my responsibility.

I owe enormous gratitude to many individuals for their constant assistance and suggestions during the many years I worked on this project. First and foremost, my thanks to Emily Roderick from Lexington who, despite knowing about the various refusals, believed in the project and in me, and to Becca Rhode Beurer and Lisa Dammeyer who helped me make it to the finishing line. Further, I am forever grateful to Jenn Clamen who answered my quest and trusted me enough to give this project Stella's approval, and to Carol Leigh for writing the foreword. Greg Nielsen and Jean-François Côté were significant in this entire process for their intellectual sustenance and genuine support. After years of editing and changes, I must thank Frances Shaver, Samantha Majic, and Isher Paul Sahni who helped me clean up the introduction and really jumpstart this project. I must thank Camilla Bellido who has been with me since the beginning and stayed optimistic despite the setbacks. I am also grateful for Salinda Hess and Penny Pasdermajian for the many editing sessions, conversations, and support in dealing with my anxiety. My thanks to Chris Bruckert and Anouk Bélanger who twenty years ago told me that I was on the right track. As for my department, I would like to thank them for providing me a private space in which to work.

Last, but certainly not the least, many thanks to Marie Prud'homme for her inquisitive mind that never allowed me to be unprofessional and Gisèle for her unconditional love. Thanks to Diane Sicotte, Gilles Laflamme, Pierre Duclot, Bettina Bouskila, Sierra Conti, Claudette Leblanc, and Jorge Briceno who gave me great encouragement and intellectual stimulation. To Dimitrios Koulis for his enormous help with the archives. Further thanks to Anthony Synnott and Neil Gerlach, who gave me the opportunity to teach my first courses; they know how important it was for me to be totally financially independent. Merci Yanik, having you back means the world to me. The largest debt I have accrued during this research, however, is to my life partner, Gordon, who always provided unconditional love and even more, the support when it was most needed.

Foreword

Margo St. James, Dolores French, Iris de la Cruz, and the handful of US advocates encountered many challenges in the earliest days of the US sex worker rights movement. One of first obstacles was getting over that hump of fear in staking out one's right to engage in sex work. Margo had come out as a "former prostitute," and I was in that generation of working prostitutes (to be true to the terminology of the times) on the brink of coming forth to demand our rights.

There was fear resulting from an ominous taboo, as well as practical considerations over the repercussions of labeling ourselves as prostitutes. The label of "prostitute" can ruin one forever. It is like a disease that cannot be cured; yes, like a Scarlet Letter that can never be washed away.

As a strong feminist, I recognized that this taboo and stigma was what kept us from claiming our truth, that we were "working prostitutes." Just to cross that line and take the risk of being branded forever had been a huge hurdle. As people came out slowly—on talk shows, in demonstrations, in print media—coming out as a prostitute became a more common stance. The fear of being branded receded in comparison to the pride one could access at having the courage to tell our truths and to do so alongside each other in the community. This pride was a new "sex worker identity," but historically it was part of the libertine identity, as historically documented in work by male writers such as Moll Flanders and "Mrs. Warren's Profession." The new identity was, additionally, a political identity. In the 50s, that aspect of the publicly sexual woman had been relatively suppressed, so the coming out that finally developed in the mid-70s was something like a dam bursting open. For many of us it felt like a revelation.

But on a practical level, prostitutes/sex workers struggled with political participation as we saw it as a direct threat to our immediate safety. My own concern was that I would be evicted from my apartment, especially because that was where I was working. I had the fortunate advantage of having previously told my immediate family; however, rejection by family and friends loomed in most people's fear of doing political work. Many felt like we would more likely get busted if we were visible politically. We weren't wrong—the police ultimately did target our local sex worker support group. These factors also underscored the importance of encompassing a wide range of commercial sex participants, including dancers, sex workers who work on the street, fetish service providers, and more. The relatively legal status of some sex workers (such as dancers or fetish providers) in the United States gave legitimacy to our position and informed public discourse about the diverse and extensive nature of sexual services.

Another obstacle in building our movement was that, as our numbers grew in the 90s, it became clear that movement participants were often the more privileged among sex workers. The face of the movement was a cis white, middle-class, and often college-educated "call girl." This alienated a wide range of sex workers. I saw class awareness in many communities of sex workers and the hierarchies could be a source of conflict among us. There was prejudice against those who worked on the streets, and many sex workers sought to distance themselves from other workers based on various levels of stigma from class, to drug use, to race, to immigration status and more. This seemed to reflect values in society, but within our small communities there was a special sensitivity to these divides. It also seemed sad and frustrating to watch discrimination at work among ourselves, when the same process was used to divide sex workers from the larger society.

When I think back to the earliest days, I see that the original leaders were fierce challengers of discrimination. They had evolved from the civil rights movement to LGBT (then lesbian/gay movements) to the civil rights–based feminism (rather than carceral based). As an early activist, I learned from Priscilla Alexander about what it means to put the interests of the most vulnerable members of our communities first. I learned about inclusion in participation. I recall the emphasis COYOTE and Margo placed on issues for people working on the streets, on meeting with people from all parts of sex work. During the early years of the AIDS crisis COYOTE helped launch the California Prostitutes Education Project, led by a community of black street-based sex workers working as peer educators within local communities. I didn't learn, however, about the importance of also supporting diverse leadership within the broader sex worker movement until a generation or so later.

As a US sex worker activist, I was introduced to Canadian sex worker activists at the 1989 International AIDS Conference and sex worker conferences in Montréal and Toronto that I had attended through an introduction by Frances Shaver. I was astounded at how advanced Canadian sex workers were. One sharp contrast was that Canadians were so smart, organized, artistic, politically sophisticated, and radical, with such cute young men, gorgeous transgender sex worker artists, kinky leather goddesses, even a seventeen year old who went on to become a movement leader. They explained why young people need to be represented in our movement as opposed to the heterodoxy of our US sex worker charters.

They seemed like a whole generation ahead of our tiny group of US sex worker activists.

Their organizations were funded by the Canadian government and they were not as illegal as we were . . . although I learned pretty quickly not to minimize the ways they were actually criminalized and arrested through nuisance laws. Canadian sex workers were a model for us.

Stella was a shining star among the galaxy of groups—bilingual and organized to support rights as well as health. Back home, most funding for social services for sex workers went to prostitution abolitionist groups, promoting the shame of our industry with the social service rhetoric that only called to get women out of prostitution by any means necessary. Our few sex worker rights social service providers struggled in that context. As we helplessly witnessed the growth of the prison industrial complex, drug users and sex workers were the primary targets.

Yes, of course, some of us idealized the Canadians. I lived in Montréal for a year in the early 70s in concert with the draft dodgers, so I had been used to looking toward Canada as the light at the end of the tunnel. Canadian sex workers reassured us that sex worker activism could be a huge movement based on the wisdom of our whore experiences. The more extreme US criminalization and values of individualism created a movement based on individual activists, yet many of us yearned for the collective action we saw in Canadian organizations like Maggie's and Stella. Canadian organizing showed us what was possible. When Francine contacted me to write the foreword for this book, explaining how she and other sex workers in Canada were influenced by my own activism, I was of course extremely honored. I appreciate this opportunity to contribute this admiring, historical perspective, and, as this book is also published in the United States, I welcome this opportunity to highlight some of the challenges that are shared across regions in our mobilizing and organizing.

I recall the shock of the organizers in my locale when the abolitionists wrote scathing condemnations of sex worker activists as pimps, with the odd claim that our circles were controlled by mafioso. The reality for all these sex worker circles involved ordinary, often left leaning and sometimes libertarian young people addressing the local progressive media. These were classic stereotypical young progressive activists, like the same queer and labor lefties that had been representing the new vision of compassionate freedom with just a bit more sex in the mix. It was so hurtful because it seemed like an obvious lie, but one that we could not correct very easily. Many of those surrounding us seemed ready to believe that sex workers reflected the biblical Whore of Babylon.

My city is one of the primary hubs of anti-prostitution activism, as this has been true since the Red-Light Abatement Act in 1913 and raids of the Barbary Coast. We are also one of the centers of the earliest US sex worker protests, a church occupation in 1917. My friends and I had been accustomed to being labeled as pimp and abusers of women by respectable newspapers when we took a step forward. The attack that Stella faced during their tenth anniversary celebration Forum XXX, when the weekly newspaper published an anti-prostitution "hate piece," was just a bit bigger. I recall that clearly, because it was framed as an article discussing the issue and validated that misrepresentation. The attack piece that was offered by our local paper was an op-ed.

I recall the hurt on the faces of the Stella organizers. In San Francisco we would have expected this, and maybe they did. It hurts nonetheless. There is just something about the fervor and time and dedication when confronted by the cruelty of how sex workers are used for sexual sustenance (i.e., pleasure, comfort, expression) and then attacked by a group of women that claims to represent the true caring spirit of womanhood.

Attacks and backlash are commonplace for all sex worker rights organizations and are within this context of disdain that we fight for our rights and weather these storms. These storms are central to the expression and day-to-day workings of the sex worker movement. Such organizations run by and for sex workers exist around the world, in various shapes and relationships to the sex worker movement. We rarely speak publicly about the struggles of our funded institutions and what it means to be tied to government support. Yet the ways that our organizations are always in the process of establishing their independence in this context, tipping the seesaw imbalance toward sex worker perspectives and rights, is vital to understanding our movement and how we survive our resistance.

Many sex worker community activities in many regions are tied to these institutional bodies—the celebration of commemorative days, a wide range of social services, building capacity of sex workers as social workers, legal experts, and more. A portion of sex worker organizations exist in this category with regional/national differences—based on how much support the governments actually offer sex workers (in the United States support is minimal) however the few organizations that receive funds to provide services are central to the movement discourse.

Often, sex worker rights organizations are seen as the enemy of "the feminist family," we embody a social evil of chaos and disruption. Gaining recognition as a movement in our own right, and doing so without the backlash of other movements, notably feminist movements, has come with so many challenges. In this book, Dr. Francine Tremblay articulates how the sex worker movement positions itself in the context of social rejection and denunciation. She addresses the difficult questions of how we maintain psychological health with the great burden of condemnation. She highlights how the condemnation, at least partly, becomes nourishment for a movement, how the censure motivates our will to survive, our courage, and our hunger (to extend the metaphor) for all that is delicious, sweet and savory.

It is crucial to emphasize that—despite its now fifty plus years, and Stella's twenty-five years at the time of this publishing in 2020—how new this movement is. Francine breaks the silence about the details concerning how we function in the midst of the organizing challenges and contradictions. She provides insight into how organizations are either made or broken by such challenges.

Since reading *Organizing for Sex Workers' Rights in Montréal: Resistance and Advocacy*, I have engaged in multiple conversations with sex workers in our community about our collective process—the process within our organizations and the relationship of individuals in our diverse communities to organizations. This book acts as a resource on how sex workers can address some delicate internal struggles that I and my colleagues have been flailing through, with conjecture and confusion. The issues of community interactions consume the largest space in our activist work, yet it is quite odd that until this book, it has occupied the least scholarly (or even activist) literature. Of course, sharing the internal workings of our movement with the public comes with its own risk, in light of all of the storms that we weather from the outside, where our personal and organizational stories are so often used by outsiders to further oppress us. Francine, however, holds this balance with grace as she identifies the outside factors that seek to continuously keep sex worker rights organizations and our movement down. Stella is a good example of how sex workers will not let that happen. And this book can serve as a reminder to all sex workers and to our organizations of the value of working through the structural and institutional oppression we experience as collectives, and the importance of maintaining our sex worker rights organizations as part of our resistance.

Carol Leigh, aka Scarlot Harlot
San Francisco 2019

Acronyms

ARRFM	Association des résidantes et résidants des Faubourgs de Montréal
ASP	Alliance for the Safety of Prostitutes
CACTUS	Centre d'action communautaire auprès des toxicomanes utilisateurs de seringues
CAS	Centre for AIDS Studies
CASAM	Centre for Advocacy on Stigma and Marginalisation
C1DBU	Corporation de développement Berri-UQAM
CD	Contagious Diseases Acts
CES	Centre d'étude sur le sida
CIQ	Comité interquartiers sur la prostitution et les intervenant-es
CLAA	Criminal Law Amendment Act
CLFM	Le Conseil Local des femmes de Montréal
CNPV	Coalition national contre la pauvreté et de la violence faite aux femmes
COCQ-sida	Coalition des organismes communautaires sida du Québec
COYOTE	Call Off Your Old Tired Ethics
CQCS	Centre Québécois de coordination sur le sida
CROWE	Concerned Residents of the West End
C-SAM	Comité sida aide Montréal

CSQ	Comité sida Québec
FFQ	Fédération des Femmes du Québec
ICPR	Comité international pour les droits des prostituées
MSSS	Ministère de la santé et des services sociaux
PAC-SIDA	Programme d'action communautaire SIDA
PAFS	Prévention action femmes sida de Montréal
PIM	Projet Intervention Milieu
P.I.a.M.P.	Projet d'intervention auprès de mineur-e-s prostitué-es
QIRG	Concordia University's Quebec Interest Research Group
STAR	Sex Trade Advocacy and Research
TIQ	Table Interquartiers sur la prostitution
RRSS	Régie régionale de la santé et des services sociaux de Montréal-Centre
UHRESS	hospital-based research units
UQAM	L'Université du Québec à Montréal
WCTU	Women's Christian Temperance Union

Introduction

The Challenges of Organizing for Sex Workers' Rights

A Glimpse into Sex Worker Organizing in Montréal, Québec

All sex workers, no matter where they fall within the whorearchy deserve labor rights, respect and dignity. We deserve to be able to organize together to form community to keep us safe, we deserve the ability to properly screen our clients without them being in fear of criminal repercussions. We deserve to be able to report an act of violence without fear of stigma, the same as Bob at subway if a client throws hot soup in his face. We must as a society be able to arrive at the conclusion that sex work is work and it is here to stay.

—Escort 2019

INTRODUCTION

Prostitution, in a technical sense, has never been illegal in Canada (Johnson 2015, 260). However, its terrain has been defined and circumscribed by a federal legal framework based on the following four laws: s210 Bawdy-house; s211 Transporting, Procuring; s212 (l) (j) Living on the Avails; and 213(l) (c) Communication.[1] In June 1983 the Canadian government requested the formation of a Special Committee on Pornography and Prostitution (SCPP), later to be known as the "Fraser Committee." The goal of the committee was to examine "the problems associated with pornography and prostitution and to carry out a program of socio-legal research in support of our work."[2] The SCPP made only one recommendation that was favorable to sex trade workers. Indeed, recommendation number 57 proposed that women work in pairs and from their homes so that they could "help each other, share the rent and help with childcare and emotional support, instead of exploiting each other" (Fraser Committee Report 1985, 538). This recommendation, however, was not unanimously agreed upon by Committee members. Andrée Ruffo, a barrister and solicitor in private practice in Montréal, was the only member of the committee who agreed with recommendation (57). Me Ruffo thought that

> persons engaged in the business of prostitution should be treated like any other person engaged in business. She feels that the maintenance of special regulations in this domain contributes to the continuation of the exploitative schemes already denounced in this part of the Report. (Fraser Committee Report 1985, 535)

Because Me Ruffo was the only member of the Fraser Committee to advocate for the repeal of section 210 (Bawdy-house laws) it remained intact; that is, allowing for the arrest of clients, sex workers, and owners of sex work establishments: "the proposals for regulation of prostitution establishments were not well received, and no provincial attorney general indicated any support for such regulation. The police also objected to the suggested repeal of bawdy house laws" (Robertson 2003). Since Ruffo was not able to convince members to change a law that would make sex work safer and "after the report was made public, Frank Iacobucci, the then Minister of Justice, introduced Bill C-49, which came into force on December 28, 1985, reinforcing the communicating law making it almost impossible for sex workers to negotiate with potential clients in a public place—including a car.[3]

The tragic consequences of the Fraser Committee's refusal to change the Bawdy-house laws were demonstrated by the disappearance of dozens of indigenous sex workers in Downtown Eastside Vancouver. The most notorious of these cases involved a pig farmer[4] from Port Coquitlam, British Columbia, who was charged with the first degree murder of two sex workers on September 7, 2002. He was charged with two counts of first-degree murder. A year later in 2003, New Democratic Party member Libby Davies, who represented the East-Side riding in Vancouver (1997–2015), demanded a revision of Canadian laws about safety and sex work. Libby Davies' motion was discussed in November 2002 and tabled on February 7, 2003. Her motion stated,

> [A] special committee of the House [should] be appointed to review the solicitation laws in order to improve the safety of sex-trade workers and communities overall, and to recommend changes that will reduce the exploitation and violence against sex-trade workers. (Davies 2003)

Davies' motion launched the Subcommittee on Solicitation Laws of the Standing Committee on Justice and Human Rights (SSLR),[5] which constituted the first systematic review of Canada's prostitution laws since the Fraser Committee. The murders and disappearances of over sixty sex workers in Vancouver alone paired with the possibility that a Liberal Canadian government might be in favor of amending sex work solicitation laws created a new and specific socio-legal context and reanimated a debate on sex work in Canada. On March 16, 2005, the Subcommittee, which was in the midst of a Canadian tour, made its stop in Montréal and met at Stella, l'amie de Maimie, Montréal's organization for sex workers' rights. I was present at that meeting and the realities presented by sex workers in the community and by allies were well represented by over forty people. Toward the end of the Subcommittee tour in May 2005, more counts were brought against the Vancouver pig farmer, bringing the number to twenty-seven charges.

The Committee presented its final report with recommendations on December 13, 2006. Called "The Challenge of Change," it offered no concrete measures to improve sex workers' safety and instead demanded that more research be done on prostitution and human trafficking. It was a disappointment to the sex worker rights community, to say the least. The next time that sex work was on the federal political stage was in 2007, when Canadian sex workers launched a constitutional challenge to three of Canada's major prostitution provisions. In 2013, these sex workers won their legal battle in *Bedford v. Canada*[6] and obtained legal recognition from the highest court in Canada. Six months later, they were hit with The Protection of Communities and Exploited Persons Act (PCEPA) that came into effect on December 6, 2014, and effectively made the sex work exchange illegal for the first time in Canada. Loaded with emotion—fear and societal disdain the spirit of the PCEPA embodies the predator/victim dichotomy so often imposed on sex work and is drafted to keep sex workers out of respectable neighborhoods (Prior and Gorman-Murray 2015, 101) and tries to eliminate sex work in its entirety. Ten years after Libby Davies' motion, and thirty years after the Fraser Committee, Canadian prohibitionists were once again able to propel a conservative/moralist agenda and align with the then Justice Minister and Attorney General Peter Gordon MacKay (2013–2015) to ignore the spirit of the Supreme Court decision. Omnipresent in the prohibitionists' narrative, the whore symbol has always been resistant to change, and once again morals trumped women's security and autonomy.

When the Supreme Court of Canada put a one-year stay on the *Bedford* decision, giving the Justice Minister one year to respond, I had not expected the state to completely decriminalize prostitution. I did, however, anticipate some recommendations that would, at least, enhance women's safety. After years of activism, Canadian sex workers' organizations and their allies were still unable to convince the Canadian government to prioritize sex workers' safety, remove police antagonism from sex workers' lives, and work toward improving sex workers' living and working conditions. Outraged by the rejection of sex workers' pleas, and by the fact that my government had once more forsaken the protection and autonomy of women, I decided to write this book.

This work is grounded in a case study about Stella, l'amie de Maimie (referred to throughout this book as "Stella"), a Montréal sex workers' rights organization, founded by and for sex workers. It explores how a group of ostracized female-identified sex workers transformed themselves into a collective to promote the health and well-being of women working in the sex industry. Weighed down by the old and tenacious whore symbol, the sex workers at Stella had to find a way to navigate the criminality of sex work and sex workers in order to do advocacy and support work and create safer spaces for sex workers to engage in such advocacy. This book is based on my dissertation, which was written at a time when I was on the board of directors at Stella and heavily involved in local activism. This Stella-supported project helps us to understand how a context of criminality impedes our ability to organize effectively.

Once the socio-historical context that gave birth to the whore symbol is reviewed, the primary goal of this book is to answer two questions: 1) what factors and processes are connected to the emergence, the organization, and maintenance of a community organization like Stella? And 2) what role does the whore symbol and other stereotypes still play in maintaining sex workers' criminality? By drawing on social movement theory,[7] this book is situated at the crossroads of sexuality, law, and gender, aiming to make sense of sex workers' struggle for legal and social recognition.

It should be noted that the legal system is not without stereotypes (Farrell 2017) and is not impartial (Jochelson and Kramar 2011, 12; Gaudrealt-Des-Biens 2001, 23) or emotionless (Nussbaum 2004, 5). The whore, a symbol imposed on sex workers by moral entrepreneurs, has proven to be a particularly enduring connection, making mobilization difficult. Criminalized and infantilized, sex workers' main claim—that sex work is a legitimate source of income generation, of work—is rejected by the Canadian state. Sex workers' community organizations in Canada, such as Stella, have not been able to shake the whore symbol. This in turn has created a situation where activists have had to mobilize within a highly unreceptive environment. Sex worker organizing deserves a fresh theoretical framework, one that endeavors to grasp the complexity of sex workers' struggle—that of navigating a particular moral and legal terrain while trying to accomplish their mandate of promoting the health of sex workers.

It is certainly true that the longevity of Canadian sex worker rights groups, such as Stella, can be explained in part by the HIV/AIDS pandemic and the ensuing financial resources from diverse Canadian health organizations. However, to analyze Stella using only Resource Mobilization Theory (RMT)[8] would offer only a superficial analysis. To suggest that Stella is simply a health promotion organization would keep the analysis at a mechanical, emotionless level—as if the intention was to gather resources and use them as tools to reach a specific goal, which once achieved would mean the end of its mandate. But Stella deserves more than an organizational analysis; hence, the present work intends to go beyond the mobilization of resources framework. Stella's goals are multifaceted, and more attention to culture and emotion are required. Therefore, my focus is directed toward the enduring symbols surrounding sex work and the influence of *emotions*—such as shame, disgust, and fear—on mobilization, which is not part of the RMT framework. Although sex workers in Montréal have been organizing since 1985 (Dumont and Toupin 2003), and, indeed, HIV/AIDS funding has been helpful in organizing and maintaining Stella, other factors play an equally large role. Drawing on social movement theory, this book constitutes the first extended effort in Canada to make sense of the transformation of a category of persons labeled as "prostitutes" into sex workers—people who sell or trade sex for money or goods. Stella provides an excellent case study to illustrate the mobilization work done by a group of marginalized, criminalized, and stigmatized women that, lest we forget, in other parts of the country brought their case to the Supreme Court of Canada and won (Johnson 2015).

Theoretical Framework

Stella, as noted, deserves a fresh look, which means an apposite theoretical framework. For that reason, the role of culture and its close link to emotions is essential to make sense of Stella's successes, struggles, and one major defeat. Older concepts such as framing, self-identity, and social identity also need to be revisited (Perozzo et al. 2016). These notions come to life when applied to important moments like the Pilot Project and the Forum XXX.

Culture

In the present work, culture is "meaning" and a "web of significance" (Benford and Snow 2000, 67)—"a collective actor cannot exist without reference to experiences, symbols and myths which form the basis of its [self-identity]" (Della Porta and Diani in McDonald 2002, 110), so in order to understand how sex workers relate to and organize within Stella, we need to explore how sex workers create, use, and maintain these meanings and how the whore symbol prevented or stimulated and sustained action (Tigchelaar 2019).

In *Dilemmas of the American Self* (1989), Hewitt argues that Mead's concepts—symbols and object—are the most apposite tools to define culture. A symbol is anything, a word, a gesture, or a sound whose function is to point to and to serve in place of something else" [. . .] object is the "that" to which a symbol points" (Hewitt 1989, 67). For example, words such as home, love, and family have become significant symbols (Mead 1922, 160) linked to a style of life of a particular group—the middle class. This linkage is shot through with a set of assumptions related to what Pierre Bourdieu has termed *cultural capital*, that is, the advantages that members of a dominant class enjoy as a result of family resources acquired in childhood, education, and social networking. These resources have enabled the middle and upper classes to consolidate and sustain their advantageous position, while at the same time allowing them to act as gatekeepers, deciding who will be respected and who will be rejected or categorized as unworthy. Clearly, marginalized members of society who have not acquired the right kind of cultural capital—such as those identified as whores—will not be listened to, and their needs will not be seen as relevant. Sex workers are not viewed as symbols of stability, morality, and normalcy. They do not point to that imagined secure place created by the middle class—the suburban neighborhood.

In her work on a Québec collective mobilizing for the right to forgo medication, Duperré reviewed 160 different definitions of culture (Duperré 2002, 78). The common thread, she stated, is the interrelation of codes and norms. From that statement, she described culture as codified relationships between individuals' meanings that "urged" people to follow certain styles of life. Thus, paraphrasing Duperré's definition, but adding an element of learning (Lavenda and Schultz 2017) and symbols, I define culture as

> Interrelated patterns of ideas, conduct, behavior and action organized around symbols, behaviors and actions linked to normative elements such as values and norms that contribute to make a group distinct. These patterns are constructed while adjusting to the external environment, and they are transmitted through teaching and social pressure.

Without a doubt, sex workers violate long-held family norms and values and in doing so their claims attract, offend, and provoke disgust. People gather around certain symbols while rejecting others—such is the situation with the expressions "sex workers" and "sex work." Therefore, I concur with Valerie Jenness that sex workers have had to engage in a massive public relations project (1993, 7); however, I add that they must also engage in such a campaign within their own organizations. The creation of the expression *sex work* (Leigh 1979) marked the linkage of highly disparate cultural products—sexuality and work.

Led by Michel Foucault and his influential study on sexuality (1976), numerous authors have debated the intimate relationship between self and sex (Benoit et al. 2018; Phoenix and Oerton 2005; Jordan 2004; Brock 2003, 1998; Parent 2001). Phoenix and Oerton in *Illicit and Illegal* (2005), Jordan in *Sex, Money and Power* (2004), and Parent (2001) underline the close relationship between sexuality and self-identity. How we "do sex" (Phoenix and Oerton 2005, 20) seems to be of great importance for the discovery of self (Parent 2001, 175). Indeed, how we have sex and with whom is linked with self-transformation and self-improvement, viz; the project of the self (Jordan 2004, 54–139).

Emotion

A relevant theoretical framework for the sex worker rights movement, I argue, is an analysis that includes the role of emotion in the formation of a collective and in collective action. Goodwin et al. (2005) first proposed the concept of emotion as a framework to help us understand what moves people to join social movements and what repels them or drives them to create counter-movements. Later on, Verhulst and Walgrave (2009) maintain that participation in collective action cannot be separated from emotion at least as an entry point. I would argue that for Stella to mobilize sex workers and allies the role of culture and emotions becomes essential.

Neglected since the 1960s, the link between emotion and mobilization is making a comeback (Rodgers 2018; Arenas 2015; Eyerman 2005; Ost 2004; Scheff 2000, 84). Once linked to madness and irrationality (Jonsson 2006), social movement scholars were not keen on including emotions in their analyses, especially the proponents of resource mobilization theory (Ost 2004, 234). Today, though, a cogent analysis of marginalized groups, such as sex workers, must include the role played by emotion.

Johanna Phoenix (1999) reports that contrary to popular belief, physical violence is not sex workers' primary concern. In London, where Phoenix's research took place, sex workers' greatest fear was to be discovered and exposed to family and friends. Thus, intuitively I am linking this fear of discovery to emotions of embarrassment (Scheff 1994, 2000), loss of status (Weber 1946), provoking disgust (Benoit et al. 2018; Curtis 2011), and unease in the presence of someone of a higher rank (Bourdieu 2000, 184). These factors are possible obstacles to mobilization. In agreement with the work of Ost (2004) and Javelin (2003), the present work not only brings emotions back into the analysis, but this time gives them a primary role—that of fuel for either action or inaction. I agree with Ivan Arenas that bringing emotions in mobilization "means going beyond a focus on the relational construction of emotions and arguing instead for their collective agency, including their power to transform participants into activists" (2015, 1). Moreover, to bring emotion to the forefront of my analysis acknowledges "that social movements *move* people, mobilizing them both physically as well as emotionally and that this has effects that reach beyond a movement's political demands" (Arenas 2015, 1122; emphasis in the original). To access people's emotions can be difficult, and to understand them quite complex

(Oberschall 1969). Still, as Melucci states, understanding emotion as "irrational" as opposed to "rational" is simply nonsense. "There is no cognition without feeling and no meaning without emotion" (Melucci 1995, 45). My years spent with marginalized people have taught me that without understanding the role of emotions, a researcher cannot understand either action or inaction. Plus, in the case of Stella and the Canadian sex workers' movement, the role of emotion sheds light on the birth of the counter-movement, that is, the particular role played by prohibitionists and neighborhood organizations. It is my contention that disgust has played a major role in the Pilot Project debacle (chapter 3) and in the prohibitionist onslaught during the Forum XXX (chapter 4). Lastly, Stella's longevity cannot be explained without the presence of emotions such as love, pride, trust, anger, and sadness, to name a few. How can one explain the presence of our allies and adversaries without drawing on such emotions as moral outrage (chapter 2)? When it comes to whether one will join a cause or not, emotions are our guide.

Framing

The relationship between meaning and action has received substantial attention within the symbolic interactionist tradition (Joas 1996, 207; Stokes and Hewitt 1976). First articulated through the understanding of behavior and purposive conduct (Mills 1940), what makes people join or start a group has come to be an important dimension in making sense of collective action (Rogers 2018; McPhail 2006; Benford and Snow 2000; McAdam 1994; McCarthy 1994; Joas 1996; Stokes and Hewitt 1976; Etzioni 1968). The link between meaning and action has developed into the concept of collective action frames (Benford and Snow 2000; Staggenborg 2008, 18); in the present work I link emotion, meaning, and action.

    To generate action, groups must perform meaning work, and the creation of meaning involves emotional labor. Actors are conceptualized as signifying agents who produce, modify, and maintain meaning inside and outside the group (Benford and Snow 2000, 613). This work, this construction of meaning, has come to be known as framing and is collective and interactive (Buechler 2000, 41). Framing is the organization of experience into something that makes sense to the actor (Goffman 1986, 10–11). As a result, meaning is emergent and past and present come together during interaction (Stokes and Hewitt 1976, 846). Culture, therefore, is frame's raw material, used to create what Mills (1940) calls "a vocabulary of motives" to mobilize members and attract new ones. If action depends on people's expectations, if action is an orientation toward things (Warner 1978, 1327), then framing for marginal and stigmatized groups becomes essential (Jenness 1993, 1995). Sex workers' organizations must convince sex workers and allies to join their struggle, and the language they use to articulate their demands must make sense to their potential members and supporters. Therefore, including the concept of frame "can offer insight into the problems that matter specifically to [sex workers' claims], where points of dispute exist, and how some discourses are privileged over others" (Hervieux and Voltan 2018, 282). The group must engage in a framing activity to convince people to join and fight with/for them. But what if a group cannot convince others to join? What would be the main reason? I have been asking myself this question for a long time. As a matter of fact, it is the question that prompted me to write this book. Why is there so much resistance from my government to do everything in its power to make women working in the sex industry safer? In the case of sex work, could it be disgust? Could it be something else? Judith Butler's *The Frames of War: When Is Life Grievable?* (2009) may enrich our reflections.

Butler argues that the way in which situations are "framed" determines whose lives are grievable. Whenever members of a particular group are defined as *the other*—whether it is because they are enemies in wartime, or because they present some other more insidious threat—they are no longer deemed worthy of care. They are depersonalized and dehumanized, so why waste psychic energy on them? While it is necessary to concede that we cannot grieve for all of humanity, it is also necessary to insist that our government offer protection and resources to all of its citizens, including those who have been marginalized. This demand for recognition and protection is at the heart of the present work.

Social Movement Theory (SMT)

What defines a social movement is contentious (Dunezat 1998) and far from being clear, but I concur with Duperré that it is important to circumscribe the notion (Duperré 2002, 59) because if we call every gathering or group a social movement, it is neither necessary nor even possible to theorize about it (Touraine 1985, 1997, 2000). The principal difference between the collective actor and the social movement is the impact that the latter has on the action system (Della Porta and Diani 2006, 20–21; Duperré 2002, 60). A social movement differs in its scope from collective action in that social movements vie for the control of historicity (Touraine 2000, 270). For sex workers the control of historicity means to resist the norms attached to sexuality; they are challenging its meaning by challenging the meaning of sexuality at its core.

Movements are disruptive forces and following Touraine (1985, 760), I wish to reserve the concept mainly to refer to conflicts that are cultural in nature. A social movement is defined by observable interrelations between opposing actors and the risks they both face. To say that sex workers' groups have been challenging the "overall system of meaning which sets dominant rules in a given society" (Della Porta and Diani 2006, 8) is an understatement. Thus, as academics conducting research on sex work, what we are observing are actors in opposition and the risks they are taking in the struggle for the control of historicity (Touraine 1985, 761)—the control of meaning. The risks that sex workers and their allies take will become quite evident in this book.[9] Paraphrasing Maheu (1983, 1991) I define social movement as collective actions that are

> Creative and innovative, linked to a situation marked by inequality or domination, which denounce and lead to freedom claims, self-determination, emancipation and democracy. These could or not lead to deinstitutionalization practices.

Self and Identity

My understanding of the self is not attached to the psychological realm. It is firmly grounded in the social.[10] Pursuing Georges H. Mead's project, I locate the genesis and the growth of the self in the social. The self is not present at birth but arises through social interaction. For Mead, social interaction takes place within three intersubjective activities: language, play, and game (Mead 1925). The focus here is on language—the words we use, that is, significant symbols and how they are indispensable to the development of self and self-identity. As humans we acquire self-awareness through interaction with others, the language our group uses to describe our actions and conduct. The word "whore" has become a meaningful symbol internalized by most if not all women—including those who are not sex workers. Many of us have been taught at a very young age about the rules of sex, that is, what to do, with whom, and when. The 60s may have somewhat liberated us to some extent (Muszynski 1999), but I would argue that the fear of being label a "slut" or a "whore" is still very much present. The symbol has become part of women's narrative.

Contemporary discourses around the self comprise three cultural themes (Hewitt 1989). First, there is an ontological preoccupation with the person. Although not expressed via religious discourse but in medical and legal terms, "the individual's state of grace [is still] a matter of both inner preoccupation and public discussion" (Hewitt 1989, 66); therefore, notions of morals and ethics are present in the definition of the self (Rose 1998). In fact, the "principle of the sanctity of the individual" does not come without instructions (Jordan 2004, 58). Medical authorities and governments may not "tell us how to fall in love and how to enjoy sex" (57), but they do define the preferable ways to live these "meaningful" experiences (Rose 1998, 79). Second, Hewitt maintains that social and generational changes enter the construction of the contemporary person and how the person is expected to transform the social context in which the individual lives and hence the sort of person the social will produce. The last theme consists of discourses about the self as either a "loyal creature of society" or a "creator of society" (Hewitt 1989, 66). This theme grounds the individual in a relationship with the social. The individual—in our case the sex worker—is neither product nor creator of the social; she is both, and the meaning of the person is found in this opposition (67). Self-identity is born inside this opposition, inside that struggle (Tremblay 2001). As the individual enters an ongoing society, that is, a normative structure, she also enters an intersubjective relationship with the social. The self is a complex design woven through culture—language, symbols, and discourse. The self does not stand still, and its construction is not linked to only one group (Cronk 1973, 327), and by this I mean that the self can be re-written by internalizing other claims such as those displayed in a sex worker's organization.

> Identity, let us be clear about it, is hotly contested concept. Whenever you hear that word, you can be sure that there is a battle going on. A battlefield is identity's natural home. Identity comes to life only in the tumult of battle; it falls asleep and silent the moment the noise of the battle dies down. Cutting both ways cannot therefore be avoided. [. . .] Identity is a simultaneous struggle against dissolution and fragmentation; an intention to devour and at the same time a stout refusal to be eaten. (Bauman 2004, 77)

In the Western world, identity became a site of confrontation during the 1960s. To be "oneself" and to "do your own thing" came to be the slogan of an entire generation (Hoffman 1991). It is the "not belonging, the social exclusion that renders discussions about identities relevant" (Bauman 2004, 12–20). Indeed, until one is met with a refusal, such as protection against violence, or access to employment or specific rights that seem to be granted to some and not others, identity may not be a huge concern. Thus, identities construction has been linked to legal, social, and moral recognition and the emergence of collectives.

As noted by Joanna Phoenix, "the term identity has been used in a number of different ways in the last few decades" (1999, 14). It is often used to indicate the "essence" of a person (Phoenix 1999, 14) or it may refer to a lifestyle, as appears to be the case for sex workers. During my research, I identified two problems; first, that "identity" has become a carry-all concept that sometimes means the individual is a member of a group or a category[11] (Reicher 2004). The second problem arises when identity is thought of as being permanent. Because "identity" often refers to a reified form, it is sometimes rejected (Drury et al. 2003, 192) or challenged (Stella 2006, 75) by activists. I reject the conceptualization of identity "as a fixed thing" (Drury et al. 2003, 192) and instead conceive of "identity" as contingent. Thus, to characterize it as a fixed state is "[. . .] ultimately impossible" (Vahabzadeh 2003, 45). Hence, I always use identity conjointly with self and it is to be understood as an ongoing project forged through experiences of nuanced power and resistance.

The Language of This Study

The sex industry is a specific branch of commerce where sex workers offer sexual services to clients in exchange for money or goods. People sell sex in a variety of venues and a diversity of ways including on the street and in indoor locations. Business owners, such as escort agencies and independent sex workers, advertise and promote different sexual services. Bars, massage parlors, hotels, private residences, strip clubs, the Internet, movie sets, and the street are all locations where sex workers offer their services. Each milieu has its own culture, hierarchy, and internal organization. Every form of sex work possesses different characteristics and each milieu has its jargon that often identifies the participants and links them to a specific form of sex work and permits one participant to recognize another.

Sex work and prostitution can be contentious terminologies. Use of the term prostitution historically carries a negative connotation and imagery of "uncleanliness," "immorality," and perversion. The term sex work, the genesis of which I describe later, is a more accepted term that originated within the community of people who sell or trade sex. For the purposes of this book, I am employing the word *prostitution* in the most historical sense, an act that indicates direct physical contact with clients. Some sex work services do not involve direct physical contact with the client, such as Webcam, erotic phone calls, and stripping. Keeping prostitution as one form of sex work is consistent with the position taken by John Lowman from Simon Fraser University, who maintains that the specific nature of such work must be recognized. Hence, I refer to prostitution as "all sexual services that offer direct contact with a client" (Lowman 2005, 1), or as Jones (2016, 231) calls it, "direct sex work versus indirect sex work without direct genital contact." As one sex worker expressed, "my breasts and my elbow are not the same!" However, I will not use the term "prostitute" which is stigmatizing and has no real heuristic value—it leads us to a theoretical dead-end. In 2004, Carol Leigh published *Unrepentant Whore*, and recently Chris Bruckert published a chapter entitled "Activist Academic Whore: Negotiating the Fractured Otherness Abyss" (2014). Equally "SlutWalks" have stormed sidewalks across the globe (Bruckert 2014). Many sex workers reuse and re-appropriate the term *whore* (Weitzer 2018, 721). When it comes to mobilization, words and expressions have the potential to attract and repel; thus, challenging stereotypes is one of the most daunting tasks sex worker rights organizations must perform, but is one that activists at Stella, and around the world, must do.

In 1979, Carol Leigh coined the term *sex work* to unite women who sell or trade sex; she wrote: "This invention was motivated by my desire to reconcile my feminist goals with the reality of my life and the lives of the women I know" (Leigh 2004, 66). The first time I heard the term was at Stella; I adopted it because it resonated with me, it made sense because it means work, it is the exchange of sexual services or sexual fantasies, and most importantly, it is a revenue-generating activity. Sex work is work that embodies the different forms of sexual services, [12] which include domination, pornography, cybersex, erotic phone sex, stripping, and prostitution, to name a few. Today, because they include prostitution, the expressions sex work and sex workers are threatening to some and sometimes divide women. Carceral or prohibitionist feminists, such as law professor Catharine MacKinnon, reject the use of the expressions sex work and sex workers. According to her, any form of sexual services cannot be work—women in the sex industry are "prostituted women" (MacKinnon 2011).

One of the problems with referring to women in the industry as sex workers appears to be with the term prostitution and its accompanying stigma, which is not surprising to anyone who has been close to the sex work milieu. Often disgraced and ridiculed, many women offering sexual services insist that they are not "prostitutes" (Weitzer 2018, 720), and this was still the case in December 2016, as I discovered during my interviews with Zoë, an active erotic dancer, and Bella, an escort. I do not resolve terminology issues in this book; I define sex workers as persons who work part time or full time doing any form of sex work or exchange of sexual services for money or goods.

Methodological Notes

This book required multiple research methods: library research, archival research of over 250 documents, and qualitative methods of interviewing and participation. A literature review was necessary to synthesize the social construction of the whore symbol aka "the prostitute" and the societal disdain around her. Lastly, an archival research was required for Montréal's prostitution terrain and the creation of Stella. Because members of Stella are conceptualized as individuals capable of acting on their environment to bring about change, a method revealing the meaning that members give to their actions was required. Hence, I based my choice of qualitative methods on three premises: (a) interviews are the only way to understand what Bedford and Snow call "meaning work" (2000, 613), which is at the core of my case study; (b) knowledge is intersubjective; and (c) the involvement of culture, that is, the principles and beliefs that influence relationships necessitate appropriate qualitative methods when the aim is to understand complex phenomena and social processes (Duperré 2002, 109; Deslauriers and Kérisit 1997, 88).

Sex workers' milieus are among the most challenging fields for researchers to access (Shaver 2005) and this book would have been impossible without the contribution of Stella's employees and allies. Without their participation the study would lack an essential aspect—the meaning sex workers give to their actions. Moreover, their continuous participation is responsible for the emergence of dimensions unforeseen at the outset. For the present work, I conducted seventeen interviews from 2004 to 2008 with Stella's employees chosen as key informants. I held the interviews for the different chapters between December 2016 and November 2018 with employees at Stella, and active and retired sex workers, eight of whom are not members of Stella.

My work is framed within a social constructionism perspective; thus, I recognize the existence of specific events and how they influence sex workers' present-day social position. For this reason, although it would be preposterous to compare the socio-political sanitary context of the 1800s with present-day conditions, it is legitimate to imagine that these events influence the way legal and health authorities, as well as the public, perceive sex workers and the sex industry today. Equally important is how the past influences the way women presently working in the sex industry see themselves—how it shapes their self and social identities (Benoit et al. 2018; Smith 2017, 344) and how it affects mobilization. According to Roger Brown, "a high social consensus [regarding social identity] defines reality" (1986, 558). If we agree with this claim, then it is no wonder that so many sex workers hide the fact that they are or were making a living in the sex industry—who wants to be perceived and treated as a minor, judged as "not too bright," a drug addict, or the carrier of diseases? Key informants confirmed these labels and the reasons why anonymity is still so relevant.

Lastly, as a woman and a retired sex worker (1969–1988), I have a vested interest in sex workers' claims for legal recognition. The decision to remain a member of Stella and to later accept the role of the administrator while doing research was well thought out, and so is my decision to come out as a retired sex worker for this book—these are ethical choices. Or perhaps these choices are also related to identity construction. The shift in my identity and self-perception is connected to my ever-increasing concern with activism. As Knowles (1996) wrote before me, I do not claim objectivity, but while following the rules of scholarly rigor, the present work remains committed and passionate, abiding by Marilyn Porter's (1995) and New Zealand politician Marilyn Waring's (1996) radical approach to social issues. Quoting American feminist sociologist Sally Hacker, she cites, "[r]esearch without action—without the potential to advance social justice—was not research she deemed worth doing. In her ceaseless effort to seek and destroy the root of oppression, Sally was radical in the word's literal, and best, sense" (quoted in Porter 1995, 426). Lastly, I wish to argue that it is by denying self-involvement that one runs the risk of lacking "objectivity"; the researcher needs what Bourdieu refers to as "self-analysis" (2004, 94).

The historical detour that I will take here is to make sense of sex workers' social identity, problems of mobilization, and The Protection of Communities and Exploited Persons Act (PCEPA). To do so it is mandatory to make sense of an enduring symbol: the whore.[13]

The Social Construction of the Whore Stigma

> The Greeks, who were apparently strong on visual aids, originated the term *stigma* to refer to bodily signs designed to expose something unusual and bad about the moral status of the signifier. The signs were cut or burnt into the body and advertised that the bearer was a slave, a criminal, or a traitor—a blemished person, ritually polluted, to be avoided, especially in public places. (Goffman 1963, 1)

In *The Prostitution Prism* (1996), psychologist Gail Pheterson explores the whore stigma that signifies unworthiness. Using Canadian sociologist Erving Goffman's concept of stigma, Pheterson reveals how a group of women came to represent everything that is judged as immoral and shameful. To be stigmatized is to be shamed; stigma is roughly the contrary of prestige in that it signals the presence of something disgraceful. According to Pheterson, the "prostitute" is the archetype of the stigmatized.[14] Although present in the British Empire (Howell 2000), this Western symbol of decadence became solidified during the industrialization maelstrom in Britain (Walkowitz 1980). Prostitution was one way for women to make ends meet, the exchange of sexual services, as favors for lodging and food existed before industrialization (Solé 1993), but it was not an industry—it was not organized. As a result, while being careful to examine prostitution primarily as a product of industrialization, this historical detour relates the events surrounding the creation of sex trade workers as a category, a symbol of national and moral decadence and pollution. Contemporary sex workers may not be referred to using the same language, but they remain linked to crime, drugs, and venereal diseases, and that in turn brings up emotions such as disgust.

Based on the seminal work of European historians Solé (1993), Corbin (1990), and Walkowitz (1973, 1980), as well as Canadian historians Lévesque (1995) and Poutanen (1998), the historical detour here and in chapter 1 is essential in understanding why sex workers' organizations are still struggling to get legal recognition and are even further away from social recognition. Also, significantly, these events have contributed to the fact that many sex workers still harbor a negative self-concept (Smith 2017), which in turn makes mobilization difficult. To be called sex workers instead of "prostitutes" has changed the presentation of self, but there is still a long way to go.

This fact may be difficult to understand unless one has been in the business long enough to witness how some have internalized all the negative implications that come with the work (Benoit et al. 2017). The construction of the sex worker as *the Other* can only be understood within the framework of past events, which contributed to creating *her* as such—*she* was created through a legal medical discursive process (Cunningham 2016, 9). Hence, the next sections examine the birth of the middle class, followed by the British Contagious Diseases Acts of 1864/66/68 and the ensuing Repeal Campaign.[15] Sex workers are born from a complex mixture of charity work and condemnation, and they are still perceived as being distinct from the wife and the mother. Female sex workers are deemed contrary to "women's essential nature" and are often perceived by legal and medical authorities as essentially different from "honest, chaste women."[16]

Birth of the Middle Class

The Industrial Revolution was the catalyst for the creation of new social classes (Deutschmann 2004). The British evangelical society, beginning in the period 1780–1790, promoted the bourgeoisie's temperance and sobriety above the aristocracy's flamboyant lifestyle. Between the years of 1820–1830, essays and sermons, novels and poems, as well as manuals offering advice on how to live, began to appear (Cott 1993), and most of the information came from the middle class. The middle-class, trying to distance itself from the aristocracy and the laboring class, struggled to assert its social identity (Cott 1993). Consequently, the middle class undertook, among other things, to define the occidental family, one that does not rest solely on blood relations and marriage but is invested with emotions and sentiments. Family life became the cradle of middle-class morality (Fox 1993, 147) and the foundation of its identity, demanding what Prior and Gorman-Murray call "landscapes associated with the sanctity of respectable domesticity"[17] (2015, 101). Districts became linked to status groups, and only members of these groups were invited to their inner circles.[18] After years of working toward accumulating wealth, an urbanized middle class demanded specific living areas within which conformity and stability would reign, that is, the safety necessary to raise a family. It was in this newly industrialized maelstrom that "the dangerous class" appeared and the poor were often referred to as "the residuum" (Jones 1971). These groups were considered weak in character and a danger to public order; hence, the evil attributed to these groups had to be confronted. The concern was understood as a moral issue; the evil to be combated was vice, drunkenness, improvidence, mendicancy, bad language, filthy habits, gambling, low amusements, and ignorance, not poverty (11).

It was within this context that concerns about prostitution emerged. Understood mainly as a moral issue, prostitution caused apprehension and these feelings of social insecurity, in turn, created a heated atmosphere which gave rise to legislation and various reforms (Jochelson and Kramar 2011).[19] In 1824, this resulted in the creation of the Vagrancy Act, a law which made begging and sleeping outdoors illegal, and the first English law using the term "common prostitute." The next law to control prostitution was the Metropolitan Police Act of 1839 (Laite 2006). This law, applicable only within London's districts, stipulated that "any common prostitute loitering or soliciting for prostitution to the annoyance of inhabitants or passer-by" could be arrested and fined. Moreover, the fine would increase with every subsequent arrest. Then in 1847, a similar law, the Town Police Clauses Act, was extended to the rest of England, allowing police to control "undisciplined" women, who often belonged to the poor working class (Laite 2006). Class is obvious in the legislation of prostitution. Prostitution was understood as a problem of the lower class, "their animality forming an instructive contrast to bourgeois self-control" (Howell 2000, 331) and systems of regulation had to be put in place. Concurrent with these social issues provoked by industrialization was England's involvement in the Crimean War. Thus, the British army also had concerns related to soldiers' habits, leading to the creation of the Contagious Diseases Acts (CDAs).[20] The alleged practices of soldiers included the exchange of sexual services for money, lodging, food, and as one can imagine companionship. Both lonely, soldiers and working women probably found comfort in each other;[21] the soldier, separated from his family and facing death almost daily, and the woman needing food and lodging. Therefore, the British army created and enforced these Acts to fight public health anxiety provoked by fraternization between "prostitutes" and soldiers on leave.

Great Britain's Contagious Diseases Acts (CDAs) 1864, 1866, and 1869

> It has become an established practice in the British Navy to admit, and even to invite, on board our ships of war, immediately on their arrival in port, as many prostitutes as the men and, in many cases, the officers, may choose to entertain,—to the number, in the larger ships, of several hundred at a time; all of whom remain on board, domesticated with the ship's company, men and boys, until they again put to sea. The tendency of this practice is to render a ship of war, while in port, a continual scene of riot and disorder, of obscenity and blasphemy, of drunkenness, lewdness, and debauchery. (Admiral E. Hawker 1821)

In 1857, a report by the Royal Commission on the Health of the Army claimed that venereal diseases were responsible for more hospitalizations than the Crimean War itself (Walkowitz 1980, 74). Five years later, in 1862, a committee was formed to investigate the matter, a procedure that, in 1864, led to the passage of the first CDA, legislating the mandatory examination of "prostitutes" from eleven garrison towns in England and Ireland (75). The first Acts (1864) were created by and for the army, specifically for the welfare of the soldiers. Working in concert with plainclothes Metropolitan Police, hospital authorities, and local justices of the peace, the War Office and the Admiralty were responsible for overseeing the administration of the Acts. Each bill (1864, 1866, and 1869) extended the domain of influence for the appointed offices.

In 1867, following a report from the Harveian Medical Society of London claiming that the incidence of venereal diseases in Great Britain was reaching epidemic proportions, doctors and authorities formed the Association for Promoting the Extension of the Contagious Diseases Acts to the Civilian Population. Following the extension of the CDAs, working-class entertainment sites such as pubs and music halls were placed under surveillance, and legal authorities had the right to arrest all "women suspected of promiscuous behaviour" (Walkowitz and Walkowitz 1973, 75). In 1869, the CDAs were again extended, this time to five additional districts, an event that tightened the surveillance of women, provided them with moral and religious instruction, and sanctioned the incarceration of women deemed "unfit for examination" (Walkowitz 1980, 86). This ultimately led to the Repeal Campaign.

The Repeal Campaign

Even though in 1867 the CDAs were extended to non-military persons, some had opposed the Acts since the beginning of the debate. Their main opponent was Florence Nightingale (Walkowitz 1980, 75; McDonald 2005, 411), who in 1862 created the venereal diseases committee. She would, until 1877, remain steadfastly opposed to regulation. For Nightingale, the problem was one of vice, not diseases. Therefore, because "vice" and "filthy habits" (McDonald 2005, 412) were the cause of venereal disease, her committee recommended that soldiers be offered "healthy, innocent and manly occupations [. . .] in barracks and on board ship"[22] (Walkowitz 1980, 75) as an alternative to sexual encounters. By providing medical examinations to "prostitutes," doctors and military personnel were making prostitution safe for soldiers, the elite, and the general population. To Repealers, mainly middle-class and religious individuals, this was unacceptable, and prostitution had to be eliminated. Not surprisingly, Nightingale's argument that sailors could be convinced to engage in healthy pastimes, such as writing poetry, perhaps, failed to persuade influential politicians! The army, the police argued, was not a moral institution, and the CDAs were designed for sanitary control in the military, not moral direction.

It was the repeal campaign, triggered by the extension of the CDAs, which shifted the purpose from hygienic to a moral one. It is clear from

Nightingale's correspondence that in the years preceding the first CDA, the central preoccupations were, as Walkowitz (1980), Corbin (1990), and Keire (2001) state, hygiene, public order, and vice.[23] The repeal campaign rested more on a desire to curb vice than on addressing the unsanitary conditions, and this approach marked the beginning of a consensus. The CDAs, interpreted as making prostitution safer, gradually became a platform to dispense middle-class beliefs and values which further solidified the "prostitute" category, because this group, if not controlled, would contaminate middle-class values. The Acts in many ways sealed the fate of women selling sexual services—they were branded as "prostitutes" and expelled from their neighborhoods. As a result, they then had no other choice but to turn to other outcasts, having lost their original communities.

The efforts of women's organizations, such as the Ladies National Association and the Edwardian suffragists (Walkowitz 1980), to repeal the CDAs inadvertently[24] produced a clear image of "prostitutes" as immoral women and criminals. The feminist prohibitionist course of action that was meant as an act of deliverance, saving these poor women from male vice, resulted in women's isolation and stigmatization. As for the groups who wished to regulate prostitution, they "ironically treated prostitutes as a separate category of women, while their very own statistics revealed that 'prostitutes' were 'very much like most women' (Gilfoyle 1999, 121). The "prostitute" became an outcast, a symbol of disorder, excess, hedonism, and lack of judgment—she became disgusting. The CDAs were suspended in 1883 and repealed in 1886. By the time the Acts were repealed, women exchanging sexual services for a fee were identified as "prostitutes" and isolated.

The CDAs had taken their toll to such an extent that between 1890 and 1914, British authorities began an anti-prostitution campaign aimed at turning public opinion against women deemed to be "prostitutes." According to French historian Jacques Solé (1993, 14), this campaign caused "the brothel as a family industry" to disappear.[25] Gradually, women who had worked from their homes were no longer accepted in their neighborhoods (Walkowitz 1980, 211). As a result, women, who had been a part of the community and relied on informal police protection, found themselves alone. Analyzing the effect of the CDAs and the ensuing criminalization of sex workers, historians Walkowitz (1980), Solé (1993), and Gilfoyle (1999) report the gradual entry and creation of the role of "the pimp" in the terrain of prostitution. According to Gilfoyle, the so-called male control, "the pimp," only appeared following the criminalization of prostitution. "Ultimately, [. . .] men and male control enter prostitution only *after* the state does" (1999, 132; the emphasis in original). It was their dislocation that caused women to turn to the so-called "pimps," for who else would associate with a "prostitute"?

For sex workers operating in taverns, drinking and rambunctious men went with the territory. In fact, because alcohol was part of sex workers' soliciting tactics (McKewon 2005, 183; Poutanen 1998, 122), many found themselves dependent on alcohol, and that may have contributed to too many arrests for disorderly conduct.[26] Thus, depicted as having a penchant for alcohol, inclined to disorderly conduct, and attracting the bad company, sex workers were deemed undesirable and unworthy of protection. These events left sex workers with no one else to turn to except other outcasts or criminals. At times perceived as victims, a threat to public health, or criminals, sex trade workers' social identity became a strange mix of prey and predator, therefore making the debate about sex work nearly impossible with prohibitionists. To this day, "nowhere is the pity/hatred paradigm more evident" (Lewis 2016, 100), and here I would suspect the concealed feeling of disgust.

This historical detour is essential for understanding the resilience of the alleged link between crime, drugs, and the sex industry that makes Stella's claims appear to be illegitimate and, according to prohibitionists, irresponsible. These historical moments leave us with a category of "the prostitute" branded and marginalized. In social science going back to historical markers is our main weapon against naturalization and its consequences, and Bourdieu call these detours *historicization* (2000, 182). For him, historical analysis is the only way to make the case against the natural view—"makes it possible to neutralize the naturalization, and in particular amnesia of the individual and collective genesis of a 'given' that gives itself with all the appearance of the natural and asks to be taken at face value, taken for granted" (Bourdieu 2000, 182). Sex workers have been conceptualized as victims of male vice, criminals, and vectors of venereal diseases. The last event that entered into the creation of sex workers as "the other"—the one who does not belong—is sexuality introduced in the last chapter.

Since the beginning of the twentieth century, the parameters of bourgeois morality have undergone a profound change, perhaps even a seismic shift. Behaviors which would have been met with outright condemnation one hundred years ago, such as divorce, abortion, and homosexuality, are now acceptable to some, if not to all, members of society. It seems that sex work is the last frontier, a site of resistance, perhaps even for those with no claim of adherence to conventional morality. The argument that the exchange of sexual services for a fee is real work and that it is worthy of respect and legal and social recognition is disgusting/threatening to many; hence, the question to be considered is: why is this so? Why is sex work the last frontier of conventional morality and the object of so much resistance and condemnation? This book is about a group of sex workers' resistance to negative labels such as "victims of male vice," "HIV carriers," and "vectors" of other venereal infections. It is about Stella's history of mobilization for legal recognition and with any luck, social change. If members of a marginalized group can accomplish this, it could be an inspiration for others.

In conclusion, it may be apposite to present the contents of each chapter to go over the main points they desired to accomplish and what are the key elements in them. Chapter 1 introduces the sex industry from 1810 to 2000 in Montréal, Québec, Canada. That the "whore" symbol has proven resistant to change and describes Montréal's ambiguous and often ambivalent relationship with its sex industry is important for making sense of the equally ambivalent position of Stella. Chapter 2 introduces the creation of Stella; it outlines Stella's history from its pre-foundation from 1992 to December 2000. Chapter 3 presents the Pilot Project, a project that Stella engaged with in its infancy and, arguably, the issues faced at the time are still very much an obstacle for sex workers' legal recognition. Chapter 4 recalls Stella's ten-year anniversary which was marked by organizing the Forum XXX. This chapter is about celebration, empowerment, struggle, and resilience. Moreover, the Forum solidified Stella's presence on the international scene. Lastly, chapter 5 is an interview with Jenn Clamen, an advocate for sex workers' rights in Montréal and beyond. Chapter five recalls the transformation of the landscape for sex workers organizing in Canada before and after the Bedford case. In the concluding chapter, I introduce two topics that I consider behind the Protection of Communities and Exploited Persons Act (PCEPA) that came into effect on December 6, 2014: sexuality and sex work as work. Sex workers have struggled to attract allies and influential people that have the potential power to change their lives. Mobilization is, as we will see, not an easy task. Arguably the most difficult undertaking and success depends on finding the right words, the right arguments. As a movement, what do we need to do? Should we highlight women's economic empowerment, women's autonomy, women's need for self-sufficiency? Sex workers' rights do not garner the public and institutional support that they should, so which framing is important to put forward? How can we convince the public that sex worker rights matters? Frames are strategic in social movements and in organizing, so at the end of the present work I can certainly raise these questions. I hope in doing so that this book inspires the public to rethink their position and potential opposition to sex workers' rights—the denial of sex workers' autonomy has real lasting consequences for sex workers.

NOTES

1. See Durisin et a. 2018 for the history of policy development.
2. http://www.justice.gc.ca/eng/rp-pr/cj-jp/yj-jj/rr01_13/p23.html#sec23, accessed September 15, 2018.
3. The new law includes: stops or attempts to stop any motor vehicle, impedes the free flow of pedestrian or vehicular traffic or ingress to or egress from premises adjacent to that place, or stops or attempts to stop any person or in any manner communicates or attempts to communicate with any person. In addition, "public place" is defined to include motor vehicles in or on public places.

4. Not naming him is voluntary.
5. https://www.justice.gc.ca/eng/rp-pr/cp-pm/cr-rc/md-tm/.
6. Source: Canada (Attorney General) v. Bedford, 2013 SCC 72, [2013] 3 S.C.R. 1101.
7. Theoretically, my work pursues the pivotal work by American sociologist Ronald Weitzer (1991), criminologist Valerie Jenness (1993), French sociologist Lilian Mathieu (2000, 2001), and more recently American Political Science scholar Samantha Majic (2014). Like their work this book recalls how sex workers' rights groups have managed to emerge, organize, and in Montréal, survive in a quasi-legal and frequently hostile environment. However, going back to the role of culture (McAdams 1994) and exploring the meaning of disgust (Lateiner and Spatharas 2017; Curtis 2011; Nussbaum 2004), my analysis includes the unspoken presence of the whore symbol. Explored by Gail Pheterson in 1996, I have no doubt that the whore symbol and its associated disgust influence the maintenance of sex workers' negative social identity, which makes mobilization difficult and, so far, decriminalization impossible.
8. A theory based on the mobilization of resources, such as money.
9. Researchers like Lilian Mathieu (2001) and Chris Bruckert (2014) in Academic Whore article would support this statement.
10. As Honneth states, Mead reverses the relationship between ego and the social world:

Such a "me" is not then an early formation, which is then projected and ejected into the bodies of other people to give them the breadth of human life. It is rather an importation from the field of social objects into an amorphous, unorganized field of what we call inner experience. Through the organization of this object, the self, this material is itself organized and brought under the control of the individual in the form of so-called consciousness. (Mead 1964, in Honneth 1996, 75)

11. Such as a woman (gender identity), a black person (racial identity), a French Canadian (national identity), a gay person (sexual identity), and sometimes the term points to a more subjective meaning, such as "personal self-identity" (Phillips 2002, 598), personal identity (Reicher 2004, 928), or simply "identity" (Della Porta and Diani 2006, 93–113; Vahabzadeh 2003, 45; Honneth 1996, 71).
12. According to Canadian sociologist Kamala Kempadoo, "[t]he definition stresses the social location of those engaged in sex industries as working people" (Kempadoo 1998, 3). Kempadoo situates the demands of sex workers within the general struggle of workers and women's demands for basic human rights. She also points out that the use of the expression sex work stresses both the differences between and similarities with other types of work. Sex work is experienced as embedded with the sense of self. Being a sex worker is "not necessarily [seen] as the sole defining activity around which their sense of self or identity is shaped" (1998, 3).
13. The sex worker is the agent that grounds the abstract idea of the whore.
14. Pheterson did not introduce the history of the stigma, which may be known to researchers but not to the general population to which this text is dedicated.
15. Solé 1993; Jenness 1993; Walkowitz 1980; Walkowitz and Walkowitz 1973.
16. The work of Cesare Lombroso and Guglielmo Ferrero (1893) on women and criminal activity is still a topic when I teach courses such as Juvenile Delinquency or Deviance. Their book *Criminal Woman, the Prostitute, and the Normal Woman* was translated again and published again in 2004.
17. German sociologist Max Weber (1946) first noted that class and status in certain neighborhoods came to be associated with the middle class. Today the same approach comes out of gentrification where people who cannot afford the new rent or do not fit the "profile" are being thrown out of *their* neighbourhood. Although the effect of displacement is not conclusive (Gobbons et al. 2018), the fact remains that some people struggle to find affordable housing once they have been displaced.
18. Moreover, it was within the mature industrial city that particular groups worked to acquire a certain social status as opposed to an economic one. These groups, or communities, as Weber refers to them, were expected to adhere to a style of life that served to identify them as members of the middle class. This style of life is shared among residents, "not a mere individual and socially irrelevant imitation of another style of life." The status groups were, as Weber

asserts, "the specific bearers of all 'conventions,'" and gradually specific civic areas came to mirror and shape "the solidarities and divisions of society [. . .]." These changes resulted in a radical transformation of the city's physical, political, and social environments, creating conflicts with older traditions—a clash of cultures. Because growth had to be accommodated, spaces came to be shared between the upper and the lower classes, creating increased social instability. Poverty, overcrowding, and unhealthy conditions affected London, in particular, causing local authorities to worry about the maintenance of order and social stability, public decency, and public health.

19. Interesting how Benoit Lauzon (2002) underlines these moments of social insecurity when citizens demand the creation of new laws.

20. Philip Howell (2000) argues that the CDAs were in effect in the colonies long before they attained Britain. According to Howell regulation happened before 1864 and is tightly linking class, gender, and race.

21. There are many references in French popular culture about relationships between women and soldiers.

22. The reader might be forgiven for assuming that Florence Nightingale had very little experience with men in general and sailors in particular. We have already seen that Admiral E. Hawker acknowledged that ships in port are "a continual scene of riot and disorder, of obscenity and blasphemy, of drunkenness, lewdness, and debauchery."

23. Nightingale's efforts were aimed at reforming morals in general and the "prostitute" in particular. Her correspondence is marked by ambivalence toward working women. It was her desire to defend "these poor creatures," to perceive them as victims while concurrently condemning their actions, that Nightingale's interventions and those of different associations contributed to the construction of the "prostitute" as a completely different woman. Reading Nightingale's correspondence between 1854 and 1871, the issue of morality becomes obvious. Her concerns were with "vice," the "evil," and "the vicious and criminal classes of women." For Nightingale, vice transcended class, but nevertheless her attention was steered mainly toward working-class men and women. Nightingale's attitude would appear to the modern reader to be both hypocritical and patronizing; however, we have to consider her epoch. These attitudes are a reflection of the times in which these reformers lived.

24. One could say that it was intentional but as Foucault and later Valverde claim I hesitate to give them intent.

25. It would be interesting to examine the sex industry in Québec in the 70s when strip clubs/brothels were owned by families.

26. Drinking with clients was still part of the job in many strip clubs and brothels until the early 70s. It began to change when the 3416 bylaw was introduced which could get a dancer arrested if she stayed too long next to a client or was caught drinking at his table.

Chapter One

Montréal's Sex Industry, 1810–2000

Montréal's geography made it an excellent port city and, akin to other port cities in England, it attracted soldiers and sex trade workers. As noted previously, war, soldiers, and the sex trade were linked, and Montréal was no different.[1] Moreover, events such as the prohibition of alcohol in the United States[2] played a significant role in establishing Montréal as a place where one could indulge in iniquitous nightlife (Bélanger 2005). So, whether soliciting on the street or working in brothels, women exchanging sexual services for a fee did not lack potential clients. The city today may be different—the once famous Lower Main is barely a memory—but a strong strip club scene seems to help Montréal maintain its reputation vis-à-vis adult entertainment. However, the city has always had an ambivalent relationship with this aspect of its character, and it remains evident to this day.

In effect to better understand the nature of this complex and nuanced relationship I adopt an approach which Pierre Bourdieu has described as *historicization*. It involves an almost anthropological "unpacking" of the past in order to make sense of the present. Therefore, I follow through on the historical detour which began in the introduction and examine Montréal's sex industry from 1810 to 1995.

The importance of this chapter resides in the fact that events in Montréal, as in England, created a specific class of women—but one without autonomy or control over their own destinies. Buffeted about as *cause célèbre* in various reform campaigns, at the center of disputes between police, judges, and diverse women's organizations, women exchanging sexual services for money were stereotyped as outcasts who at worst inspired only pity and disgust. At best they were victims who could only be saved by authority figures graced with special wisdom. In many ways, as one of Stella's mobilizations will make clear, by the year 2000, Montréal's authorities still held an ambivalent approach to the sex industry; that is, a blend of criminalization, regulation, and medical intervention. Moreover, in some neighborhoods, the whore symbol remained intact.

Montréal was not spared the turbulence brought about by industrialization and urbanization. Indeed, the Montréal of the nineteenth century was the scene of profound social, demographic, and economic transformations; intensified immigration, the decline of traditional commerce (most famously the fur trade), unemployment, and epidemics of cholera had important repercussions for all Montréal inhabitants, especially those who were struggling (Poutanen 1998), notably working-class women. And so it was that for many working-class women, prostitution was often the best option. How different societies have managed prostitution has varied according to the epoch and locations, but how they dealt with it has always depended "upon the ordering of three factors—economic, moral, and hygienic circumstances" (Pivar 1973, 13). Montréal is no different, and political leaders and city officials developed policies in harmony with the culture of neighborhoods, the city, or the legislating nation. Indeed, as we will observe, the combination of Montréal's French and English cultures gives the city a unique identity. The way the city navigated the sexual landscape in social, moral, and legal terms has been unique as well. The work of historians Mary Anne Poutanen (1998), Andrée Lévesque (1995), and Danielle Lacasse (1994) allows for a description of Montréal's prostitution terrain from 1810 to 1870, help making sense of the reforms that occurred from 1865 to 1925, and criminologist Jean-Paul Brodeur (1984) sheds light on the confusing status of prostitution in Montréal.

MONTRÉAL'S SEX WORK GEOGRAPHY 1810–1850

By examining court depositions, historian Mary Anne Poutanen (1998, 102–24) observes that in 1810, brothels were operating over the entire city of Montréal.[3] Streetwalkers, brothel owners, and residents had an unspoken "code of conduct." By consulting these court archives, Poutanen reaffirms that if brothel-keepers did not attract attention to their house, for example by disorderly conduct, the police did not press charges against them, nor close the establishment.[4] The separation between private and public spheres was not part of the sex trade worker's experience. The street was paramount in her trade; it was a place where she met with other sex trade workers, raised her children, and a place where women helped one another. Consequently, soldiers met sex trade workers wherever they lived, and it seemed that for some military personnel, to be seen in public in the company of a "working lady" did not matter. Already the sex trade was two-tiered because although brothel prostitution was not entirely different from street prostitution, as women were moving between the two spheres, the criminal justice system did not treat them the same way because whenever they were working outside they were treated differently. Street sex work was the main irritant. Moreover, male civilians, if seen in the company of a sex worker, were arrested, while soldiers were simply taken back to the barracks (125). Geography did not circumscribe Montréal's sexual landscape. Commercial sex was not limited to red light districts,[5] but was mediated between neighbors and sex trade workers (102). Gradually, however, public places became symbols of class and gender. At the beginning of the nineteenth century, "male spaces" such as public halls and theaters (103) emerged in Montréal, and by the mid-1800s "proper" neighborhoods were reserved for middle- and upper-class women, thus obliging working-class women to share public space with sex trade workers. With the events that brought soldiers to Montréal and certainly provided more clients for street "prostitutes" and brothels, the old city became an important area for streetwalkers. By 1836, Montréalers were complaining that disgusting scenes prevented them from enjoying the old part of the city.

As in England, Montréal sex trade workers preferred specific areas—such as waterfronts—where the military barracks were usually located and where sources of entertainment were available (103). Between 1839 and 1854, more than a thousand soldiers resided in the barracks. Because the army sanctioned marriage for only 6 percent of the soldiers, they sought sex through other forms of relationships. Prostitution was an obvious choice, so it was not unusual to see sex trade workers and soldiers together. The relationship between soldiers and sex workers was more than financial. Soldiers were protectors and companions and, at times, even provided shelter. With Montréal's winter weather conditions, it is not difficult to imagine that this side of the relationship was particularly important. Thus, as in England, soldiers and prostitution went hand in hand (Poutanen 1998, 125–26). Caught between trying to survive and being hounded as a public nuisance, life for streetwalkers was extremely difficult. Poutanen (1998) reports instances of "women of ill repute" discovered dead, half-dressed, and frozen. In 1850, trapped in an unstable situation, sex workers were gradually directed toward a red light district (Brodeur 1984, 61). Poutanen's research reports that in 1842, seventy brothels were present in Montréal's red light district, which at the time was situated on the Lower Main.[6] An examination of Montréal prostitution reveals the irresolute attitude of the city and legal officials regarding the red light district, and this attitude reflected the incessant struggle between groups proposing solutions for prostitution—either legalization or abolition. The history of Montréal's various reform campaigns, which will be discussed in the following section, highlights these inconsistencies.

MONTRÉAL AND THE REFORM CAMPAIGN 1869–1925

As in England, Canadian social reformers' primary concern was prostitution (Lowman 2001, 1). Tolerance of prostitution was far from unanimous, and by the end of the century, Montréal witnessed the emergence of the regulationists and prohibitionists (Lévesque 1995, 90). In moral matters, English Canada inherited the English Protestant approach to prostitution (Valverde 1991, 81), which was to eradicate it. In Montréal, because of its French Catholic heritage, however, the city authorities did not adhere as strongly as English Canada to the temperance and reform movements[7] (Bélanger 2005, 19). Therefore, in Montréal, there was open dissention regarding prostitution and friction remained constant between regulationists, whose goal was to manage prostitution, and prohibitionists, who wanted to see it disappear. The lack of consensus surrounding prostitution reflected gender and class differences as well as the Francophone and Anglophone language division (Linteau 1998) as did the prohibitionist and regulationist positions (Brodeur 1984; Lacasse 1994). Police and judges would in turn favor prohibition and regulation. Police would arrest madams and the judges would free them the next day.

In 1869 and 1870, hygiene and venereal diseases were the central preoccupations of the regulationists and, as in England, Canadian authorities feared for the health of soldiers and civilians. In that context, the Canadian Institute of Montréal[8] suggested that the regulation of prostitution would be useful (Lévesque 1995, 89) and twice in 1869 and 1870 members of the institute pondered the need to regulate prostitution. It was in this spirit that Judge De Montigny in 1878, Montréal's recorder,[9] recommended that prostitution should be tolerated.[10] This recommendation must have been applied considering that, circa 1888, *Montréal by Gaslight* published an article admitting a losing battle against prostitution. The article announced that this was in part due to police laxity and concluded that regulation was the more logical option (Lévesque 1995). This issue remained a topic for the next ten years.[11] However, beginning in 1904, different groups, judges, police, clergy, social workers, women's groups, scientists, health professionals, and citizens contested the solution to prostitution, which had been to tolerate brothels.

The next inquiry, in 1909, was the first to be organized by citizen committees. Judge Cannon presided; the inquiry, also the first to be designated as a "royal inquiry," came to be known as the Cannon Inquiry (Brodeur 1984, 20). The inquest comprised 115 public sessions and produced, along with recommendations, a morality squad (22). The Cannon Inquiry denounced police tolerance vis-à-vis brothel owners, and for Montréal as critique of "open-mindedness" would remain constant throughout every other inquest.

Anticipating the imminent end of World War I (1914–1918) and the return of soldiers, Montréal authorities demonstrated an interest in morality in general, and toward prostitution in particular. Montréal's Catholic and Protestant churches united for a war against vice and the target was prostitution (Lévesque 1995, 95). That summer, Police Chief Joseph Tremblay ordered the search of 350 known brothels and that same night 200 people were arrested. Later Tremblay wrote to Robert Laird Borden, then Québec's Premier, that some houses of ill repute seemed to enjoy some form of protection. Upon hearing about the event, Judge Geoffrion harshly criticized Tremblay for these arrests. Again, this type of altercation illustrated the expression of a profound division between the bench (judges) and the police in their views of prostitution (96).

At the end of 1918, a citizens' committee, Comité des Seize, dedicated to the abolition of vice in Montréal, produced a report that fascinated the public (Lévesque 1995, 93). Indeed, the Committee produced the results of a New York study on Montréal's sex trade industry, which demonstrated the level of exploitation suffered by women working in brothels (96). Women were forced to work long hours for little pay, some were using their daughters to increase family earnings, and one-third of the women working in brothels were under the age of eighteen. The Committee's main conclusion was that although commercial sex might be impossible to stop, the third party, that is, brothels and pimps could and must be stopped. And so, the prohibitionists, not unlike the Ladies' Associations in England, cultivated a discourse that linked vice to the degeneration of the city and the decline of specific populations.[12] In fact, the prohibitionists believed that vice and mental illness were related and if left untreated could "trickle down" six generations (Lévesque 1995). The Committee attributed crime, illegitimate births, and diseases to the "prostitute" (97) and demanded that institutions, such as group homes, be placed at the disposal of the "diseased prostitute" to protect both the city and "the prostitute." As a result, the approach to prostitution was a combination of prevention, rehabilitation, and repression (98).

Prevention was founded on educating the public; hence, Canadian middle-class women accepted a responsibility to help and to be intolerant of a situation which, if left alone, might degenerate. The causes of prostitution, they believed, were poverty, unsanitary conditions, overcrowding, and uncontrolled leisure time mainly for "the young domestic" (99). Supervision began in the home, and for the Committee, children of alcoholic parents left without supervision became targets for pimps. Despite their own diagnostic, the committee did not attack issues such as poverty and low salaries; they chose to work within the existing social conditions (100), and again the underlying issue was a personal weakness. Women exchanging sexual services for money were perceived as fallen women and beginning in 1919 became objects for rehabilitation. In Montréal, women's organizations, such as the Conseil local des femmes de Montréal (CLFM), demanded the creation of reform schools for women coming out of jail. There were reform schools for girls but nothing for women. These reform schools were intended for "prostitutes" who, according to the CLFM, could find redemption through work. The committee relied on the same discourse: Montréal needed institutions for adult women coming out of jail or those who were simply victims of Montréal's immoral environment (100). Montréal's Police Chief Joseph Tremblay did not believe the chances of rehabilitation were high. Most of the organizations worked with the full knowledge that they would achieve only a small degree of success, especially in helping women to find work. Even in the domestic help trade, the risk of being fired because of one's past was very high. Rehabilitation remained difficult, and repression became the Committee's primary activity.

The lofty vision of putting an end to prostitution was not easily accomplished. Times of prosperity such as those brought about by the end of the First World War did not slow down activities linked to prostitution. In 1917, to the contrary, Montréal had at least 200 to 300 brothels. By the following year 350 brothels were known to exist on the island of Montréal with 50 percent of prostitution occurring within their walls (Lévesque 1995). In 1918, the worldwide Spanish influenza epidemic forced health authorities to order the closure of most public places; the brothels doubled their business (Lévesque 1995). That same year, the Committee published its first report on prostitution and attracted some media attention. The report was made into a booklet and widely distributed (101).

Le Devoir, a perennial Montréal newspaper, supported the Committee and decided to circulate the report. The paper linked prostitution to other social concerns, such as the influx of rural dwellers to the city and people's indifference concerning commercial vice. However, *La Patrie*, a Montréal popular newspaper founded in 1879, disagreed with the Committee and *Le Devoir*'s decision to publicize the report. Montréal's Anglophone press supported *La Patrie* and, along with Montréal mayor Médéric Martin, deplored that by disseminating vulgar events, which should have remained hidden (Lévesque 1995, 102), the Committee had promoted Montréal as a city of vice. The disagreement, however, did not stop the Committee and in February 1919 it launched its campaign against brothel owners. The Committee won its first battle when article 781 of the criminal code was amended so that brothel owners could be arrested with no chance of making bail if arrested twice at the same address. A case was brought to court and lost, rendering all the Committee's efforts worthless and once again illustrating the opposing positions between the bench and the police regarding prostitution (102–3).[13] It soon became clear to reformers that the abolition of prostitution was not as straightforward as they had thought.

In January 1923, the Committee published its fourth report and Dr. A. K. Haywood held a conference focusing on the commerce of vice and narcotics. He concluded that since the Committee's first report, in 1918, prostitution remained prevalent in Montréal. Therefore, he demanded the collaboration of Montréal's recorders to help him eliminate this vice, believing that nothing less would suffice. Following this conference, Montréal witnessed a concerted effort to abolish prostitution. The Committee reminded the authorities that laws existed, and these must be applied. In 1923, the city of Montréal registered the most significant number of arrests since 1920 (Lévesque 1995, 106). The number of arrests may have increased, but they did not target clients and brothel owners who usually paid less than the fines demanded of sex trade workers.

As in England, Montréal's women had a special mission in society's restoration. After all, women, considered to have superior morals, were always to be consulted regarding social matters (106). Protestant leaders asked for increased public participation by women to instill morals. Moreover, Reverend McManus, an Anglican minister, suggested that order in the city would not be re-established until women sat at city hall. The Methodist church joined the demand. Parallel to these efforts, the bench ridiculed women and the prohibitionists, and despite their hard work, according to Lévesque, by the end of 1923 Montréal's brothels were thriving. In 1924, Mayor Médéric Martin, who supported the idea of a red light district, was defeated and Charles Duquette was elected, but to no avail—the sex trade still flourished (108). Once again reformers, police, and the bench disagreed on how to control, manage, or eradicate prostitution.

In 1924, the Comité des Seize once again called in specialists, this time from Chicago, New York, and New Orleans, to study the state of Montréal's "moral downfall." In March 1924, two young Chicago detectives, one an ex-marine, investigating the situation in Montréal declared it "the most wide, the most open town I have ever seen . . . the rottenest town I have ever been in" (Lévesque 1995, 108). Both men reinforced what the Committee had been trying to say. The same year, following a murder in the red light district, suspecting judicial and police corruption, prohibitionists demanded an inquiry. On October 6, 1924, Judge Louis Coderre became the president of what came to be known as the Coderre Inquiry. The commission issued its report on March 13, 1925, and for the next six years, the Committee prolonged its efforts, giving conferences, producing a press release, and publishing different reports to sway public opinion and stop commercial vice (94).

The prostitution issue was particularly offensive to French Canadian judges. Concerned with the moral and biological effect on the French-Canadian race, Judge Coderre recommended the elimination of prostitution (Brodeur 1984, 31). Moreover, resting on the Committee's conclusions, Judge Coderre maintained that medical examinations of street sex workers gave the public a false sense of security. As well, like the English Repealers, he was against mandatory testing. In his report, the judge remained ambivalent, knowing full well that refusing to change the bylaw encouraged underground prostitution, and the proliferation of venereal diseases (35). He nonetheless agreed with the prohibitionists and demanded the complete elimination of prostitution in Montréal; he did not see the advantages even for health reasons to maintain a red light district. He recommended a firm suppression of prostitution and upheld that it was the only way to save the "prostitute" from exploitation. It was also necessary to save the French-Canadian race from collective suicide by venereal diseases and eliminating police corruption (Lévesque 1995, 113). The reaction was immediate. Police officers were offended and tried to annul the report, the media coverage was massive, and public opinion was excited. Women's groups were satisfied with Coderre's recommendation and offered their support. These events that tarnished the city's reputation were without consequence, and in 1926 Médéric Martin and the entire executive were re-elected (114). Protected by the police force, the brothels continued to thrive; their numbers had not diminished since 1923. Lévesque's (1995) synopsis corroborates the findings of Shaver (1996–2009) and Lowman (2001–2001), who both maintained that by 1920 the Canadian Social Purity Movement started to wane, and prostitution was no longer a public issue. Shaver maintains that from 1920 to 1944 the sex industry in Canada continued to operate without public interference (Shaver 1996, 212–214; see also table 9.2). As for Lowman, he suggests that in Canada the lax attitude regarding prostitution was maintained until 1970. However, Lacasse, in *La Prostitution féminine à Montréal 1945–1970* (1994), challenges Lowman's claim by stating that, in Montréal, the concerted effort to control venereal diseases came in 1944 and, as in England, it came from the military.

MONTRÉAL 1944–2000: THE MILITARY ROLE IN THE GRADUAL DISAPPEARANCE OF THE BROTHELS

Montréal's brothels survived the Great War, the economic crisis of 1929, and the Second World War (1939–1945). Although under constant surveillance and attack from diverse moral organizations, the brothels remained at the heart of the red light district. In 1940, about 100 brothels were still operating between Saint-Laurent, Craig, Saint-Denis, and Sherbrooke. Lacasse reports that location and prestige went together. The brothels open for the public were inside the red light district. Outside the red light district were semi-open houses and these were by referral from a regular patron, or by taxi drivers who brought their clients. Lastly, also situated outside the red light district, were the very private, completely closed houses reserved for the wealthier clientele (Lacasse 1994, 63).

In January 1944, the Canadian Army sounded the alarm regarding venereal diseases (VD). Major E. J. Renaud revealed that 16 percent of the soldiers stationed in Montréal suffered from VD (Lacasse 1994, 47; Brodeur 1985,

50). Consequently, on February 2, 1944, Renaud sent a letter to Montréal's City Hall. The letter threatened to forbid soldiers to be stationed in Montréal if authorities did not take the necessary measures to fight prostitution (Brodeur 1985, 50). So, after being in operation for almost one hundred years, from 1850 to 1944, the red light district "disappeared" overnight! Three significant inquiries,[14] public outcries, and repeated scandals had not succeeded in altering the conduct of brothel owners, much less forcing them to close (61). This resistance makes it hard to deny the link between some judges, police, and brothel owners again demonstrating the city's ambivalence toward prostitution. Some brothels still operated without much trouble; nevertheless, the situation was troublesome.

On February 26, 1945, the Hygiene Commission of the city of Montréal demanded that a special committee be formed to study the state of sexually transmitted disease in Montréal. Camilien Houde, the mayor at the time, seven doctors, the chief of police, and an army representative comprised the committee. Federal, provincial, and municipal health services became involved in the autumn of 1945 (Lacasse 1994, 48). Concerning venereal diseases, health services held the brothels responsible for their spread because they served the highest number of clients and suggested the cleanup should begin there. The following year, the Fédération des Ligues du Sacré Coeur, in existence since 1883 to fight intemperance, held an inquest into certain public places they suspected were harboring "prostitutes." Their first target was the red light district where prostitution was most visible (Lacasse 1994). Following the visit to the district, a member of the Fédération attacked the permissiveness of the police and the way these places were protected (39). As in England, women exchanging sexual services for a fee became the primary target and *they* became the problem detached from social causes. Newspapers played a major role in the next inquest, one that would change Montréal nightlife forever.

Beginning on May 8, 1948, *Le Devoir* published a series of articles written by a young lawyer named Pacific (Pax) Plante. The series, titled "Montréal under mafia's rule," ended on November 28, 1949, and, according to Brodeur (1985, 52), these articles were interpreted as a call to establish an inquiry. In January 1950, after being made aware of foreign articles praising Montréal nightlife, a religious committee[15] demanded action against immorality. On February 7, 1950, the Fédération began a crusade against vice. By March 1950, within the framework of the *Ligne d'action civique*, thirty-five Montréal associations, including the Jesuits, demanded an inquiry. On May 11, 1950, Me Jean Drapeau, another young lawyer representing the different associations, officially requested an inquest. Forming a team, Drapeau and Plante proceeded to do away with brothels, blind pigs (after hours bars), and organized crime (Bélanger 2005, 21). Thus, on May 31, 1950, Judge Tyndale ordered an inquiry. As with the Cannon Inquiry of 1909, the investigation aimed to examine the status of gambling and prostitution in Montréal; however, it essentially investigated police actions (52). Repeated inquiries had not succeeded in eradicating Montréal's sex industry which raised suspicions and ultimately launched the largest inquiry ever: the Caron Inquiry, 1950–1953. This inquiry gave Montréal's nightlife its *coup de grace*; the city's sex and adult entertainment industry would never be the same. After this last inquest, Montréal's brothels slowly vanished, to be replaced by another form of sex work: the strip clubs, which until that moment had not been the authorities' primary target.

From 1890, in North America, burlesque entertainment presented women displaying their bodies, but not removing their clothes (Bruckert 2002). In 1910, disrobing behind a screen began, followed in 1920 by stripping. The costumes were elaborate and the choreography extensive. The focus was the tease, not the nudity. In Montréal, the uncontested star remains the legendary Lily St-Cyr (DiNardo 2007). Tall, blonde, and beautiful, St-Cyr embodied the strippers' mystique. She presented her act at the Gayety Theatre, today the Théatre du Nouveau Monde, on Sainte-Catherine Street. Performing in Montréal from 1940 to 1955, arrested in 1951, St-Cyr was a "casualty" of Judge Caron's inquest (Bélanger 2005).

The Birth of the Strip Clubs

In the late 1960s strippers were not that different from the *posture molls* of eighteenth-century London, "who stripped naked and mounted on the table to show their beauty" (Burford in Bruckert 2002). Posture molls would excite their clients, but never sexually satisfy them. They, as with the strippers or go-go dancers, carefully differentiated themselves from "prostitutes" (Bruckert 2002). In 1967, the York Hotel, under the management of Olivier Lamoureux, introduced Montréal's first go-go dancers as an integral part of the club. Dancers, wearing pasties, performed all day to the sound of a jukebox; and they continued all night between live entertainment and shows given by a guest stripper, the star of the evening. In 1972, club owners asked dancers to remove their pasties; dancers accepted an action that set a precedent. The York burned down in 1973, but not before establishing the strippers and go-go dancers, as workers. Continuing what the York Hotel had started, Montréal witnessed an explosion of bars, hotels, and taverns all offering go-go dancers, strippers, and live music. Strip clubs were businesses with punch cards and paychecks. Gradually, strip clubs eliminated the strippers and hired go-go dancers who progressively showed more nudity. The clubs also included porn movies and speciality acts such as the *erotic couple*. Next came table dance, and as the clothing fell, so did the salary.

Like escorting, the field of stripping has changed drastically over time. Gone are the days of teasing clientele with a flirty grin and the slow removal of one's bra top. Today strippers must take it all off leaving nothing to the imagination; VIP rooms are now the location where all forms of sexual acts occur, despite not being advertised as the case. In the 1990s, dancers were not remunerated at all, but had to pay a fee for the right to use the premises to work. Strippers today must pay to dance, unlike in the past when the clubs compensated them for their time which should have continued. Many customers choose to take advantage of the situation, coming into the clubs to gawk at the strippers without compensating them for their time and getting off on watching them for free. At least before, there was a salary to pay for slow days. Although the sexual geography was somewhat different, Montréal still maintained its reputation vis-à-vis adult entertainment, and the same uneasiness persisted at the time of Stella's creation in 1995.

At the end of this chapter, it is evident that Montréal mayor Jean Drapeau's and his partner Pacific "Pax" Plante's fixation on changing the city's reputation created a vacuum that changed the city's sex scene and produced an unplanned and different environment—the night club. The openness of the nightclub scene allowed strippers and go-go dancers to meet one another, and also allowed health officials to find them. At the end of the chapter I cannot but use the words of Alex Tigchelaar because I am reminded how "sex workers may make visible the idiosyncratic state of providing vitality to a city's history while simultaneously being excluded from its living present" (2019, 15). Attracting flocks of tourists during the US prohibition, showgirls and women exchanging sexual services in brothels, bars, or soliciting on the street were carrying the same stigma—the whore stigma. They were stereotyped as vectors of disease, such as syphilis and HIV, or as drug addicts who were linked to criminal activities. In 1992, it was these same women that the health branch of our government mandated to combat HIV. Strippers, street-based sex workers, recovering drug addicts, and escorts agreed to be identified and began the massive task of mobilizing their troops to be part of a pilot project that became one of the strongest sites of resistance in Canada. Mobilizing people is already quite a task; mobilizing underground, criminalized women is a considerable endeavor. The next chapter recalls this venture.

NOTES

1. The War of 1812 between Britain and the United States, and the revolt of the Patriots against colonization resulting in the Rebellions of 1837 and 1838, had increased the number of soldiers stationed in Montréal.

2. 1920–1933.

3. This analysis concerning the practice of prostitution is new because until recently most historians took the mid-1800s as their point of departure. Historians such as Solé, Poutanen, and Gilfoyle changed that. They offer an analysis beginning before the creation of red light districts. Poutanen maintains that such was the situation in Montréal during the first half of the 1800s.

4. As a matter of fact, Poutanen reports that madams could count on police help without fear of being arrested.

5. Criminologist Jean-Paul Brodeur maintains that red light districts appeared in 1850 (1984, 50).

6. Sanguinet, Saint-Laurent, and Saint-Catherine and Craig Streets.

7. See Valverde (1991) and Bélanger (2005) for a discussion on the reform as both argue that Protestants and Catholics approached the issue of prostitution differently. The temperance and reform movement emerged from England.

8. Institut Canadien de Montréal.

9. Keeping records—archiving.

10. In 1881, even as Montréal became Canada's capital, the improved economy notwithstanding, all was not well in the city. Concurrent with its economic growth, the city's population doubled in the following ten years, increasing the ever-present health concerns.

11. However, Judge De Montigny's decision and the recommendations from the aforementioned publication were insufficient to bring about a public consensus (Lévesque 1995). Consequently, Judge Dugas interpreted De Montigny's suggestion as too lax, and one that might encourage police corruption since the police could fine certain establishments while ignoring others (Lévesque 1995, 90). In 1894, suspecting police corruption, Deputy Mayor Rainville called for an inquiry (Rainville Inquiry), which disclosed the complicity between police and brothel owners (Brodeur 1984, 16). Eventually, another judge ordered a further investigation. This time the bench placed some brothels under surveillance in order to discourage corruption.

12. The Social Purity Movement did not have the same hold in Montréal, where according to sociologist Caroline Knowles and historian Andrée Lévesque social issues were debated in biological terms (Lévesque 1994; Knowles 1996). Both researchers report that Carrie Derick, a professor of botany at McGill University, used her scientific expertise to demonstrate that 60 percent to 75 percent of "prostitutes" were somewhat deficient and this was the cause of their downfall. Derick's analysis coincided with Lombroso's theory about sex trade workers (Phoenix 1999). This particular discourse was well received in English Canada (Knowles 1996), but remained a controversial issue in Montréal, where economic circumstances entered the analysis. According to this narrative, "prostitutes" were victims of economic circumstances and they needed to be protected and rehabilitated (Lévesque 1995, 98).

13. Following this judgment, it became clear that landlords could rent to whomever they deemed appropriate and brothel owners operated without too many restrictions (Lévesque 1995). In 1920, the Committee, through the provincial legislature, succeeded in the adoption of an Act allowing the bench to order the closing of "les maison de désorde" for one year. Once again it was almost impossible to apply the law. Houses were owned by holding companies, and this fact made it difficult to trace their owners' manoeuvres. Moreover, not being on site, owners denied any knowledge concerning the use of the premises. In Montréal, the "vice commercialisé" seemed to be well established and that fact was demonstrated when members of the Comité accompanied representatives of the Montréal morality squad and the Montréal public security division for a visit to the red light district. Indeed, members of the Comité noticed that the "madams" continued their daily tasks seemingly undisturbed by the visit of officials (Lévesque 1995). In what seems to have been a last attempt, the Comité called upon social workers to quantify the profits made by landlords, brothel owners, and the city.

14. Deputy Mayor Rainville—Rainville Inquiry (1894); Judge Cannon—Cannon Inquiry (1909); Judge Coderre—Coderre Inquiry (1924).

15. Le Comité diocésain d'Action catholique.

Chapter Two

Stella

The Story Recalled and Analyzed from 1992 to 2000
Within the Socio-Medical and Cultural Context

In Québec, the Rochon commission created on June 20, 1985,[1] allowed for the formation of diverse community groups which focused on the issue of harm reduction. These included Séro Zéro (HIV/AIDS) and CACTUS (IV drug users). Without being named as such it is fair to say that "women at risk" (Bilodeau et al. 2002, 39) in the report signified sex workers. Once again, in the gaze of health officials, sex workers joined Dr. Catherine Hankins, nurse Sylvie Gendron, and sociologist Frances Shaver from Concordia University on September 1993 to create a pilot project to empower women to take care of their health. From the start it was clear that for sex workers to participate, the project had to meet certain criteria. This chapter recalls the founding of Stella l'amie de Maimie by a group of women who refused to be labeled and how this refusal drove the creation of Stella. In 1993, sex workers launched what Mélançon (2018) and Toupin (2009) call a movement of dissent. They rejected labels forced on them by the state (Mélançon) and prohibitionists and in doing so demonstrate that the undoing of the stereotypes is central to the organization's emergence, maintenance, and longevity.

PLANTING THE SEEDS FOR STELLA:
ALLIANCE FOR THE SAFETY OF PROSTITUTES

In 1980, in Vancouver, a group of primarily "high-profile, white, upwardly-mobile men and women, led by a gay man Gordon Price, formed Concerned Residents of the West End (CROWE)" and began organizing to eliminate prostitution from their neighborhood (see Ross and Sullivan 2012 for a history of CROWE). In 1982, sex worker Sally de Quatros joined forces with Marie Arrington to form the Alliance for the Safety of Prostitutes (the Alliance) in Vancouver, British Columbia. By 1984, the group was holding protests when CROWE's campaign turned into harassment of sex workers.[2] That same year on June 20, twelve members of ASP occupied Christ Church Cathedral[3] to protest CROWE's violence as well as an injunction by the attorney general banning sex work west of Granville Street in Vancouver (Ross and Sullivan 2012, 613). In 1985, ASP organized to challenge the new communications law that made most street sex work illegal in Canada. The result of the amendment was Bill C-49 that revised Criminal Code section 213 (solicitation law), which "criminalize[d] communication in a public place for the purposes of engaging in prostitution or of obtaining the services of a prostitute" (Criminal Code of Canada–House of Commons 2006, 42). Adopted on December 20, 1985, and in application across Canada on January 10, 1986, this new law targeted street prostitution. The Alliance argued against the changes made to these solicitation laws (Bill C-49), because for the Alliance it opened the door to arbitrary policing and repression. Two members of CROWE left the group because of the attitude of some white middle-class women, and instead helped sex workers to organize, giving birth to a network (Dumont and Toupin 2003, 617). A branch of the Alliance was born in Montréal a few months after the adoption of the bill and lasted one year; however, despite its short life, in May 1986 Montréal's ASP branch sent an open letter to Montréal magazine *Communiqu' ells* (616–21). The letter was published the same year. The following paragraphs outline the content of the letter that recalls the ASP position regarding prostitution and the laws circumscribing it.

According to Dumont and Toupin (2003), the Alliance did not imagine prostitution as a choice, but as an activity imposed on women mainly for economic reasons and their social position (2003, 617). The general goal of the Alliance was to create a society where women did not have to resort to prostitution and although ambivalent regarding prostitution, the group maintained a strong conviction that sex workers should be safe. For the Alliance, decriminalization of prostitution was not the final solution because it did not address the underlying causes of prostitution and so they recommended the creation of services to help eliminate circumstances leading to prostitution.

The Alliance rejected the rationale behind the criminalization of prostitution. The group did not give credence to municipal authorities who asserted that they could dissuade women from exercising their craft on the street by applying criminal law. The Alliance contended that for many street workers, nothing would keep them off the street. They did not fear going to jail or being ticketed. Some women had accumulated close to $2,000 in fines, making it impossible to leave the sex work milieu and their source of income that would pay those fines. The Alliance denounced the application of criminal status as being responsible for the illegal situation and the increased violence. Forced to work in isolation, more sex workers were relying on third parties—often referred to as "pimps"—to ensure their security. The Alliance argued that targeting street prostitution was not a solution and by targeting the most vulnerable women it could limit their efforts to change their circumstances. Therefore, although the Alliance was not supportive of the existence of prostitution, per se, they still attributed blame for violence and the lack of safety in sex work to the legal system, that is, the criminalization of prostitution.

The Alliance made an important distinction between decriminalization and legalization, stating that decriminalization would offer, on a short-term basis, the opportunity for women to work safely and under conditions that would increase their control over their lives. Legalization, however, would cause women to work within a structure where women could be exploited. The Alliance was against legalization such as in Germany's Eros Centra where women advertise in windows, something that they found degrading and imposing constraints on women. Decriminalization, on the other hand, would allow women the space needed to work at their own pace and perhaps leave the sex work milieu without a criminal dossier. As far as people who worried about the possible effects of decriminalization, such as noise and public nuisance, the Alliance answered that municipal laws were sufficient to control these matters.

The Alliance questioned the government's decisions to invest money into repression that was cruel and did not work. Why was the same government not investing in programs offering true alternatives, instead of investing in cruel and useless repression? Why not attack the real causes of prostitution (Dumont and Toupin 2003, 620) such as poverty and lack of real choices? Instead of arresting sex workers, the Alliance argued, government agencies should be developing a referral list to help women obtain necessary services.

At that time, the Alliance translated a booklet from Calgary entitled *Towards an Understanding of Prostitution*. Often ridiculed and insulted by the public and prohibitionists, sex workers are repeatedly dismissed as being a part of the underclass, and defenseless victims or in collaboration with patriarchy and exploited. This of course is a simplistic analysis which denies women the recognition as actors; hence, the Alliance suggested that myths should be exposed, and that dialogue should be opened. Clearly aware of the "whore stigma," the Alliance was committed to changing the myths that separate women into groups of "good" and "bad" and the group offered workshops to educate and undo this social attitude that separates women (Dumont and Toupin 2003, 621).

The Alliance's discourse was making the same claim as that of Call Off Your Old Tired Ethics (COYOTE), who without celebrating the sex work milieu stated that keeping prostitution underground causes a continuation of violence against women who work in the sex industry. In fact, in its brief life in Québec, the Alliance challenged the whore stigma and the laws, that is, they fought the conceptualization of sex workers as victims, and the useless, dangerous, and biased nature of the communication laws. Although the group held a critical stance regarding prostitution, it did not back away from denouncing violence and they produced Montréal's first Bad Trick List (*Con-Stellation* 2005b, 102). The Alliance may have theorized prostitution not as a choice but rather being forced onto women. However, it is clear from the writings of Dumont and Toupin (2003) and Stella (*ConStellation* 2005b) that the Alliance always treated sex workers with respect, attesting that women's groups can disagree and still place women's security first. As Brock (1998) states, prostitution is not a social problem but a social issue that must be understood and discussed. The Alliance was one of the first groups to organize in Montréal; while they did not exist for long, they planted the seeds for other local sex workers to mobilize, such that they were ready when a window of opportunity opened in 1988. The context for sex worker organizing has been ripe throughout the years, and before the creation of Stella, Montréal sex workers were mobilizing in formal and informal ways.

Parent (2001) posits that the socio-political-cultural context of the 1960s had been a receptive environment for sex workers. The Cultural/Sexual Revolution was at its peak with the feminist movement and the burgeoning gay rights movement heralded the beginning of a new era. In fact, COYOTE in the United States, the De Rode Draad[4] in Amsterdam, and le mouvement des églises in France all took advantage of cultural change in the 60s to articulate their first claims and begin organizing. Canadian sex workers' groups emerging in the 1980s and after operated in a relatively different socio-political and health climate than that of COYOTE, De Rode Draad, or le mouvement des églises.

Precondition of Stella's Emergence: Socio-Medical Context, 1970 to Late 1980s

In November 1979, Québec medical authorities diagnosed the first case of acquired immune deficiency syndrome (AIDS) (Bilodeau et al. 2002, 25).[5] In Montréal, HIV/AIDS was first identified within the Haitian population and among homosexual and bisexual men. The media coverage of the new illness and its probable causes resulted in its association with the gay community and was not perceived as an overall public health concern. Therefore, in 1982, the first organization, a Québec HIV/AIDS Committee (CSQ),[6] targeted gay communities but not the general public. One year later, in October 1983, medical authorities officially declared HIV/AIDS a disease and two years later the idea that all people are at risk of contracting HIV became more widely understood. It was in this context that in 1985, with the release of provincial funds following the recommendation of the CSQ, the first community groups began to formally organize. Accommodations and support were offered to victims of HIV/AIDS (see Bilodeau et al. 2002 for a complete list of these resources).

In March 1987, the CSQ was dismantled, and the Ministry of Health and Social Welfare (MSSS) announced phase I of its plan to fight HIV/AIDS. Former members of CSQ worked along with the MSSS to build the basis for Québec policies in terms of HIV/AIDS. These measures were made in preparation for phase II which aimed to inform and educate the public. The MSSS announced these prevention measures on December 1, 1988, during the first World HIV/AIDS Day. In Québec, most community groups were created between 1987 and 1992 during the implementation of phase II, which recommended that financial assistance to community groups be increased.

Collective action is usually triggered by historical conditions, and the creation of Stella is no different. Stella was formed during phase III of the Rochon commission. It is important, however, to recall the main events that led to its creation and of a few other community organizations commissioned to reach and inform different populations on HIV/AIDS prevention in Montréal.

Health Canada was, without a doubt, the quickest institutional actor to respond to the HIV/AIDS pandemic and to favor community involvement in program development and application. In 1989, MSSS created the HIV/ AIDS coordination center, the Centre Québécois de coordination sur le sida (CQCS), whose function was to coordinate all that was being done in Québec in terms of HIV/AIDS programming. Also, in 1989, the MSSS subsidized the creation of hospital research units (UHRESS). During that period, the gay population contested the presence of the CQCS, maintaining that the HIV/ AIDS pandemic should not be approached as a "gay problem" but as a civilian one. In order to harmonize the relationship between the MSSS and the gay population,[7] the CQCS decided to adapt its program. Considering the nature of the problem, which was understood and analyzed as risky sexual practices, the CQCS decided to call upon community interveners,[8] recognizing that they should participate in the development and coordination of the project. In recognizing the creation of a community resource, the MSSS acknowledged the expertise of community workers. As part of an advisory committee, Séro Zéro, today called Rézo, became the first coordinated effort to establish education and prevention programs. Starting with small private donations, Séro Zéro soon became a major player in the fight against HIV/ AIDS. Its mandate was and remains HIV/AIDS prevention.

Following the creation of Séro Zéro, the 1990s witnessed the creation of Québec community organizations whose common goal was the fight against HIV/AIDS. In 1991, these community groups formed a coalition called the COCQ-sida. That year, a community action SIDA (PAC-SIDA) was already sustaining numerous non-governmental organizations (NGOs). In that year alone, different Canadian health agencies funded 119 projects. Health Canada was responsible for the first injection drug users' program in Québec when in 1989 the health departments of two Montréal hospitals, Montréal General and Maisonneuve-Rosemont, created CACTUS.[9] At this point, I must underline that in Canada, HIV/AIDS was diagnosed as a health issue, not a moral one. Therefore, in Québec, Health Canada's role was mainly at the financial and project planning levels.

A Window of Opportunity: 1990s

Between 1988 and 1989 researchers from the Centre for HIV/AIDS Studies (CAS), the Montréal-Centre Regional Public Health Team, CLSC Ahuntsic, the Bureau of Laboratory and Research Services, and the Department of National Health Canada, led by Catherine Hankins, MD, examined the connection between needle use and sexual practices to HIV[10] among incarcerated women. This research was conducted in Montréal, and 394 women participated. Women volunteered for an HIV test and then responded to a risk factor questionnaire. Through the questionnaire, researchers were able to identify three risk-taking activities: 1) injecting drugs, 2) having unprotected sexual relations with a partner who injected drugs and/or had HIV, and 3) engaging in prostitution as a major source of revenue. The study concluded that the risk of HIV transmission increased with the first two risk-taking activities, that of injecting drugs and/or having unprotected sexual relations with a partner who injected drugs (Hankins et al. 1994, 1637). Most importantly, it was not necessarily the activity itself that the study identified as a risk factor but rather the conditions under which sex workers are laboring and living that placed them at higher risk for HIV—notably criminalization, stigmatization, and discrimination of sex workers, their work, and the people in their lives. Their study was pivotal to the creation of Stella and the holistic approach that Stella took to safe sex, health, working conditions, and overall safety for sex workers. Stella placed sex workers at the center of the struggle against HIV and recognized the surrounding structural factors that contributed to HIV transmission.

Led by Hankins, researchers from the CAS demanded and obtained a grant to study the feasibility of setting up some sort of intervention program that would disseminate health information specifically to Montréal-Centre's street sex workers. A grant from the Regional Health and Social Services Board of Montréal-Centre led to consultations with sex workers and diverse organizations who were in contact with them (Stella 1996a, 2). The programs, initiated in 1990, followed the recommendations of the Rochon commission from 1988. During the first three years, programs subsidized by the Ministry of Health and Social Welfare (MSSS) focused on gay and bisexual men. In phase III of the program of the CQCS and the MSSS "money was made available for gay and bisexual men, users of injectable drugs, young people in difficulties and women at risk" (Bilodeau et al. 2002, 39). The variable of "women's lifestyle"—particularly that of the street sex workers— appeared and it was within that conjuncture of public health concerns that the Centre of HIV/AIDS Studies planned a program specific to sex workers. The HIV/AIDS pandemic and the ensuing public health concern created an opportunity for sex workers to formally form community, to mobilize their knowledge of safer sex practices, and to educate one another on how to take care in a context of social, state, and legal repression. This was not the first time that sex workers would care for each other and their community this way—there are numerous undocumented and unrecognized mobilizations of sex workers in a context of an HIV epidemic, poverty, homelessness, and other social issues where sex workers organized. The attention, however, from public health provided an opportunity for sex workers to organize in a different way, and with more resources (Clamen and Crago 2013).

Projet Stella: The Ground Work—1992–1995

In April 1992, Projet d'intervention auprès des mineurs dans le prostitution (P.I.a.M.P),[11] a harm reduction service organization for minors in the sex industry, organized a seminar at l'Université du Québec à Montréal (UQÀM). The meeting included psychologist Gail Pheterson, sex workers from Montréal, and other feminists and academics. As the meeting concluded, a new sex worker rights group was born in Montréal—the Association Québécoise des travailleuses et travailleurs du sexe (AQTTS). In Montréal, the AQTTS framed its demands as the International Committee for Prostitutes Right (ICPR)[12] had done, with demands for law reform, better working conditions, and access to better health services and resources. By demanding the decriminalization of sex work, the AQTTS grounded its mandate in the criminalization of sex work, and that sex workers' criminal status was the main obstacle to obtaining safe working conditions, which in turn affects sex workers' health. As their work began in 1992, they sought to organize with sex workers for participation in a harm reduction project.

The first meetings were located at the Public Health Unit of the Montréal General Hospital. These meetings included three members of the Centre for HIV/AIDS Studies (CES), Catherine Hankins, Sylvie Gendron, and Caroline Ford, Claire Thiboutot of AQTTS, Robert Paris of P.I.a.M.P, Thomas McKeown from CACTUS, a center helping intravenous drug users, and Frances Shaver of Concordia University.[13] The main objective of the meeting was to explore the feasibility of an HIV/AIDS prevention program aimed at supporting street sex workers in Montréal-Centre (CES 1993a). At the first meeting, the team identified three main safety considerations for sex work and challenges for safer sex practices: criminalization regimes, barriers to safe drug consumption, and safer sex practices in non-sex-work-related sexual relationships. According to Shaver, Thiboutot, Paris, and McKeown, harassment from Montréal police had also intensified at this time (CES 1993a, 2). In addition to criminal laws, sex workers were overpoliced by municipal laws and general law and order mandates, although being residents of the neighborhoods they worked in, they were often regarded as a public nuisance and overpoliced as a result. A second obstacle was the barriers to safe drug consumption such as clean equipment, needle, pipes, and other drug paraphernalia. Shaver, who had just completed research with downtown Montréal sex workers, identified risks such as intravenous drug use as related to HIV risk. Hankins et al. (1994) also confirmed this through their research. A third challenge for sex workers was that while sex workers may use condoms at work, they were less likely to wear them with their intimate partners, because they considered condoms as working tools (CES 1993a, 2).[14]

During that first meeting, the AQTTS raised their fear around relying on HIV/AIDS funding alone.[15] Their concern was justified: sex workers have long been constructed as vectors of disease, despite sex workers being the first to protect their bodies as their working tool. The context in which sex workers live and work, however, create conditions that compromise their health and safety, notably, criminalization of sex work, sex workers' relationships, and the capacity for sex workers to have access to the working materials they need to keep safe. These barriers to HIV prevention and overall health care are important issues for sex workers but often ignored. While sex workers navigated this difficult space, the general population maintained as its common belief that sex workers were vectors for HIV and other sexually transmitted infections. The use of HIV/AIDS funding to debunk these myths, to address the structural factors that lead to HIV transmission, and simultaneously encourage safer sex practices in sex working communities was part of the challenge that lay ahead. It was clear by the end of that first meeting that an HIV/AIDS intervention program needed a holistic approach which included addressing the criminal status and socio-economic environment of sex workers—the conditions under which sex workers were working increased vulnerability to HIV and hindered their capacity to act securely (CES 1993a, 4). Collective action frames and framing processes have become essential in comprehending and explaining collective action. Sex workers' challenges were often perceived as individual problems, and the structural factors that rendered sex workers vulnerable to arrest, incarceration, homelessness, etc. were often ignored. This new project centered on these structural issues and on sex workers' agency and their capacity to address them. During these meetings, Shaver often reiterated the need for a project that would address the issue of working conditions (CES 1993c, 3). She stressed that it was not about modifying their work but rather changing their working conditions. Women must be informed of their rights when they face the police (CES 1993c, 4). These exchanges among members of the team revealed their ethical identity[16]—where they stood on sex work. The main concern was the health and safety of sex workers and the point of departure was the environment, not the individual. That was highlighted again in January 1994 when, during the fourth meeting, Hankins underlined the fact that although the grant application needed to meet the objectives of the sponsors, that is, public health agencies, she was aware that a program focusing on the individual would not be successful. Her position reflects empowerment principles which demand an awareness of the intersection between the individual and the structures which she inhabits.

The AQTTS wanted their pilot project to resemble Maggie's in Toronto,[17] the first Canadian, government-funded sex worker–led project founded in 1986.[18] Sex workers around the table wanted their work to focus on the protection of and access to rights, including labor rights—this would include a holistic approach not only to providing services, but to be a group focused on action and social change.[19] All those involved stressed the importance of improving the working and living conditions for sex workers; this included education for sex workers about their rights as residents when they face the police (CES 1993c, 4) and around health and safety in these contexts. Morality of sex work was not the issue.

On February 23, 1994, the founding group held a meeting in the old red light district, in an attempt to make it more accessible for sex workers who wished to join the group; they functioned as an advisory committee to set up the project. It was fundamental that the project be informed by the needs of people working in the industry—sex workers had to be involved every step of the way. On April 20, 1994, the group decided on the project's name: It would be called Stella, and from then on was referred to as Projet Stella (CES 1994c, 3). The name of the projet was inspired by a similar resource in Montréal founded after World War II by Maimie Pinzer (pen name), a former sex worker from New York (Stella 2005b, 19). Stella Phillips (name change) was Maimie's protégée (Pinzer 1977)[20] and for Maimie she was "the handsomest girl [that I] ever seen" (248). The project would later be officially deemed "Stella, l'amie de Maimie"—Stella, a friend of Maimie. The first funding application was for an eighteen-month pilot project grounded in the concept of empowerment, where sex workers' agency and capacity to make decisions were centered, and the role of sex workers in service provision was prioritized.

The projet soon hired its first coordinator and shortly afterward, in October 1994, the advisory committee—CACTUS, CASM, and AQTTS—met with community and public organizations from Montréal-Centre and Centre-Sud to present Projet Stella and its philosophy of service provision and action, as well as its focus on female-identified sex workers in the industry, including cis and trans women.[21] A mission statement, a philosophy, and a charter were written with a view to incorporating the project and ensuring its autonomy. Next, sex workers and members of the committee had to decide where in the city they wanted to locate, and which area was best suited for the site. It was reiterated that Stella was to serve as a meeting place where sex workers can connect and exchange, that is, a drop in not a service center (CES 1994i, 1). Projet Stella received its first funding from Health Canada— $40,000 for three years—in November 1994 (CES 1994f). There was no money allotted for rent and maintenance of Stella's local, rather only money to spend on service delivery. The budget had to take this fact under consideration, and other financial resources had to be found (CES 1994f, 1). And Stella for awhile used the Québec Federation for family planning (FQPN) charity number to obtain funds. Later, in the spring of 1995, other monies came from the MSSS—Québec's health minister.

In February 1995, the first round of interviews began, and Stella's first outreach workers team was created (Stella 1996a, 2). The appellation Projet Stella disappeared from the minutes in March 1995, and the organization was referred to simply as Stella (Stella 1995a). The phone line was set up, the logo was designed, and business cards were printed. Sylvie, one of Stella's first outreach workers, recalled the story behind the logo:

> In the 1980s, in order to dance in Ottawa, you needed to have an ID card if you wanted to go out to the bars after work (not even the dogs outside have tags!). My card was a nice little card. Beside my picture, they wrote that I was an artist. I was so touched; I wasn't just a "stripper." I was an artist! Also, on the card was a beautiful woman with a boa who made me feel sexy and proud. In 1995 I was hired at Stella, because of my experience. They were looking for a sexy logo, so I thought of my dancer's card. The image stuck, and it's been Stella's logo ever since. We are proud, sexy and in solidarity. (*ConStellation* 1999, 16)

The task of finding a location was not an easy one. Over a half dozen locations were rejected due to cost and accessibility (Stella 1995a). Stella's first report underlined that finding a suitable site was more difficult than anticipated (Stella 1995a). The City of Montréal did offer a place, but it was not suitable. A site was found in mid-March. On April 19, the founding group met at Stella for the first time, and the center opened on April 27, 1995, which became Stella's official birthday.[22]

Foundation and Emergence: 1995–1999

The first site was located at 1433 Saint-Laurent,[23] and at the time the address was confidential. At first, the office was used for private meetings and as a storage place for sex workers' personal belongings. The kitchen and living room were common ground, open for discussion and rest. The center was open Monday to Friday, from 2 to 8 pm (Stella 1996a, 5). It was closed during the weekends, but outreach workers were available to meet with sex workers and to promote Stella or give references concerning other resources. Everything was in place for Stella's new outreach team and in March, with the help of two community organizations, Passages and CACTUS, it began what soon became its regular rounds in Montréal's legendary red light district (*ConStellation* 2005b, 114). From 1995, Stella's representatives had already been invited to join working committees such as Prevention Action Women HIV/AIDS of Montréal[24] (PAFS) and to speak at Concordia University's Simone de Beauvoir Institute and the national workshop on women and HIV. Moreover, Stella's team was invited to participate in a workshop held in Toronto by the Canadian HIV/AIDS Society. While in Toronto, two people from Stella met with Maggie's team and received materials, supplies, and information for the project. This information was used as resources for Stella's focus groups. Lastly, Stella's representatives met with police at Station 33 to inform police officers about Stella, and to confirm their agreement to let Stella do its work in peace.[25] The chief of police at the time, Michel Sarazin, awaiting an alternative to repression, agreed to this (Stella 1995a, 5).[26] The Montréal media was equally receptive to Stella's opening—the magazine *Perspective* and journal *L'itinéraire* wrote articles to announce the arrival of the new project (Stella 1995a). In August 1995, a precursor to Stella's Bad Trick List, a communication tool that sex workers used to warn each other about violence, was written by hand and then photocopied for distribution to other sex workers (*ConStellation* 2005b, 114)—this tool was inspired by similar ones in other parts of Canada and would become one of Stella's most important communication tools for sex workers to use for violence prevention and community building. This tool was and continues to be developed through reports from sex workers about bad clients or aggressors encountered at work and aims to provide sex workers in Montréal information about potentially dangerous individuals. In a context of social and police repression, sex workers rely on this tool and others like it as a way to communicate and look out for one another. By October 1995, the first official list was distributed to downtown sex workers and was translated into French and English. It contained seven descriptions of bad incidents with clients, as well as health and safety tips (*ConStellation* 2005b, 114).

In November 1995, Stella's charter was created. It included seven points aiming to improve working and living conditions for sex workers and change public perceptions about sex work. It read: 1) Provide support and information to sex workers in their efforts to live and work in safety and with dignity; 2) Encourage the sharing of information between sex workers so that they can create links between them and develop actions in response to their needs; 3) Facilitate the exchange and the sharing of information between sex workers and existing resources on their psychosocial needs, including their health and HIV prevention needs; 4) Work in partnership with community resources; 5) Encourage the participation of sex workers at all levels of the organization; 6) Encourage knowledge and respect for the differences between women (differences of language, class, and race), and facilitate the creation of alliance between sex workers and non-sex workers; and 7) Receive donations, bequests, and other contributions of the same nature in money, securities, administer such donations, bequests, and contributions, campaigns subscriptions to raise funds for charitable purposes (Stella 1996a, 4). By framing sex work as a legitimate means of income generation, Stella created an opening for women to recognize their own legitimacy and the legitimacy of the way they decide to earn money. The practice of safer sex and rights go together: the right to protect oneself, the right to have access to services that provide help to do so, to take the time to negotiate a service, and the right to refuse a service. As it was made clear during a protest against police brutality, "violence is not a part of my job."

Empowerment and Collective Action

Stella's grant application made clear their mandate to create an empowering space for sex workers, allowing sex workers to take control of their health and safety (Stella 1998b, 1), thus making empowerment the cornerstone of Stella's existence. Similar to Nina Wallerstein's (1992) and Ronald Labonté's (1990) work, Stella described empowerment as a process that requires the right environment (Stella 1998b, 5). With Wallerstein's (1992) writings as a guide, Stella's founders defined empowerment as a social process promoting individual and collective power (Stella 1998b, 5). Popularized in the 1980s by Paolo Freire, the notion of empowerment is described as follows by Wallerstein:

> [. . .] Empowerment is a multi-level construct that involves people assuming control and mastery over their lives in the context of their social and political environment; they gain a sense of control and purposefulness to exert political power as they participate in democratic life of their community for social change. It is an ecological construct that applies to interactive change on multiple levels: the individual, organization, and community. (Wallerstein 1992, 198)

The notion of empowerment cannot be detached from social structures (Labonté 1990, 67) that some activists have the tendency to deny (Cohen 1985). So, based on this argument, Stella had to become comfortable acting concurrently in both personal and structural dimensions or risk losing sight of the simultaneous reality of both. If Stella focused only on the individual, and only on crisis management or service delivery, they risked overlooking the social structures underpinning poverty and powerlessness. But if Stella only focused on the structural issues, then it would have mystified the plight of people in crisis. Outreach workers and coordinators had to think within both dimensions simultaneously, and from the outset, the founding members were aware of the need to address both dimensions.

> We feel that it would be irresponsible to support sex workers' sense of control over their environment to encourage them to address their health and safety needs without ensuring that the larger context in which they operate is sensitized. We represent sex workers at the Table interquartiers sur la Prostitution and the City of Montréal Task Force on Street and Juvenile Prostitution. These groups bring together municipal officials, police officers, community workers, sex workers, researchers and citizens to address problems associated with prostitution. Through these activities, we have developed close collaborations with representatives of Alerte Centre-Sud and Tandem Montréal. Our participation encourages those involved to explore the impact of prejudice on the ability of sex workers to access safe, healthy living conditions. Our task with the Coalition for the Rights of Sex Workers ensures that sex workers' needs are represented adequately. This work has both served to raise public awareness on many aspects of sex work, and will, we hope, adapt public policy to the degree that sex workers will have more control over their work and health. (Stella 1998e, 11)

Contained in the notion of empowerment is the humanist premise that humans have the capacity, the agency, individually and collectively, to shape their destiny and modify their social and physical surroundings (Swendeman et al. 2015). This capacity, referred to as agency, "is the actor's capacity to reinterpret and mobilize an array of resources in terms of cultural schemas other than those that initially constituted the array" (Sewell 1992, 19). This definition is inspiring and offers us the possibility of hope, but it also assumes a universe of almost unlimited possibilities which the actor/agent may manipulate at will. Therefore, I sometimes feel that our capacity for agency is overestimated. Nonetheless, it is linked to empowerment; hence, to fulfill its mandate, Stella had to create choices (through working for decriminalization) and mobilize sex workers to identify and act upon these choices (Kabeer 2001; Swendeman et al. 2015; Cornish 2016). Stella had to prepare the ground for sex workers to become recognized social actors. Stella's team was conscious that:

> [c]ertain conditions [had to] be met to promote empowerment. [. . .] Members of a community must have a common history and share certain values and beliefs. [. . .] A trust relationship must be established through continuity; mutual interaction needs to be maintained, and options for solving problems should be provided to individuals. (Stella 1998b, 5)

Collective Identity

The creation of a common history is the foundation of a collective identity, a process that includes emotions (Melucci 1983; Della Porta and Diani 2006), self-identity, and political environment (Eisinger 1973). Melucci calls this process an action system: a process that refers to a network of active relationships" (Melucci 1995, 45) with all that this entails—feelings, passion, and power. Indeed, these are difficult but essential to the creation of a collective identity.

I often wonder if researchers and activists realize what it takes to build a collective—how difficult it is to make someone comfortable and create trust. In fact, Stella's 1996 annual report highlights that the discrimination and prejudice sex workers experience from the general public are sometimes reproduced within the community itself, presenting a challenge to creating trust. Internalized stigma around "good" women and the "whore" made it clear that education within the community about different kinds of sex work and sex workers was equally important for promoting community values. These challenges made it important for the Stella team to constantly evaluate the extent to which they were successful in involving a diversity of sex workers. The original stated goal was to work with and create community among street sex workers (Stella 1996l, 5), but this was often a challenge since many street workers were trying to survive and attend to their most basic needs. This was and continues to be a delicate balance as Stella provides a space to recognize the role of race, class, and type of sex work as contributing to how sex workers can participate in the organization. Indeed, in a 1997 report, Stella's coordinator Karen Herland stated that "finding time [to take care of oneself] is a challenge many of us have difficulty meeting" (Stella 1997m, 11). Herland understood that sex workers' participation in workshops, part of which results in breaking isolation and, according to Cornish (2006) and Kabeer (2005), is an essential measure of empowerment, is far less urgent than basic survival needs. For street sex workers, the challenges may be even more acute. Few people appreciate the difficulties experienced by street sex workers; highly visible, these workers are most likely to be the most stigmatized and marginalized, the most overpoliced, and the most socially and legally repressed (Benoit et al. 2018). Stressors also included increased competition among workers, in part due to police repression and a poor economy, as well as from outside, from the police and from their neighbors.

Another challenge for Stella's new team to mobilize sex workers into community and to promote safer sex practices was the historical stigma around sex work, and how this stigmatization impacted safer sex practices.

> By regularly providing HIV/STD information, we offer prevention informa-
> tion in the context of daily concerns. In the first months of operation, many of
> those who use the resource refused condoms and denied that they were in-
> volved in sex work. [Creating a space for sex workers] allows sex workers to
> be more honest about their relationship to it, and the issues they face. Sex
> workers who originally denied their involvement in the trade now openly
> discuss clients and no longer refuse condoms. (Stella 1996a, 3)

Gradually, more and more women involved in the industry came to Stella to
get information and safer sex materials. Empowerment of a community is a
process and requires intimate knowledge of that community's struggles. Involving sex workers directly in service provision was fundamental to Stella's
mandate.

Efforts made to encourage street sex workers to join the fight or, to
paraphrase Benford and Snow (2000, 615), to get them from the streets to the
barricades, was difficult, particularly in a context of police repression. In
February 1997, Montréal's morality squad was implementing a zero-tolerance plan for prostitution and was demanding the support of all local organizations (Stella 1997i, 2). Stella produced a document reiterating their mandate and highlighting how police repression impeded creating community
and safer and healthier conditions for sex workers. During a board meeting in
April 1997, Stella members concluded that it was clearly impossible for
Stella to participate in a zero-tolerance approach. That summer, Stella was a
constant presence in their denouncement of a constant and unwanted police
presence in sex workers' lives and the impact on sex workers in general.
Certainly, the constant avoidance of arrest interfered with sex workers' capacity to negotiate adequately with their clients around services and safer sex
practices.

It is important to underline how Stella's outreach program, drop-in center,
and workshops contributed to give meaning to these situations of injustice
and to attaching emotion to the situation. People act toward objects that have
meaning for them;[27] hence, Stella's work gave meaning to sex workers'
experiences. A language that has evolved at Stella is the one framing the
notion of injustice, of being marginalized, or, as Honneth states, "the refusal
of an intolerable social situation" (1996, 139). Hence, the one frame that
should be "culturally resonant to their historical milieu" (Benford and Snow
2000, 619) is the one that revolves around the issue of rights, and it deserves
to be recognized as a master frame. But what if too many women working in
the sex industry have been taught to believe that they do not deserve to have
their rights protected and respected? What if they are taught to have shame
about the exchange of sexual services? What if they are taught to behave a
certain way because there is a social expectation regarding how sex workers
should feel about their work (Tonkens 2012, 196)? It is in this context that
the role of emotions assumes its significance. This was a challenge for Stella:

How could Stella create a community for sex workers to be empowered in this context? How could sex workers in Montréal fight for their rights as workers in a context where their work is not recognized as legitimate work, and they are, instead, expected to be ashamed about their work?

The By-and-For Challenge

Having an organization led by people working in the sex industry was fundamental to the success of Stella, but it did not come without its challenges. People who work in the sex industry may not be accustomed to the standard 9 to 5 work day. The working conditions and the demands of the work are also structured differently from mainstream work. These differences are even more pronounced when working in public spaces, not to mention the criminalization of sex workers' lives and work and the role that criminalization plays for people also doing "straight" work in addition to their sex work. The skills and experiences of negotiating all of this was essential to the skill set that sex workers brought to the job as a member of Stella's outreach team. Part of the challenge of an organization run by and for the community it serves, however, meant that the organization hired sex workers who were struggling with the very same human rights violations, poverty, homelessness, and other challenges that the organization sought to address. Moreover, the by-and-for model became even more complicated when sex workers occupied various roles in the organization, such as being both a participant that is a "service user" of the organization and a member of its board of directors (Stella 1998b, 11). Navigating this ethical terrain was and continues to be something that the staff, the board, and the membership at Stella must constantly engage.

Another challenge to creating a community of sex workers was working across diversity and difference—sex workers arrived at Stella with different levels of experience in non-sex-work jobs and different levels of education. From the beginning, Stella struggled to balance and open space to the diversity of sex workers involved with Stella; indoor sex workers needed to understand and center the realities of street sex workers who were more heavily pursued by law enforcement and simultaneously experienced higher levels of poverty, and street sex workers needed to learn the skills sometimes only offered in academic settings like the administration requirements of a board of directors (Stella 1998b, 10). This delicate balance required a lot of skill sharing and learning for everyone involved. All these activities were occurring in a context of criminalization and imposed shame on sex workers' lives and work. Tasks that may appear to be small to institutions, like scheduling meetings, maintaining a schedule, or working with a team, were challenging for the staff and members of Stella.

Many sex workers who endured precarious living conditions were not able to create an activist community with other sex workers. Years of reflection and reading about other sex workers groups (Weitzer 1995; Mathieu 2001) helps explaining some enduring challenges with the by-and-for model:

> The mistrust and individualism of sex workers, particularly those on the street, was underestimated at the outset to this project. Sex workers on the street are there because they reject existing structures. Several have told us that they could not see themselves in "straight" jobs because they would be unable to operate within a framework, with a boss. That coupled with the disorganization that rules their lives (addictions, poverty, violence, and legal problems) makes active participation in groups difficult. (Stella 1997m, 11)

Sex workers do not form a homogeneous group and empowerment does not mean the same thing for all and for some this required a lot of support. The meaning and practice of by-and-for remains a constant negotiation but is necessary for the survival and integrity of a sex worker rights group like Stella. Often interpreted as a reproach, discussions around empowerment are important to illustrate the enormous task that Stella had to face during its inception. As Zoë Dodd wrote in the context of drug using community organizing,

> What [we are] saying about the "good" peer worker is really about organizations hiring workers whose lives are not as "chaotic." The worker who isn't as marginalized anymore and whose lived experience was a long time ago. Workplaces often want these types of workers—not the one that are currently in it. There are many organizations that recognize that those workers with current lived experience are incredibly valuable to an organization and should be employed, but the problem with a lot of organizations is that we're not built to support people who have been the most impacted by the systems of oppression. (Michaud et al. 2016, 191)

Reviewing Stella's Mandate One Year Later

In May 1996, Stella celebrated its first anniversary with a picnic for its members and later for the benefactors, volunteers, and partner organizations (Stella 1996e, 5). At the time, Stella's revenues came from three different sources: Health Canada, the Ministry of Health and Social Welfare of Montréal-Centre, and the CQCS (Stella 1997, 5).[28] Despite the success of the magazine *ConStellation*, a prize from the Sécurité des femmes décerné par le Comité d'action femmes et sécurité urbaine de la Ville de Montréal for the Bad Trick List, Stella's team reported that their first year was challenging. The team struggled to adjust and respond to the many needs that sex workers had while also fulfilling the mandate of creating community and increasing sex workers' input in civic life. The difficulties involved in creating a by-

and-for organization, that is, an "organizational context where the direction and management is also comprised of individuals coming from the same population or community" (Michaud et al. 2016, 187), were stark.

At the time of this one-year review, Stella had five paid employees including its coordinator (Stella 1997b, 5). In line with Stella's philosophy, its coordinator had a strong community outreach background, and the others were from the community of sex workers and/or drug users. At the end of their first year, the team realized that the first-line workers were overwhelmed, and that the way the outreach program was structured was unmanageable. The inclusion of services such as food distribution, clothing services, and active listening plus other forms of assistance were too demanding. Employees and outreach workers soon realized that the basic services like food and clothing distribution were beyond what Stella could provide and that they were needed not only by sex workers but by other women occupying public space. In the face of these demands, Stella workers had very little time to reach sex workers and develop approaches aimed at increasing their input, let alone develop programs intended to increase community participation/empowerment (Cornish 2006). In addition, during the first year, it became apparent that hiring former sex workers as outreach staff and encouraging them to be on the board created challenges. Indeed, of the eleven administrators, six were former or current sex workers.[29] Of these six, despite the support of members of the board with more experience, three were not able to fulfill their mandate (Stella 1997a, 3). The administrative tasks were often overwhelming for these members. Therefore, that year, following that philosophy, the board began to think about the mechanisms needed to address these challenges. This involved looking at the composition of the board, how Stella works toward achieving its mission, and the elements of the outreach program.[30] There was also the realization that Stella employees needed more support to do their work (Stella 1997a, 3; Stella 1997b, 6).

The staff and members of Stella were aware that a by-and-for model is not easy to attain and although all levels of participation were open, only a few were able to take an active role:

> Although all levels of decision-making within Stella (like our Board of Directors) have been open to participants, few have taken an active role. [. . .] Survival issues sex workers face on the street make it difficult for them to participate in meetings [. . .]. Those whose personal lives were less turbulent [. . .] avoided Stella because they had no need for its front-line services. [In the end] we realized that we were trying to do too much [so] we returned to our original objectives [. . .] designed to reach and support the widest possible number of sex workers. (Stella 1997a, 3)

An ad hoc committee composed of the administrative board and community organizers decided to rethink the outreach program. Following a long process that began in November 1996, Stella's team proceeded to a reorientation of some of its services—it eliminated offering food and clothing and focused on information sharing and referrals and the development of community between sex workers (Stella 1998c, 4). Going back to its original charter, Stella's first mandate was to offer support and information to sex workers in their efforts to live and work in safety and dignity.

Another change was the use of the space itself: the drop-in center had been closed while outreach teams worked on the street. The board realized that this situation did not properly accommodate sex workers and that it was an obstacle to their participation. More time and energy had to be spent to invite and attract sex workers to come in and talk about issues that affected them and their work; these changes jump-started a whole new approach. The board decided that the drop-in center would be open once again, including the hours when outreach workers were on the street. Thus the focus of Stella shifted—rather than offering services such as clothing distribution and daily meals, which were discontinued, the team would encourage sex workers to come together and share their experiences in a safe space (Stella 1997b, 11).

One of the ways in which members share their experiences was through its famous (or perhaps infamous) publication *ConStellation,* launched on September 27, 1996. The Bad Trick List, which I mentioned earlier, permitted sex workers to communicate violent incidents to one another (Stella 1996j, 5). Following Stella's mandate, these two publications allowed a space for sex workers to express their opinions and positions on issues that matter to them. The group has, since the first issue of *ConStellation*, been recognized for its creativity in the development of tools that, while promoting the use of health and social services, also fight stigma and other prejudices (Stella 1997b, 4). Each *ConStellation* has been written by-and-for sex workers. The magazine launches were successful and brought together allies and sex workers representing every area of the sex industry. And, as mentioned briefly earlier, in February 1996, Stella was awarded a prize for the Bad Trick List (Stella 1996d, 4). The prize was awarded by the CAFSU,[31] a coalition of women's groups, municipal police authorities, and the Regional Health and Social Services Board (Stella 1996a, 4).

Toward Collective Action: Community Organization

The year 1997 was a turning point for Stella (Stella 1998d, 1). First, in June, having borrowed the charity number from FQPN and the bank account from P.I.a.M.P, Stella was able to become independent (Stella 1997d, 2). In May 1997, Stella held a workshop with sex workers in the community inquiring about the ways that sex workers could get involved in the organization.

Participation in these kinds of workshops is what Cornish calls empowerment, that is, "something to be qualitatively specified, in terms of a concrete domain of action [. . .]; it is not a mental state or a feeling of confidence but 'the ability to take an action' (Cornish 2006, 305). Then after major staffing changes, Stella was required to move to a temporary location and seek out a new one that suited their needs. In July 1997, Stella took possession of new quarters (*ConStellation* 1999b; *ConStellation* 2005) and it had *pignon sur rue*—a storefront with glass window. Situated on Saint-Laurent Street in the heart of the old red light district, the location was mythical. People walking by were able to buy the *ConStellation* magazine, see art created by sex workers, and peruse documentation. The center also had a hidden walk-in for sex workers who wanted confidentiality and privacy. The new location was more adapted to Stella's goal, that of community building. Indeed, the new place had one large common room instead of many small ones (Stella 1997m, 7). The place was popular, and volunteers brought snacks, sat around in the main room, and made sure that there were always conversations going on. The place was alive and buzzing. Stella created a place where sex workers could participate. The move was successful but added financial stress, since the rent was more than twice the previous. Following these changes, the team noticed that more women were coming to the drop-in center, that they were coming more often and staying longer. Also, women were more involved, as measured by their participation in organized activities. According to the team, these data represented a connection that was taking shape at two levels—between sex workers themselves and between sex workers and Stella's management and outreach workers (Stella 1998b, 11). The mandate was reaffirmed—Stella was there to support without judgment and encourage sex workers to undertake their own education to increase their capacity to respond to imposed institutional and societal pressures (Stella 1998b). As Ms. Pat wrote in autumn 1997, Stella's location was important to street sex workers:

> I, like most of you I spoke with, felt deserted after last winter [but] Stella has moved back to St-Laurent and has found [itself], and is again offering the chance to find ourselves. So, don't be bitter and don't be shy. Come back to Stella and give it a try. [. . .] Again, Stella is: Seriously Together Enjoying Living Laughing Again. (*ConStellation* 1997, 4)

The workshops enabled sex workers to be open about their work. Sex workers explained that the fixed site was a place where one could feel secure, a *lieu de vie* where sex workers came together to exchange ideas and find solutions for their common problems. It was a place where they could develop a sense of solidarity (Stella 1998d). As a group, they began to attend workshops and to get more involved in the conversations that took place at

Stella—about health, about work, about living and working conditions. Some began to take better care of their health and to have more contact with the CLSC than they had before (Stella 1998b, 16). Increasingly, sex workers came to Stella to participate in workshops, to get condoms, and to get the Bad Trick list. Sex workers were participating in the development of projects, and the organization was supportive of their efforts. They were involved in learning and had a hands-on attitude toward their work (Stella 1998c, 4; Stella 1998d, 1). The Stella space was newly focused on collective participation rather than basic service delivery and permitted the involvement of more sex workers in the day-to-day functioning of Stella (Stella 1998c, 4).

Outreach workers promoted Stella's goals and were pivotal in informing other Montréal organizations about sex workers' needs. Stella's coordinator, together with a psychologist from St-Luc Hospital, supported the outreach workers, and a special committee was in place to support and supervise the outreach program. Also, in 1997, Stella began to extend its outreach and connect with bar owners (Stella 1998d, 4). The antagonistic relationship with the police sometimes made this work challenging, but some police stations were more cooperative than others (Stella 1998d, 7). The desire to participate in Stella was complicated by a fear of being arrested, a situation that was also noted by Cornish's (2006, 302) analysis of sex workers in India.

The momentum of sex workers coming together to create Stella also created a space for the creation of other collectives and sex worker rights initiatives, working in tandem but distinct from Stella—the Coalition in 1996 and the Lilis in 1997 (*ConStellation* 2005, 116). In September 1996, in Montréal, Concordia University's Québec Interest Research Group (QIRG) organized a three-day conference entitled When Sex Works: International Conference on Prostitution and Other Sex Work. Stella was present at the conference, and on the last day, city officials announced their intention to form a committee to examine street and juvenile prostitution. Following this announcement, a group of sex workers founded the Coalition for the Rights of Sex Workers. Thus, on September 29, 1996, Stella witnessed the birth of what came to be known simply as the Coalition (*ConStellation* 2005b, 115). The Coalition was formed in response to the creation of the mayor's committee on street and juvenile prostitution. The Coalition, although independent of Stella, benefited from its full support and part of its membership (Stella 1998b, 11–12).

Also, in 1997, after a workshop Stella organized for strip club dancers, they formed their own group called the Lilis (Stella 1998b, 13), a group that aimed to change strip clubs' working environment. In November 1997, after raids in strip clubs, Stella provided a brief training on how to approach the media. The training stressed the importance of a collective versus a personal message (14). Les Lilis was short lived, but the media training was important to the sex workers who continued to do activism for dancers and other sex workers in their community. Framing their claim, stating that sex work is a victimless crime, they said, "if we are criminals, who are the victims?" and the right to "dance proud, work safe" were the slogans used (*Place Publique*, janvier 1998).[32]

Although more sex workers were coming to the drop-in center, forming community was still quite a challenge. Successes were often individual and fleeting for many, because of the challenges of social and legal environments (Stella 1998b, 2). Following this assessment Stella trained five volunteers to be spokespersons around sex workers' issues. The organization also tried to ensure that sex workers were more involved in Stella's programming. In September 1997, four volunteers became full-time employees with contracts and more responsibilities, and at this time additional efforts were deployed to hire more people (1998b, 11).

The Coalition organized a fundraising event and assembly in October 1997. The event collected almost two thousand dollars for Stella and increased Stella's visibility. It provided an opportunity for the organization to reach more sex workers in a different context (Stella 1998c, 10).

Stella was working hard to maintain and intensify its contact with its partners, and that year the organization was, for the first time, invited to take part in a march, Take Back the Night,[33] a project that denounced violence against women. Stella also participated in Ça Marche, a march in support of HIV/AIDS organized by the Farha Foundation, no longer in existence (Stella 1998d, 9). Stella's participation permitted the organization to establish links with other community organizations and in doing so expanded sex workers' access to a variety of resources and possible allies. Sex workers were also located through partner organizations such as CACTUS, Passages, CLSC, and hospitals (Stella 1998d, 1).

Judging by the far reach of their own magazine, *ConStellation,* and the visibility of Stella in public milieus, Montréal sex workers appeared to be emerging as a collective. Stella's collective identity was strong, and the mood was high, but at other times the task of building and maintaining a collective was difficult. Efforts were made to increase women's participation and bring them together; however, the competitive nature of the industry and the fact that most sex workers were focused on working not doing activism remained a challenge for maintaining a collective (Stella 1997a). The one-year Stella report concluded by stating that the barriers standing between sex workers and the methods of protection against HIV/AIDS and other sexually transmitted infections were diverse, but still the team at Stella recognized the great role that legal and social forces played in shaping sex workers' attitudes toward their work. The road to empowerment and participation was a difficult one, and more so when sex workers were still perceived by police and neighbors as criminals and outsiders. Toward the end of the year in their application for a charity number, Stella reiterated the societal factors that complicated the ability of sex workers to protect themselves, including rejection, legal and social repression, isolation, violence, addictions, and poverty (Stella 1997c, 1).

> We feel that our role to ensure equal access to health and social services, support and referral for a marginalized segment of the population must be understood as positive for the public and has been interpreted as such for other organizations. [. . .] Our activities relate to the rights of sex workers and sensitivity trainings we provide to different sectors of the community [such as police] through media and various table and partner organizations. [. . .] Stella's role falls within the health promotion model of Health Canada to provide information and tools for marginalized populations to improve their ability to access health and social services and to benefit from their "rights" to these services as do other citizens. (Stella 1997c)

At the end of 1997, Stella reported an increase in contacts and attributed this to a change in its approach. The presence of Stella's outreach workers increased its ability to reach sex workers and significantly helped sex workers increase their self-esteem, self-worth, and skills (Stella 1998a, 4). This could be interpreted as participation and collective building. Stella staff understood offering services that engaged with sex workers' lives as a first step in community building, to recruit members and participants. Moreover, I agree with Samantha Majic that by dispensing services Stella was, as other groups have done, "indirectly politicizing sex workers by providing a space where marginalized populations can come together and share information in a protective environment, which brings a lot of self-efficacy and social capital development as a result of feeling and being part of a community" (2014, 57).

Charity Number

Since September 1994, P.I.a.M.P was designated as the organization to act as a fiscal agent to Projet Stella (CES 1994f, 1), which allowed Stella to receive donations (CES 1994i, 1). P.I.a.M.P. became Stella's trustee. Funding was available but limited if a community organization was not a registered charity, particularly in the context of health promotion, homelessness, and other social issues; often private donors and foundations require a charity number. Discussions about obtaining a charity number were raised at various moments with the Stella membership (Stella 1995c; Stella 1995d), and in February 1996, they began the lengthy process of their application (Stella 1996a, 7; Stella 1997i).

Stella's November 1996 request for charitable status was refused on the basis that the organization was perceived as only a rights defense group (Stella 1996o, 1). Despite Stella's role "to ensure equal access to health and social services, and support and referral for a marginalized segment of the population must be understood as positive for the public as a whole, and has been interpreted as such by other organizations" (Stella 1997c, 1), they were told that they did not fulfill the requirements for a charity number that stated "an organization must be 90 percent to 100 percent aimed at charitable action." Almost a year after its initial demand, Stella was still trying to obtain its charity number. The main problem for Mr. Juneau of the Charities Division was that "to help sex workers to come together to enable them to exchange [information] and to increase their sense of community is not necessarily a charitable activity" and was no doubt interpreted as political in spirit. Therefore, Stella reiterated the relationship of creating community to public health goals in their next application for charitable status. Sex workers constantly needed to justify how political needs were entrenched within personal needs, and that human rights were integral to public health approaches. Framing its argument as a public health issue, and using a rights discourse, as other organizations had done, Stella wrote another letter demanding charitable status. It was a hard-fought battle; it is difficult for community organizations like Stella to navigate the institutions that determine what charity work looks like. But on January 22, 1998, during a special General Assembly and after years of correspondence with Revenue Canada, Stella obtained its charitable status (Stella 1998a, 1).

In September 1999, a group of sex workers gathered in Charles-Mayer Park demanding nothing less than reserved working zones (Journal de Montréal 1999) and launched a new edition of *ConStellation* magazine—one at a local bar called City Bar (*Ici* 1999) located on a popular sex workers' stroll where sex workers would congregate and find clients, and the other to celebrate its fourth anniversary.

In 1999, at the new location, the outreach team, pursuing their mission, began to gain credibility and trust in their community, and this hard work proved beneficial as sex workers began to be aware of services and participated in other activities and movements. One such project was the HIV Vulnerability Project at work since 1996, which allowed sex workers to validate the factors that put them at risk. The project reiterated the fact that discrimination, criminalization of sex work, and constant rejection impeded sex workers' capacity to fully implement health and safety strategies (Stella 1997a, 2).

Stella and the Fédération des femmes du Québec (FFQ)

Situated firmly in a feminist analysis of women's labor and human rights, Stella has also worked hard over time to find allies in feminist movements. Founded in 1966 by Thérèse Casgrain, the Federation of Quebec Women (FFQ) is an independent feminist organization that works to transform relationships of domination in all spheres of life, with a view to fostering the development of the full autonomy of women. The FFQ is the largest women's association in Québec. Beginning in January 1999, Stella's team, in collaboration with the FFQ, worked to inform the Québec women's movement about sex work (Stella 2001g, 11). This following section introduces a crucial moment in the women's movement, the Women's World March in 2000, and recalls Stella's participation.

After the first Bread and Roses march (1995), an FFQ initiative that aimed to address poverty, activists who had participated expressed their desire to organize another event, but something connected to the global women's movements. At the end of 1996, the National Coalition against Poverty and Violence against Women (CNPV) sent 500 letters to women's groups across the world. The response was positive, and in May 1997, the FFQ unanimously adopted a resolution to organize the World March of Women (Marche mondiale des femmes) scheduled for October 2000. Demands were numerous, and women from South America, in particular, insisted that the issue of violence be added to that of poverty (World March 2001a, 7).

The objectives of the World March were to 1) inform and educate women on the national and international stages regarding women's poverty and violence toward women; 2) lay the foundation to create an international network aimed at worldwide collective action while respecting diversity of cultures and of strategies; and 3) make national and worldwide demands to influence the decision makers and provoke some significant changes for women (World March 2001, 8). The committee in Québec created two large workshops: one on violence against women and one on poverty. Stella joined the first workshop, and representatives gave themselves the task of informing and educating participants about the reality of sex workers' experiences with violence.

The CNPV developed criteria for the formulation of demands. They had to be feasible on a short or relatively short-term basis, and they determined that every woman must recognize herself within at least one claim. Finally, these claims had to be conducive to mobilization. The debate regarding demands lasted from January to October 1999. Most claims quickly reached consensus, but two were a source of tension: lesbian relationships and their access to artificial insemination or parental rights and sex work. The CNPV realized that some groups, such as lesbians and sex workers, experienced many levels of discrimination. The committee met with different lesbian groups, and after a few meetings, which clarified certain issues, groups began to understand one another. In the end, more organizations were able to support their claims and participate in the World March (World March 2001, 16); however, in Québec, the claim that sex work is legitimate work was one that unmistakably unsettled the committee. Because the claim was not introduced at the very beginning of the development of the World March, but proposed later within the violence committee, the sex work claim disconcerted many (FFQ 2001a, 16). From the beginning, Stella's director recognized resistance to the issues concerning sex work (Stella 1999a, 2). She noticed that some feminists were ambivalent when it came to sex work; therefore, it was difficult to engage in dialogue around sex work with the World March leaders. Since it was impossible for the committee to reach a consensus on sex workers' demands, the CNPV realized that more information and debates were necessary and chose to produce a document that would raise the issues for sex workers' rights. It was decided that the FFQ president at the time, Françoise David, would tour the province to discuss sex work with its members (Stella 2000b, 5).

The exchange between the FFQ and Stella, although somewhat open, stumbled around messily. Nonetheless, this confrontation in the CNPV opened a dialogue between them, and following the World March, the FFQ's president and Stella's director prepared a document that permitted this provincial tour dedicated to educating women's group on the realities of sex work. In June 1999, the violence committee of CNPV prepared and published The Fundamental Rights of Sex Workers, creating a position, which denounced the double exclusion such as being black and lesbian and triple exclusion if we add sex work (CNPV 1999, 3).

Regarding sex work, the CNPV demanded the decriminalization of sex work and better working conditions for sex workers. The committees adopted a demand in connection with the discrimination and violence endured by sex workers (CNPV 1999, 8). Throughout the meetings, many local and regional organizations underlined the difficulty in supporting demands made by lesbians and sex workers publicly. These issues, still taboo, created a malaise within larger groups. Nevertheless, during meetings women did talk about these issues in smaller groups and ultimately according to those present these discussions were good for the growth of the women's movement (World March 2001, 17). All members of the committee agreed on the necessity of continuing their reflections after the World March. Although at the time, Stella's team reduced its involvement in the organization of the World March (Stella 2000d, 3; World March 2001, 7), they did participate in the march. The event brought some gains. Among others, the World March permitted Stella to showcase its creativity while articulating its claims, something that is typical of contemporary collective action (Melucci 1983).

> One sex worker that I interviewed had this to say about the march: [The March], was an event that was very important in Stella's life. It was an event that I think has mobilized us. It did us good after all the events that followed the failure of the Pilot Project.[34] For sure, it was hard but also rewarding. . . .
> We sat there on a Committee then [our Director] did a lot of work to get women to propose the decriminalization of sex work. And, finally, it was not accepted at all. But, with the World March Committee, we arrived at a consensus, [we arrived] at common claims where everyone agreed to combat discrim-

ination against sex workers, particularly in their rapport with social services and the police. It was the big claim that the World March of women brought here in Montréal [. . .]. So, it was our first experience in the women's movement. [We] decided to engage in a collective action within this March. [. . .] The March would pass in front of Stella's [headquarters]. So, [. . .] we decided to transform Stella into jail. [. . .] This mobilization was super important for Stella, and it was very, very positive. There were a lot of people [. . .]. It was an interesting experience, [. . .] and one that helped us heal from everything that happened, from the pain that we experienced after [the Pilot Project]. Yes, [sex workers] were enthusiastic about the activities that Stella organized.

The stage built around Stella's quarters for the World March was indeed quite colorful and innovative, and this creativity remains at the core of Stella's visual identity. People marching down Saint-Laurent Boulevard that day were met with sex workers wearing black sensor strips over their eyes to signal confidentiality and clandestinity, others standing on painted cement blocks; one woman was nursing her child while another one was chained to a target, arrows surrounding her with the words hate, prejudice, and laws. The Stella locale itself had been transformed into a prison—the windows now had bars and women were handcuffed to them. Inspired by an action by sex workers in Lyon, France, in 1975, a banner hung from Stella's third floor window that read "On ne veut plus nos sœurs, nos mères, nos filles, nos blondes, nos amies en prison." In Stella's tradition of wanting to connect with other sex workers around the world and commemorate their actions, this banner translates as "We no longer want our sisters, our mothers, our daughters, our girlfriends, our friends in prison." As part of their action to occupy the St-Nizier Church, sex workers in Lyon had rolled out a similar banner. On the balcony, across Stella's headquarters, giant puppets personifying a sex worker, a policeman, and a "bad trick" were simulating an altercation. As one participant said, "women in the march cheered on Stella and the sex workers who were hitting the policeman with a giant inflatable bat, and a spirit of solidarity stung the air." That whole *mise en scène* was just one of many created by Stella. At another memorable gathering in 2001 was a scene created especially for the new mayor under the banner of the Coalition for the Rights of Sex Workers. Sex workers gathered at Montréal City Hall and tainted the fountain water red and invited the mayor for a plate of puttanesca pasta (*ConStellation* 2005). Adorned with red boas, they waited in vain. The mayor did not join them for lunch. Asked about their artistic representation or performance, a former board member says, "Yes, we are a community organization, and yes, it could be very boring, straight but [Stella] is filled with people used to living in marginalized spaces. [We] have graphic designers and artists at Stella who develop amazing projects. [. . .] We love to get messages out that way—yes always with humor." Even though the FFQ and Stella did not agree on sex work, at the time it was productive to tour Québec with the FFQ to discuss sex work, and at the very least provide visibility to a group of working women so often ignored in feminist discussions.

Indeed, Stella's participation to the World March was of great importance. After years of sex workers' organizing efforts, it became impossible for the global feminist movement to ignore them (Lamoureux 2005, 79). In Québec, Stella had been a member of the FFQ, and although the relationship had been somewhat tense, the fact remained that as long as Stella was present in the FFQ, discussions about sex work would continue within their membership.

In 1999, Stella's new director Claire Thiboutot published an article entitled "Are Sex Workers Politically Correct?" (*ConStellation* 1999b, 5). She expressed how unfortunate it was that important words like "sex work" and "sex worker" were being interpreted as "politically correct" instead of being taken seriously as words that signify women in a context of work instead of as criminal or a moral aberration. Thiboutot's article is highly significant because it highlights the relationship between meaning and action (Stokes and Hewitt 1976; Joas 1996, 207). Symbols have the capacity to attract and repel, and Thiboutot is attempting here to fight for the expressions that sex workers themselves employ, to replace derogatory language. As mentioned in the introduction to this book, Carol Leigh's 1979 coining of the expression "sex work" was purposeful—it was the first step in dismantling the whore stigma and invited others to join the fight: "This invention was motivated by my desire to reconcile my feminist goals with the reality of my life and the lives of the women I know" (Leigh 2004, 66). According to the Global Network of Sex Work Projects (NSWP), Leigh's expression marked the beginning of a movement.[35]

Symbols and people's relation to them have important consequences for sex workers and for sex workers' rights groups. Whereas culture and action are interwoven (Stokes and Hewitt 1976; Warner 1978; Hewitt 1989; Joas 1996; McPhail 2006), one of sex workers' groups' main activities is to challenge cultural symbols.

Culture plays an important role in understanding action (Mills 1940, 905; Stokes and Hewitt 1976; Warner 1978; Hewitt 1978; Buechler 2000; McPhail 2006). By articulating their claim—the social and legal recognition of their revenue-generating activity—sex workers' organizations have entered a conversation (Mills 1940, 905) with different groups; each of the parties defines the situation differently. Since the 1970s, sex workers' groups have conversed with different interlocutors—government, factions of the women's movement, legal and medical authorities, and resident groups. Addressing these parties has demanded a constant reassessment of strategies around health, as well as of moral and legal terrains because groups differ in their strategies and their capacity to address sex workers' realities and definition of the situation and, with this difference, frustration emerges differently which in turns creates motive for the organization. How the issue is defined is important. For Stella, the main driver that initiated their movement was health and safety, and addressing the health and safety required the collaboration of the different institutional, social, and other players in the environment. For the police, sex work is defined as a legal or criminal issue that necessitates arrests and for Montréal authorities, sex work is a social problem created by prostitution and the solution rests on Stella to resolve it. The decision as to how sex workers will act in a given situation is consistent with Mead's pragmatic approach, that is, adjusting one's strategies in keeping with real-life situations, rather than only reacting from some psychological impulse such as "desire" (Mills 1940, 906). There is a link between emotion and action. Being pragmatic means adapting action to possibilities. Stella constantly has to review and adjust their movement in an effort to find solutions.

For "prostitutes," enduring symbols of decadence and victimization, the solicitation law is still perceived as the only way to control prostitution, protect "prostitutes," curb their addiction, and maybe convince them to leave the trade (Le Pard 2006, 69). The "whore" symbol has become a significant symbol. It is safe to infer that until the emergence of sex workers' groups—and even afterward—"the whore" publicly signified a fallen woman—to be feared or pitied. Integral to the struggle for sex workers' rights is the use of language and the decisions in how to use these words and symbols.

The cultural elements—the symbols—that make people join or start a group have come to be an important dimension in making sense of collective action (Etzioni 1968; Stokes and Hewitt 1976; Joas 1983, 1997; McAdam 1994; McCarthy 1994; Benford and Snow 2000; McPhail 2006). The link between meaning and action has developed into the concept of collective action frames (Benford and Snow 2000; Staggenborg 2008, 18). Again, Stella must constantly check their frames and if they have resonance—do they still mean something to their base?

As noted earlier, to generate action, groups must perform meaning work. Actors are conceptualized as signifying agents that produce, modify, and maintain meaning inside and outside the group (Benford and Snow 2000, 613). This work, this construction of meaning, is known as framing and is collective and interactive (Buechler 2000, 41). Framing is the organization of experience into something that makes sense to the actor (Goffman 1986, 10–11). To women working in the sex industry, the expression sex work should be meaningful; it should mean work. Leigh's goal was to reframe the "prostitute" symbol to "sex worker." Was this enough to get sex workers mobilized in the struggle for safer working conditions? Criminality prevented them from always doing so but it most definitely garnered support for a global movement that is still growing today. In fact, the sex worker rights movement has taken on enormous proportions with over 250 sex worker rights groups led by sex workers across the globe (www.nswp.org).

Meaning is emergent: past and present come together during interaction (Hewith 1976, 846). Stella created that place of interaction but was it enough? The young organization had to battle stigma and the fear of arrest that at times proved to be a formidable obstacle. Stella needed the neighborhood to join in their struggle, they needed the cooperation of Montréal's mayor and its police, but even though the Stella mandate was legitimized by financial support from the Canadian government's Public Health Agency of Canada, respect for sex work and the work of sex workers had not yet been achieved.

Culture frames are the raw material used to create what Mills (1940) calls "a vocabulary of motives" to mobilize members and attract new ones. If action depends on people's expectations, and if action is an orientation toward things (Warner 1978, 1327), then framing for marginal and stigmatized groups becomes essential (Jenness 1993, 1995). I also consider Leigh and Thiboutot's statements—that sex workers be recognized as workers—the cornerstone of the sex worker rights movement. Recognizing women in the sex industry as workers is the first step to undo the whore stigma and to alter the emotion. The driving emotion that prevents support for the sex worker rights movement is often associated with immorality and disgust—notions of "disease" embedded in sex work, HIV, drug use, immoral sexuality, and homelessness drive hatred of sex workers (Oaten et al. 2011, 3438).[36]

Stella was founded on the principle of empowerment and the recognition of sex workers' agency. As Cornish (2006) states, sex workers organizations create spaces where women can make their own decisions, take control of their lives, and act. But how can Stella assist street sex workers to do this when police, city officials, and prohibitionists want to see the sex industry, and thus sex workers, disappear? How can Stella create a safe environment for women when all the institutional and social forces around sex workers promote arrest and surveillance? How can a group of stigmatized women convince their social and political environment to create space for them to be heard? The historical meaning that has created the symbol of the "prostitute"—as impure, diseased, and criminal—is difficult to erase and her place in society is still the site of intense and often violent debates.

For Stella and the sex worker rights movement to be successful, social conditions for sex workers need to be rendered visible. As McAdam (1994) and Honneth (2004) state, leaders of any social movements must convince their troops that the situation is unacceptable. Awareness of structural inequalities is important for all marginalized, stigmatized groups. In the case of sex workers, it is crucial. To be criminalized, to live in fear of being discovered, because you are stigmatized and deemed not worthy of protection is objectionable. Thus, the first step of empowerment is consciousness-raising:

identifying the injustice and revealing it as a common social issue, not an individual problem. Uniting with the people who live with the same injustices and appreciate the importance of collective action is crucial because the seeds of political action are sown through such transformative experience. Political action begins with a) the refusal of an intolerable social situation, b) extends into a fight against the group interested in the permanence of this social situation, and c) aims at equity. Empirically, however, only if the means of communication for a collective are available "can the experience of disrespect become a source of motivation for acts of political resistance" (Honneth 1996, 139). Honneth's insights are certainly applicable when one considers Stella's mobilization plan, which was founded on the recognition that we can only change our living and working conditions when we realize that these are unacceptable because

> [only] a person who is supported may understand that her living conditions are unacceptable and only then may the person take steps that are necessary to make changes. Realizing that she is not alone in her situation, she will recognize the importance of acting on a collective level by identifying solutions to common problems with other people who experience the same injustices. This process involves several steps which are not linear. (Stella 1998c, 5)

Moreover, as underlined by Honneth (1996) and Demazière and Pignoni (1999, 126), the realization that one's suffering may have social causes may favor the formation of a collective, which in turn helps political efficacy.[37] The social, legal, and institutional risks and consequences of being out as a sex worker make it nearly impossible to claim rights as individual workers. For most sex workers, "coming out" is risky. To do so without any support of community can be even riskier. Hence, Stella's point of departure was always an individual grounded in the social and acting within a collective. Getting sex workers to form a collective and to unite for the legitimation of their work was and continues to be the most important and often the most difficult task.

Collectives must engage in core framing tasks (Benford and Snow 2000, 615) such as diagnostic framing and prognostic framing. The former introduces the problem and attributes blame, and by doing so creates a target, and this, according to Javelin (2003), is crucial for mobilization. For Javelin, the role of leaders is to render a vague, unclear target more precise (2003, 119), to give the group an *Other*. And for Ost, it is possibly the most important task facing activists (2004, 241). Who is responsible for the injustice? The more precise the assignment of responsibility the more chances for protest. Identifying who is to blame in a supposed democratic society is often a difficult task and the leader must be able to identify the one who caused the problem and the one who failed to resolve it (Javelin 2003, 107). It is not about "being right"; it is about making an enemy visible. According to Javelin (2003), this is even more important than political opportunity because "[. . .] divided elite [. . .] signifies weak and vulnerable leadership" (2003, 120.)

Blame attribution feeds emotions such as indignation and anger (Javelin 2003, 108). Successful blaming does not rest on accuracy but on the capacity to convince the group as to who is responsible for the situation. A protest without a clear target is always costlier (110) and may trigger a "what's the use" attitude. In *Blame Attribution*, Javelin (2003) concludes that it is easier to protest if one believes the protest to be effective and this is done when the culprit and solution are in sight. Next, the group must propose ways to resolve the problem—prognostic framing—and from that frame create consensus so the group can get to the task of building a "mobilization pool" (Buechler 2000, 41). Now the group has one final task, motivational framing (617), how to get "people from the balcony to the barricades" (Benford and Snow 2000, 615). The answer may very well be given to us in part by Javelin's work: by tapping into people's emotions—anger, hurt, and/or indignation. Blaming is about getting together and fighting the one responsible for one's suffering. Stella and their allies were clear on one of the main causes to blame for the harms to sex workers' health and safety—criminalization. Their task was then to demonstrate the players that maintained this system of criminality and how to dismantle it.

Stigmatized groups need to accomplish three tasks—gather, defend, and mobilize (Demazière and Pignoni 1999, 169); hence, from its inception, Stella has endeavored to gather and unite sex workers and to create a place that would favor solidarity, cohesion, and mobilization. Stella's team was aware that for sex workers, empowerment was a process that must begin with recognition of and respect for differences. Since it was imperative that sex workers be involved in every aspect of the organization, the team had to remain vigilant and do everything to try to break the barriers that kept sex workers away from one another and from participating. Indeed, from the outset, Stella encountered some of the same obstacles described by Pheterson (1996, 132), that of class and hierarchies between sex workers and non-sex workers and within the sex industry itself. Early in the project, during a meeting held on June 21, 1995, members of Stella underscored that solidarity was difficult to achieve (Stella 1995d, 1998). Stella, despite all the obstacles, managed to finish the year 2000 on a high note when they received the Idola Saint-Jean prize from the Fédération des Femmes du Québec, a prize that underlined Stella's contribution to the women's movement at large (Lamoureux 2005, 81). The prize came with a special mention: "guts and determination" (Stella 2001g, 11). The year ended well, and members and Stella staff felt encouraged, which makes the struggles and the Pilot Project debacle described in the next chapter even more dreadful.

NOTES

1. The Commission was named after its chair, Jean Rochon, former Dean of Medicine at Laval University. In 1985, Rochon was invited by the Québec government to study Québec's health and social services. Rochon's report built on the Castonguay–Nepveu Commission of 1967–1970, which had recommended a decentralized structure of departments of community health based in hospitals and local community health clinics. The mandate was to assess the functioning and funding of the health and social services system, to explore the possible solutions to the various problems facing the system, and make recommendations to the government which would ensure the maintenance and development of health services and related social services. For the report see Commission d'enquête sur les services de santé et les services sociaux (Commission Rochon), Rapport, Les Publications du Québec, 1988, p. 63–64, http://www.bibliotheque.assnat.qc.ca/guides/fr/les-commissions-d-enquete-au-québec-depuis-1867/7685-commission-rochon-1988.

2. Please see the documentary *Hookers on Davies Street*.

3. Reminiscent of French sex workers in 1975 when they occupied a church in Saint-Nizier le movement des églises.

4. http://www.amsterdamredlightdistricttour.com/news/de-rode-draad-association-prostitutes-went-bankrupt/, accessed December 3, 2017.

5. This section is based on Bilodeau, Lefebvre, and Allard. 2002. See their complete report on HIV/HIV/AIDS and the creation of community organizations in Québec.

6. Comité sida Québec.

7. The results of the research had been validated by the steering committees. The actors can now make another reading of the situation. Angèle Bilodeau, October 19, 2018.

8. Later this will become known as peer or the by-and-for model of community organization. While this is a problematic formula, that is, the focus on risk and certain populations was current at this time, the limits and issues associated with this approach will be discuss at the end of this chapter and revisited in chapter 5.

9. Centre d'action communautaire auprès des toxicomanes utilisateurs de seringues. The same year Health Canada subsidized another center Pic-Atouts also managed by the same two Montréal hospitals Montréal General and Maisonneuve-Rosemont.

10. Dr. Hankins is referring to HIV and not to the final stage which is HIV/AIDS.

11. The Prostitute Minors Intervention Project (P.I.a.M.P.) is an autonomous community organization aimed at responding to young people aged twelve to twenty-five who exchange or are likely to exchange sexual services. The P.I.a.M.P. also offers information and training to individuals involved in prostitution and to those who surround these young people: parents, friends, caregivers, educators, etc.

12. http://www.nswp.org/members/europe/international-committee-the-rights-sex-workers-europe-icrse.

13. People of Action sida Montréal—Femmes (CASM) and Passages, a woman group, were invited but absent.

14. This situation has not changed—condoms are related to work. Plus, often the request may be equivalent to a lack of trust in your partner.

15. The AQTTS demanded the decriminalization of all aspects related to sex work (Thiboutot 1994, 15). In doing so, the AQTTS engaged in what Benford and Snow (2000) identify as the core framing task, that is, to diagnose a situation and who was to blame for keeping the laws in place. The fight needs to make sense to people, in our case sex workers and allies. Before a community can organize and mobilize its troops it needs a cause; the community needs to frame its call to arms. And the language used needs to be appropriate and meaningful to convince the community to join the cause. Framing—the creation of meaning—is the cornerstone of collective actions and the creation of social movements.

16. Ethical identity is born from taking a stance on matters such as euthanasia, abortion, and the death penalty. These decisions are ethical and spiritual in nature (Taylor 1989).

17. http://www.nswp.org/featured-member/maggies-toronto.

18. By-and-for groups are for the majority state-funded projects to face drug, HIV, and violence issues (Michaud et al. 2016, 187). I will address the distinctions and tensions related to the by-and-for and peer models later.

19. AQTTS demands were framed as rights issues, a frame which throughout the years has acquired cultural significance with sex workers (Majic 2013).

20. In the Maimie Papers (Pinzer 1977) in summer 1915 Stella is recovering from venereal disease and Maimie describes her as having grown "stout and beautiful" (364).

21. Soon after Thiboutot suggested that she and another person would go to Maggie's in Toronto to gather information as to the functioning of the organization, Danny Cockerline, one of the founding members of Maggie's, accepted to help Projet Stella write its constitution (CES 1994g, ii).

22. Even before the official opening, the project's co-ordinator (CES 1995, 2) was invited to link up with CACTUS and other community organizations such as TANDEM to join in 1995 the Neighbourhood Committee on Prostitution (CIQ) that eventually put together in 1996 the Neighbourhood Table on Prostitution (TIQ). Representing Stella, the co-ordinator began with "the notion of respect between us is a good starting point. Our positions may be different, but the respect should lead to collaboration. A city like Montréal must inevitably face questions like the one that concerns us. Please understand that prostitutes do not feel that they have the same rights as the other citizens. Can a prostitute, a victim of sexual assault, bring her attacker to court?" (CIQ 1995).

The CIQ was composed of city officials, police officers, community workers, sex workers, researchers, and citizens (Stella 1998, 6). In doing so, the CIQ respected the empowerment philosophy: sex workers had to be included from the outset. "It was noted that the awareness campaign should be undertaken in consultation with the prostitutes" (CIQ 1995, 3).

23. I was not able to locate the apartment number.

24. Prévention action femmes sida de Montréal.

25. The police were aware of Stella well before the doors opened, including a commitment from police to not visit the site, set up nearby to watch who used it, nor to follow people to the site. Police could come only if invited if a sex worker wanted to lay charges against a bad date, under a series of special circumstances (private communication with Karen Herland, September 2017).

26. Concerning the needle exchange Stella's co-ordinator voiced her reservations (Stella 1995b, 4) and a policy was adopted in June 1995 (Stella 1995d): Stella was not a needle exchange site but would help in emergency situations. I can imagine how difficult it was to get accepted as a community organization helping "prostitutes" without adding "junkies" to the list!

27. See Stokes and Hewitt 1976; Warner 1978; Hewitt 1989; Joas 1996; McPhail 2006 for discussion on the role of meaning and collective action.

28. Québec coordination center for AIDS.

29. It is not clear who among the board were Stella's paid staff members.

30. Following Stella's efforts to restructure, Stella had to move to a new location where a community police station was located across the street. The proximity of the police, combined with their efforts to clean up the neighborhood, made it very difficult to attract sex workers to Stella. The team met with police officers many times but to no avail. The situation remained difficult, making sex workers harder to reach and some more aggressive (Stella 1997m, 6). At this point, Stella decided to move to a smaller place away from the police station and away from residential areas.

31. A women committee for safety.

32. https://atsa.qc.ca/revuepresse-97-9.99.

33. https://takebackthenight.org/.

34. In chapter 3.

35. http://www.nswp.org/timeline/event/carol-leigh-coins-the-term-sex-work.

36. Philosophical Transaction of the Royal Society B (2011) 366, 3433–52, doi:10.1098/rstb.2011.0095.

37. See also Bourdieu 1999.

Chapter Three

Sex Work and the Metropolis

The Pilot Project Initiative

While still in its infancy, Stella was compelled to take on the oldest and most unsettled disputes: street prostitution. To prohibitionists, prostitution was a "social problem" created by sex workers which, in turn, demanded that it be resolved by them. This chapter as the previous one is situated within the years 1996 and 2000; however, it deserves its own place as it recalls the events surrounding the planning around a pilot project aimed at finding solutions to the tension created by street prostitution. Instead of finding answers, the project reinforced the presence of the whore symbol/stereotype and propelled the creation of resident organizations and brought back the conflation of sex work with human trafficking, which I consider the most damaging for Stella. Trying to find an alternative to legal repression, the project came to be referred to as the Pilot Project and was the perfect occasion for the city of Montréal and Stella to work together to address concerns around street prostitution and what the city refers to as "its accompanying irritants." Unfortunately, the project was a complete failure and makes visible the role of public opinion in policy making.

Having been accused of collusion with criminal organizations and glamorizing prostitution, members of Stella struggled to achieve credibility in the public eye and public momentum for sex workers' rights claims: to create an empowering space for sex workers, so that sex workers could take control of their health and safety (Stella 1998b, 1). Understanding the adversity that Stella encountered during this period, however, requires an introduction of background and context, key moments that are useful in making sense of the resistance and at times outright refusal by prohibitionists and municipal officials to accept Stella's mandate—to promote the health and well-being of women working in the sex industry (Stella 1996l, 5).

THE PILOT PROJECT: THE GROUNDWORK

> An individual is stigmatized when they possess some signs which lead to them being permanently avoided by members of the larger society within which they reside. (Oaten et al. 2011)

In 1993, the atmosphere in Centre-Sud—where street sex work was concentrated—was tense. Residents were angry about the presence of prostitution in the neighborhood and took out their frustration on street sex workers themselves. The discontent with women soliciting clients on the street had been simmering since the 1950s and finally reached a boiling point in 1993 with what had been called "witch hunts" by Stella. Confronted with the escalating situation, Alerte Centre-Sud, a local organization, called for people from different community organizations, police, residents, and outreach workers to help them find solutions to ease their frustration. Hence, in 1995 the group created the Inter-District Table (TIQ 1996, 1). Community organizations including Stella sitting at the Table demanded that the role of outreach workers be recognized, stressing the fact that outreach workers, more than any other groups, were needed to engage with sex workers (TIQ 1996, 4–5).

Sitting at the Table, Stella framed its argument not only as a rights issue but also as a public health issue (Stella 1998a, 7). People at Stella were aware of the effect that the zero-tolerance policy had on their health mandate and sex workers' safety. The socio-legal atmosphere had to be taken into consideration because it influenced Stella's outreach work. In these moments of heightened resident frustration and consequential heightened police presence, outreach work was made more difficult. Police sweeps and different forms of harassment prevented outreach workers from establishing meaningful relationships with street sex workers, rendering sex workers more vulnerable to violence. The practice of safer sex and health promotion programs was also compromised, thus interfering with Stella's mandate. For Stella, the Table was about finding solutions to the anxiety produced by street sex workers. Unfortunately, no real solutions were put forward, and in 1996, with tensions rising once again in Montréal's east side around street prostitution, the city announced the creation of the Montréal Committee on Street and Juvenile Prostitution (MCSJ) (Stella 2005, 115). After the announcement, people from diverse organizations such as CACTUS, Séro-Zéro, Passages, and the Coalition met with municipal and legal authorities and public security. These diverse groups were willing to work together once again to find solutions to the ongoing social tensions brought about by street prostitution, and Stella would be involved insofar as its mandate would be respected (Stella 1996o,

2). The committee became official in December 1996 (Sansfaçon 1999) and called upon Montréal's official representatives to review what was often referred to as "the perennially unresolved issue" of street prostitution (Sansfaçon 1999, 7). Stella was present at the meetings and, in June 1998, its representatives began to participate, hoping that city officials and the police would understand that Stella's mandate, which consists of educating the public and empowering sex workers, required their cooperation. Stella anticipated an outcome that would grant sex workers safe working conditions (*ConStellation* 1998, 5).

An optimistic atmosphere reigned at Stella: "hopefully our presence and participation will result in a substantial improvement in the conditions of work, health and safety of sex workers" (Stella 1998a, 7). Another member of Stella sitting at the MCSJ table explained her reasons for being there:

> I aspire to dignity, total respect for my rights. I am against the stigmatization of sex workers or any other group or minority workers. This openness to dialogue, made possible by the Committee, could allow me to express myself without shame or feeling demeaned in my job [. . .]. Here again, I'm not dreaming, but I aspire to one day feel protected by my neighborhood police as are all [non-prostitute] citizens. (*ConStellation* 2000, 6)

This member framed her claim as a rights issue, a stance that demonstrated her own empowerment and insistence on autonomy. And she extended these rights to other minority-stigmatized groups; she trusted that the committee's recommendations would work if based on recognition.

The MCSJ completed its work in June 1999 with nine recommendations. After three years of at times tense discussions, the committee came to a fragile consensus that turned out to be the fourth and key recommendation of its report—the Pilot Project (Sansfaçon 1999, 63). The MCSJ's goal was understood as an endeavor to find an alternative to legal repression. The alternative was a project of non-judicialization—this would mean that police would refrain from using the criminal law against adult sex workers working in a defined area. The project would not begin until certain conditions had been developed and approved:

• Signature of a protocol binding those involved in the actualization of the project;
• The re-organization of work, if needed;
• The provision of human, financial, and material resources;
• The formation of interveners; and
• The installation of a permanent advisory committee.

The Pilot Project was presented for the first time on March 14, 2000, in the borough of Ville-Marie. After the meeting, Rosaire Théorêt, an involved citizen, wrote a letter in the local newspaper, the *Quartier Latin*, stating the position of his organization (*Quartier Latin*, November 1999). Linking the "prostitute" to organized crime and drug consumption, Théorêt argued that the project might attract "prostitutes" from other regions, including the United States. Doubting the benefit of the project, he wrote that "the only one [who may benefit] from this whole operation will be scavengers who exploit human misery." The committee's mandate, according to Théorêt, should be to help them leave the sex trade. "Do we want them to leave the street or maintain them there? No civilized country would accept that their people would be involved in this 'work.'" Adding to the fire, a Montréal newspaper, *Le Devoir*, published two letters by academic Yolande Geadah that highlighted issues of freedom of choice, concerns about victims in the sex industry (*Le Devoir* 1999a), and human trafficking (*Le Devoir* 1999b). These letters fed the tensions created by the Pilot Project, once again exciting public opinion and creating more fear.

The first MCSJ public meeting brought together 300 people. The president of the MCSJ, Madame St-Arnaud, stated that the committee had consulted residents regarding the "everyday irritants" related to street prostitution and that together they had decided on the Pilot Project, but to no avail. Residents did not believe her—"no brothel in our neighborhood" was the unanimous response. Even Sammy Forcillo, a city councilman who was one of Stella's supporters in 1994 and who sat on the MCSJ committee, was against the Pilot Project. The second meeting on March 16 was also fruitless and it ended with a bomb threat aimed to stop the meeting and the city pulled out of the initiative. One member of Stella recalls: "I remember the surge of prejudice, hatred, urban legends, disregard, and psychological violence. I remember a sex worker who at that time was chair of the board of directors, who had the courage to stand up in front of an angry mob and go to the microphone. Stella was well represented."

Years of education did not change the public perception of women working in the sex industry, particularly those working on the street. According to Canadian sociologist Daniel Sansfaçon, who at the time was the committee spokesperson, the project failed for three reasons. First, the title lent itself to misinterpretation. The use of "de-judicialization" in the title may have signified a "free for all" attitude in a neighborhood already struggling with poverty and petty crime. Second, there were internal tensions in the MCSJ, and third, the committee did not make good use of the public sphere to denounce the fact that those opposed to the project did not have a constructive solution, just opposition to the project (Sansfaçon 2000, 20). As the Montréal police inspector acknowledged at the time, "the way in which the case was presented to citizens immediately raised shields." The main issue was "why in our neighborhood, why not in upper-class neighborhoods such as Outremont or Westmount?" Despite the fact that it was obvious that prostitution was concentrated in this particular region, no one at the time could answer that question, and as Sansfaçon later said, it was a difficult argument to counter. Serge Bruneau, the coordinator of the MCSJ, admitted that he had been surprised by the reaction: "I do not hide that we were shaken, admits Bruneau. As is the case with any project, we expected some dissent or mis-understandings. But honestly, I didn't expect such a strong outcry" (*Le Devoir*, August 6, 2000, A5). A member of Stella described the atmosphere as follows:

The room was divided into strict camps, with the large majority so angry with prostitutes and with Stella that they were resorting to boos and angry jeers. It was incredibly violent. The poor committee on the stage was trying to keep it together, answering the questions as they could, but seemingly trembling from anger and disappointment. Bang. Welcome to the Centre-Sud. [. . .] I was totally naive, and Stella taught me almost everything I know about politics, community work, harm-reduction, mediation, strategy, feminism.

The Project ended in what Stella called "Les jours de la haine" (days of hatred) (Stella 2000b, 3), with increased acts of violence toward street sex workers (Stella 2000h, 14). Stella found itself having to deal with violence and its ensuing effects on the team, most notably stress.

Cathy: [. . .] a lot of residents had become fanatical . . . completely crazy and decided that they were going to impose their own justice. But it was not about decriminalization. It was about no longer handing out tickets. For this woman going to prison for "tickets" or unpaid fines! [. . .] Her life conditions deteriorate because she loses her house while she is there. [. . .] As for the project, it was something which responded to our needs and offered solutions that were interesting for the sex workers in these neighborhoods. [. . .] In any case, it was terrible. The increased level of violence on the street during this period was horrifying. Fear of customers, "attackers" [in quotes] but also the fear of residents. They were being screamed at by the residents. In any case, it was real hell. Really it was extremely difficult.

The Pilot Project died before it even got off the ground and created an atmosphere of greater intolerance vis-à-vis street sex workers (Stella 2000h, 14). In the aftermath, Stella's team was knocked off balance, and although never truly welcomed, street prostitution became even less tolerated. The event marginalized and drained the team, making other projects difficult to accomplish and outreach work more complicated. At one point, the situation got so tense that Stella had to close for a week. Windows at Stella's local were broken, and members of the team received anonymous aggressive phone calls. Stella's mandate depends on its outreach work, reaching sex workers where they work and having sex workers come in to Stella. For one year after the dreadful evening of March 16, the work of Stella's outreach team was difficult. For marginalized populations, this kind of disruption is particularly burdensome, and Cathy had this to say:

> It was very difficult for a year following [the Pilot Project]. At the street level, there was major intolerance on the part of the police . . . it was difficult in the neighborhood; women had to work harder because they needed money. Over time, there were some who moved from the Center-Sud closer to Hochelaga Maisonneuve [. . .] then, for us, it was difficult, [. . .] the [lack] of confidence, nervousness, tension on the street, it had an impact. [. . .] The events certainly traumatized us. It's like. . . . I think a big injury to Stella. For a long time . . . then it's as if we retreated [. . .]. It was hard on the street during this period—when you have a "cleaning" operation going on [. . .]. Because of the Pilot Project, we had a big increase of violence [. . .]. We held a press conference with the Fédération des femmes du Québec and with public health officials about the increase in violence.

Following the debacle of the Pilot Project, the National Coalition against Women, Poverty, and Violence (CNPV)—which was somewhat reticent about the idea that sexual services could be work—nevertheless adopted a motion denouncing acts of violence against street prostitutes in the Centre-Sud neighborhood, against people and groups who represented sex workers, and their allies. Stella and the Fédération des Femmes du Québec (FFQ) may have had a divergence of opinions/positions regarding sex work, but in this crisis, the FFQ and Stella had one voice. Françoise David, who at the time was the FFQ president, commented on the ensuing violence:

> I knew, after consultations, what was the situation [at Stella] that week, all the acts of violence that had been reported in the newspapers. When I heard about it, I was really devastated. I found this appalling! It was from that moment that finally, the National Coalition of women against poverty and violence [. . .] adopted a resolution of support. We're not in agreement with the manifestations of intolerance and hatred towards sex workers. We have remained very vigilant. If this happens, there will be complaints from us. This is unacceptable, that's all. (*ConStellation* 2000, 8)

Moreover, in June 2000, women from the Centre-Sud held a press conference calling for peace and dialogue. In August, the FFQ and Stella participated in a press conference denouncing the surge of violence against sex workers (FFQ 2001). Françoise David and Dr. Réjean Thomas, president of Médecins du Monde (*Voir* 2000, 23–29), both denounced the violence. Plus, David labeled police sweeps in Centre-Sud as violence toward sex workers (*Le Devoir*, August 24, 2000, A4). Nevertheless, in September, two residents' organizations came into existence and joined the prohibitionist movement, becoming a huge obstacle for Stella to achieving sex workers' rights. The first of such organizations was C1DBU, a development corporation attached to l'Université du Québec à Montréal (UQÀM) and the second was the Association of the Residents of the Suburb of Montréal (ARRFM). The ARRFM gathered two hundred residents of the districts of Saint-Jacques and of Sainte-Marie. The members were involved in the district's affairs. Of interest to them was the beautification of the district's parks and streets. Residents who, in the winter of 1999–2000, protested the Pilot Project founded the ARRFM in April 2000. Sex workers were not included in the "beautification" project. This Pilot Project constituted a good lesson for the residents, who decided to get involved in matters concerning their environment.

RESIDENT ORGANIZATIONS

According to a municipal employee, after defeating the Pilot Project, residents of the targeted neighborhood vowed never to be caught off guard again. C1DBU and ARRFM immediately received support from police stations number 21, 22, and 23, and they wrote a letter thanking the commander for his continuous efforts to eliminate "prostitutes" and their customers (C1DBU 2000, 2). The group asked the police not only to keep up their crackdown vis-à-vis customers, but to intensify it. They asked Madame Saint-Arnaud, who at the time was responsible for public security, to support police intervention and do so without restraint "to stop street prostitution as well as other phenomena of criminal delinquency, which harms our citizens and the good reputation of our neighborhoods" (C1DBU 2000, 3):

> The shenanigans of some pressure groups and some individuals don't impress us. We know their tactics; we know how they manipulate the information, this is a science of which they are masters. The way they do it is to make the public believe their iron-clad argument, while there is nothing substantial in their comments and their testimonies are based on nothing that we can control (3) [. . .] We have undertaken actions which are successful, and which are in line with our laws. We hope that you won't be distracted or intimidated by people or pressure groups that encourage the continuation of illegal actions. (C1DBU 2000, 5)

It is quite insidious that Stella was not named among the pressure groups mentioned in the letter. The language of "shenanigans" and "intimidation" by "people or pressure groups that encourage the continuation of illegal actions" used in the passage above underlines the fact that Stella and sex workers in Montréal were, at best, not recognized at all and, at worst, were labeled as a deceiver and manipulator of information and criminals. Even Stella's public health mandate was not recognized as legitimate, much less its role as an advocate for sex workers. For most residents, age-old stereotypical symbols

attached to sex workers continued to resonate. Street prostitution was perceived as an activity related to crime, morbidity, and immorality, making the
mobilization of allies very difficult.

> [. . .] stop taking us for fools. [. . .] The increasing violence against street
> prostitutes result from several factors such as the rise of violence in society in
> general, as well as [prostitutes'] own actions such as stealing from their cus-
> tomers, plus the behavior of these pressure groups which ensure that street-
> prostitutes will not complain to police if they are victims of violence or rape on
> the part of their so-called clients. [. . .] Street prostitution cannot be separated
> from the current context of the whole street-specific issue. The criminal world
> is omnipresent. It is important to know if it is drugs that lead to street prostitu-
> tion or vice versa, but one fact remains: the two are intimately related and
> bearers of violence. (C1DBU 2000, 6–7)

The group was far from impressed with Stella's press conference in August
(C1DBU 2000, 5) and went as far as accusing Stella of discouraging sex
workers who were victims of violence from going to the police. C1DBU
demanded police intervention to protect women and maintain order:

> Stella and its acolytes are alarmed about the increase in violence against street
> prostitutes. [We have no doubt] that street prostitutes are victims of physical,
> verbal and psychological violence. [However] we want to emphasize that this
> is only one aspect of violent behavior. We believe [that such incidents in fact]
> exceed the 24 cases reported by Stella. [Along with] physical battles [. . .] the
> verbal abuse [there are] struggles for the control of space of sidewalks which
> vary according to hours and days. [In addition], the street prostitute interacts
> with many people: her pimp, her pusher, her shylock, her lover and her clients.
> In short, she is an object in the hands of individuals who have no respect for
> humans.

These observations are intriguing because they provide an example of how
prohibitionists effectively turn Stella's argument about the need for protection on its head; they assert that since sex work is intrinsically violent and
dangerous, it is not only the workers who need protection but the rest of
society as well. This attempts to justify their need for greater control and
increased police presence. However, such a rigid position prevents any opportunities for what Axel Honneth calls moments of "reciprocal recognition"
(1996, 108)—when both parties recognized each other's autonomy and are
willing to open a dialogue. Sad, because as Jonathan Haidt writes, "when in
conflict with a person or group, an incredibly valuable tool is to acknowledge
where others are right because in almost any conflict each side is right about
something" (Hoggan 2016, 39). That moment was clearly impossible. And
with the gentrification of "hot neighborhoods," the situation was far from

being resolved. A city official comments on the relationship between residents and community groups after the Pilot Project debacle:

> [. . .] we are no longer speaking of the same residents as five years ago, now they are professionals who have a settled and very articulated world and make political representations according to their needs. And then it is certain that the dossier is highly politicized also because [of the Pilot Project]. The entire backlash demonstrates how this case has become highly political. When any community attracts investors, resident associations are there to represent the interests of community members. [. . .] They, in turn, put pressure on politicians to solve problems, and they will inevitably ask them—what are you doing about it? So, this is a new and ongoing dynamic that did not exist as recently as 99. [. . .] And then it joined [the city's] mission where we encouraged the communities to take ownership of their development, by working together. So, you know, it's the very basis of our mission in social development. This is to ensure that the associations of residents take responsibility for the community in their own hands. Thus, we have the same agenda.

Their agenda did not include Stella's presence in their neighborhood ensuring the safety of street sex workers. Both C1DBU and the ARRFM rejected the expression "sex work" used by Stella, an expression used to underline the importance of the work dimension and which contributes to finding solutions to sex workers' struggles (*ConStellation* 1999, 5). The resistance to the Pilot Project exemplified the whore symbol almost to perfection. All the tools used to delegitimize sex workers' claims were present in the letters from the C1DBU and ARRFM—language of the pimp, disparaging language about drug use, and the presence of organized crime.

The whore symbol, and the morality that it is shrouded in, has proven to be resistant to change. The imagery and language that are used to describe "the whore" prevent outsiders from perceiving sex workers as anything other than victims or criminals, and delegitimizes sex workers' rights frames. The source of violence was contested: Stella claimed that criminalization gave potential aggressors free rein; prohibitionists maintained that violence is intrinsic to sex work. When asked if another Pilot Project was possible, a Montréal civil servant had this to say:

> [. . .] Oh no! We must forget the idea of [bringing fewer workers to court]. In the context where we live now it is not possible, and then you won't see [the idea of bringing fewer cases to court] appearing in the 2004–2007 action plan. [Residents] are very well organized now and then I would tell you that today's residents are not the same residents. They have a well-organized network; I would say that [they have a voice now], and we can't go around them.

While residents and prohibitionists were forming a coalition, Stella and community partners were planning an event aimed at assuaging some of the

tension created by the Pilot Project debacle. The project was called Projet
Milieu and included Alerte Centre-Sud, a community organization; CAC-
TUS, a support organization for drug users; Passages, a woman's shelter;
Séro-Zéro, an HIV prevention organization; Spectre de rue, another support
organization for drug users; and Stella. Projet Milieu's main goal was to
encourage people concerned by street prostitution to come together and find
solutions. Everybody would be included. The first order of business was to
find influential people from the community, to educate, open a dialogue, and,
using innovative practices, create a space to promote the empowerment of all
those concerned. The project was planned for August 2001 until March 2003
and was supported by the mayor's committee designated to find solutions to
social issues (Stella 2001). Although much effort was put into the project by
members of Stella, there was difficulty in coordinating the six organizations
involved in the project.[1] Nonetheless, an outreach worker from Stella organized picnics in different parks, and these were well attended by Stella members and residents. Moreover, a get-together between daycare workers and
mothers and sex workers was initiated, and the result was positive. Efforts
were made but were not enough to alter the tensions experienced daily as
Stella's team was trying to nurse itself back to health because in the middle
of efforts to ease tensions in the neighborhood, prohibitionists launched a
media blitz. Indeed, in 2002, Sisyphe.org, an Internet site for the abolition of
prostitution, published eleven articles between September and December.
Some of these pieces were written by Richard Poulin and Micheline Carrier,
two known Canadian prohibitionists, and Gunilla Ekberg, well known for her
prohibitionist stance on the global stage.

According to members of Stella, what were framed as "debates" around
sex work were not neutral, but actually promoted a prohibitionist perspective
and was thus prejudiced. Prohibitionists' strategies included: fiercely maintaining the link between human trafficking and prostitution, opposing any
distinction between voluntary and forced prostitution, fighting against all
attempts to present sex work as work, demanding the criminalization of
clients, and insisting on grants for groups opposing prostitution and working
with "prostituted" women and survivors. For Stella, any prohibitionist strategies, including those criminalizing clients and so-called pimps, contribute to
maintaining the sex industry underground and thus increase the possibility of
abuse (Stella 2002, 2).

The goal of the ARRFM was to recognize and promote the residential
character of the district and to propose solutions related to the problems of
"narco-prostitution," and in 2005, the ARRFM submitted a paper to the
Canadian Standing Committee on Justice, Human Rights, Public Safety and
Emergency Preparedness. The title of the paper was "Narco-Street Prostitution and Neighborhood Life" (ARRFM 2005) and in its text, the ARRFM
claimed that the expression "sex work" did nothing but standardize one real-

ity, which was certainly not theirs. The term, they claimed, was disconnected from the meaning shared by most of the people outside the sex industry. The content of the submission testified to the experience of the residents and their desire to see the end of prostitution. The ARRFM stressed that the practice of prostitution has an impact on residential districts, particularly because in their view, street prostitution is closely related to the sale and use of drugs, which in their view was clearly a bad thing. The following passage describes what has come to be known as "narco-prostitution" (van der Poel 1995) and underscores the mentality that has prevented any form of dialogue. From the outset Stella's empowerment philosophy and framing sex work as work were rejected completely:

> The role of the organized crime behind the narco-street prostitution is always obscured. [. . .] Community groups only report to their donors and to their members. The community at large is ignored. Each community group sees "its trees and ignores the forest." Studies, documentation, and, knowledge of the characteristics of customers of prostitution services, are almost nonexistent, while [these clients] are an integral part of the phenomenon. There are no organizations and or programs to help customers. About 150 prostitutes take our neighborhood hostage. (ARRFM 2005)

Outreach Work: Stella's Everyday Presence on the Street

Outreach workers and social workers have different mandates, and they do not approach street outreach the same way. "The tensions we found [between outreach workers and social workers] relates to the ignorance of street work and the difficulty [of social workers] in identifying the specificity and the relevance of this mode of intervention" (Duval and Fontaine 2000, 51). Outreach for an organization is non-directive and grounded in developing a relationship and making space to respect the decision-making process of sex workers. Outreach is about valorizing people, recognizing their autonomy, making connection—all which are essential to the process of empowerment and participation (Benoit et al. 2017). The struggle between social workers and outreach workers revolves around two important issues: social workers often see their mission as rescuing sex workers from the street or attempting to change their course of action, whereas Stella's outreach workers meet sex workers where they are and focus on whatever is priority for the sex worker. However, it must be emphasized that empowerment is a process which requires a community of like-minded people who understand and support each other. Without it, the process is not possible. It is not about rehabilitation which is often the mandate of the social worker. Stella's work is about fostering agency/autonomy and self-respect. Empowerment begins where the person is, physically and emotionally, not where social services might wish them to be. Clearly, some women are struggling with family violence, drug use, homelessness, and undernourishment. Outreach workers offer guidance in these situations, and to do this effectively they need resources, which at times are lacking. They need the time, the money, and the space but for outreach workers to negotiate these demands remains difficult because to this day there is little recognition of their mandate (Winters 2016).

The last annual report presented at Stella's Annual General Meeting before the Pilot Project stated that the organization was attaining credibility; sex workers, diverse organizations, and public services seemed to work together. The report stated Stella's capacity to act as a collective (Stella 1998c, 10). Stella was a site where sex workers came to discuss, to learn, to debate. It was becoming a milieu de vie, where getting services and information came hand in hand with a growing sense of belonging. It is clear from this quote that the atmosphere at Stella was optimistic: "[. . .] the links that we were able to establish help us support sex workers' efforts to improve their life and health. [For] sex workers, the name Stella now refers to respect, recognition of rights and their ability to act and to achieve solidarity" (Stella 1998c, 10).

The report acknowledged that Stella's efforts at demystifying sex work seem to have led to an improvement in the social position of sex workers in Montréal. Indeed, Stella was invited to participate in the Table Interquartiers and the MCSJ followed by the Pilot Project. These events were pivotal in Stella's life—highly significant for their collective identity, their recognition as workers, and their self-worth. Each one of these events necessitated a great deal of organization and mobilization. Despite the popular belief that sex workers are victims, sex workers continued to resist, and with their participation in different committees, especially the Pilot Project, Stella's team began carving out its place as a political actor in Montréal. Stella was coming out in the public sphere. These events attached themselves to members' narratives, again feeding Stella's history, identity, and feelings of belonging. This period thoroughly positioned Stella as a community organization producing meaning and countering the victimizing narrative on "prostituted women" and prostitution. To use Stuart Hall's expression, Stella engaged in "the politics of signification" (in Benford and Snow 2000, 613) and for a stigmatized and criminalized group, this is essential. Thus, began what Melucci (1995, 43) identifies as the creation of a collective through self-definition and relationship with the environment—allies, city and health officials, and prohibitionists.

Stella worked three years with the MCSJ, and as painful as the failure to alter people's conception of Stella was, the disappointment contributed to the formation of a "we" by helping members clarify their goals and identify areas of possibilities and their limits. Indeed, early in 2000, Stella published three editions of *ConStellation*, one of which was the political edition.

Without a doubt, the MCSJ witnessed Stella's coming out as a force to be reckoned with, but this visibility created unanticipated consequences. Based on the 1998 Annual General Meeting report, it was clear that Stella's representatives and sex workers in the community were optimistic and felt they were being listened to by Montréal authorities and people responsible for creating changes. Pregnant with anticipation, the Pilot Project boomeranged and created a new adversary—neighborhood committees—and in addition, revived the conflation of sex work with human trafficking. The positive atmosphere described in the 1998 report was shattered, and as they came to the MCSJ with great expectations, it made the debacle even more painful. As an enduring presence in the metropolis, sex workers were a concern for policy makers, neighborhood organizations, police, and moral entrepreneurs. The Pilot Project represented a possible solution, so what went wrong?

CAN WE TALK ABOUT STEREOTYPES: THE POLLUTING EFFECT OF MISREPRESENTATION?

Sociology as discourse and metanarrative is reflexive: it reflects back on the sociologist who plays an important part in the production of sociological knowledge, a part which [I] confess rather than conceal. (Knowles 1996, 23)

My standing as a social scientist would be pointless if my concluding analysis of the Pilot Project debacle was simply an activist-motivated rant—it could very well be interpreted as such since from the very beginning I have positioned myself as activist/scholar. This may be contested but all sociological questions are grounded in the subjective, in personal concerns and values and interests. So at this juncture I wish to drive home two points. First, although a clear link between policies and public opinion has not yet been conclusively established (Page 2006), there is nevertheless ample evidence that policy makers have an intimate relationship with the community (Johnson 2015) and that the failure of the Pilot Project is a highly apposite example of distortion by stereotypes. The project failed because the residents brought up the most damaging stereotypes that directly and detrimentally impacted sex workers organizations' struggle for legal and moral recognition, namely, human trafficking and drugs. What follows then is my own informed position/reflections regarding the failure of the project—the seeds of this reflection were planted in 2001 when I worked with Fran Shaver as a research assistant on the Sex Trade Advocacy Research project (STAR)[2]— and do not necessarily reflect Stella's position.

The MCSJ and the ensuing Pilot Project recalled Montréal's unclear approach to prostitution—some participants were willing to try something other than criminalization and some, such as the neighborhood organizations, wanted to see it disappear. Debates surrounding the legitimacy of sex workers' claims are contentious, and framing processes have become essential in comprehending and explaining collective action and the success of the collective. A superficial look at the demands of Stella evince how these confused the public; it did not make sense to residents that people who were considered "criminals" could demand rights and safety or recognition and space for outreach to this criminalized community (TIQ 1996, 4–5). Everything about the project, to them, was wrong, especially the timing 1998–2000[3] and the location—in a neighborhood already struggling with poverty and petty crime.

Although Montréal's reputation as a relatively liberally minded city still holds, years of zoning and what Anouk Bélanger calls "rehabilitation" (2005, 23) had changed the surface of the city's sexual landscape. Indeed, years of police and social repression have reduced Montréal's red light district to a mere memory, and I cannot help but speculate, as Cameron did, "where they think the activity [has moved] to" (2004, 1651). The answer, as in other cities, is that street prostitution has moved to residential areas already struggling with poverty. After multiple campaigns and the introduction of zero-tolerance policies, sex work continues to be present in Canadian cities, and street prostitution remains an "irritant" to the cities' residents and authorities.

Stella's mandate conflicted with other resident interests, namely, removing of prostitution from residential neighborhoods. The outreach workers at Stella were focused on improving the living and working conditions for sex workers, and in order to do this they placed the sex workers' expertise at the center of this intervention. This meant following the sex workers' lead rather than offering prescriptive directives. Stella's mandate was to build relationships of trust and to inspire women to take care of their health. As a member of Stella's team said, "we're trying first and foremost to create links of confidence in people. We don't have a mission, a goal with this person here. If you have a goal, it is to develop a relationship of trust [. . .] this isn't to pick up and rehabilitate." This philosophy of empowerment/participation came to be interpreted as promoting sex work by prohibitionists and residents' organizations, which was a clear rejection of Stella's actual mandate. The ARRFM argued:

> We believe that some community organizations dedicated to defending the rights of prostitutes are not helping them to get out of prostitution. Rehabilitation and detoxification are non-existent most of the time. The [group headquarters] is not located in the neighborhood where solicitation and street prostitution takes place. They show no sympathy for the problems experienced by residents. Harm reduction and empowerment are the "buzzwords" of community groups which themselves are self-proclaimed undeniable experts on prostitution, drug addiction, and prevention of HIV/AIDS. (ARRFM 2005)

The rejection of Stella and its mandate by residents and neighborhoods amounted to a rejection of Stella's participation in finding solutions for harmonious neighborhoods. Resident groups came to view Stella itself as a problem if the organization refused to encourage women to leave the industry altogether.

I was only able to make sense of what had happened years after the fact during an interview with a city employee that resident members who were a part of the Pilot Project Committee had erroneously created an expectation that Stella would be "exiting" sex workers from prostitution. And here it is important to remind ourselves that "[the city of Montréal] is not just a web of organizations and actors," but also a web of understanding about the proper classification and configuration of those organization and actors" (Mayrl and Sarak 2016, 9). What I consider central in making sense of the failure of the Pilot Project was Stella's classification—an awkward mixture of victims and a criminal group. This categorization presupposes the existence of margins, lines, or divisions between those who can define the situation, those who can label, and those who cannot. Indeed, Stella stood at the margins, a space where one is defined as an outsider a criminal—one that does not belong.

Following the sex work conference in Montréal in 1996, sex workers became more visible. Indeed, in October 1996 Stella, the Coalition, and the Association québecoise des travailleuses et travailleurs du sexe (AQTTS) sent a letter to City Hall demanding the inclusion of sex workers on round tables analyzing the state of street prostitution in Montréal (Stella 1996k, 4). Every committee that emerged in Montréal between the years 1996–1999 included sex workers. Not everyone rejoiced in Stella's visibility. Sex workers became more vocal, more present. For the police, a service group was acceptable, but my interview with a city employee confirmed that Stella was only seen as credible if they were "rehabilitating" sex workers. However, while the MCSJ may have given Stella a seat at the table, they never accepted or recognized Stella's mandate. It was clear that for the resident organizations the whore symbol was quasi-intact; sex workers were stereotyped as drug addicts, linked to criminal gangs or organized crime, immature, and incapable of autonomy.

The Rebirth of an Old Conflation: Human Trafficking and Sex Work

Defining trafficking has become a challenge for politicians, the courts, and academics (Hauck and Peterke 2010), but what does it mean for sex workers' organizations such as Stella? Because it was brought up during the Pilot Project disaster, Stella was forced to deal with the revival of human trafficking discourse. This conflation of children and adults elicits anxiety and disgust in the general population; language that conflated youth with adults had made its way into the Pilot Project and was reinforced by the relentless prohibitionists' narratives that amalgamated the sex industry with human trafficking. At this point, the role played by human emotions is significant, and for marginalized groups such as Stella, they had to contend with not only attracting resources, allies, funds, and positive media coverage but also with countering the stereotypes and confusion that emerged from forced conflation of human trafficking and sex work. According to historians, the seeds of this conflation were planted during the Industrial Revolution. So once again a short historical detour is needed to attempt to clarify the events that have linked sex workers' organizations to criminal activities (Walkowitz 1980).

The Old and the New Entangled

It is in England during the 1880s, amid the syphilis epidemic and the ensuing Contagious Disease Acts and Repeal campaign, when influential essays and newspaper articles began to appear about white slavery and child prostitution (Walkowitz 1980; Corbin 1990). The event that galvanized the public occurred on July 26, 1881, when Lord Snagge, a member of the British Parliament, published a report detailing the trafficking of "thirty-four young Englishwomen including virgins" (Corbin 1990, 276). Newspapers reported that the trade occurred between England and Brussels, and its purpose was to provide children and women for brothels in Europe. The next key event was the publication, in the summer of 1885, of a series of five articles by W. T. Stead, "The Maiden Tribute to Modern Babylon," in *The Pall Mall Gazette*. These articles were an exposé of child prostitution and reported that ". . . virgins were sold to old aristocratic rakes" (Walkowitz 1980, 246). Following this newspaper report, a court in Belgium concluded that such traffic had in fact happened; however, not to the extent that some social reformers insisted. As for the presence of young sex workers on the streets of London, historian Judith Walkowitz found evidence of their existence, but again, not to the extent reported in the press or depicted in historical research on prostitution. Without trivializing the issue, Alain Corbin and Judith Walkowitz show that public officials and the media exaggerated the phenomenon.[4] Both historians analyze the white slavery matter as a social coping mechanism. The 1870s provided fertile ground for generating moral panic; rapid social change brought on by industrialization had created a febrile atmosphere.

It did not matter whether the concerns were justified or not; the publication of "The Maiden Tribute" brought about the 1885 Criminal Law Amendment Act (CLAA), which increased the age of consent for girls from thirteen to sixteen, thus effectively increasing legal control over the sexual behavior of young women. Moreover, it made both procurement for the purposes of prostitution and brothels illegal, carrying fines and the possibility of jail time. As fear around the "white slavery trade" grew, the Vagrancy Act of 1824 was amended again in 1898 to include a provision that resembled trafficking and addressed what today is referred to by the general public as "pimping." The concern about trafficking and the ensuing debates came back to haunt sex workers' organizations in the 1980s and early 90s and, according to Chris Bruckert, resurfaced in 2002, resulting in most of the work done to make some headway once again being almost washed away.

Contemporary Sex Worker Organizations and Human Trafficking

Tackled in the 1980s by seasoned feminists such as Kathleen Barry, Andrea Dworkin, and Catharine Mackinnon, the violence/slavery/prostitution combination has turned out to be one of the most complicated arguments that sex worker rights groups have had to face. Barry and MacKinnon were instrumental in the conflation of trafficking and prostitution; it is a link that has become more entrenched over the years. With a Ph.D. in Political Science, and as a professor in the faculty of Law at the University of Michigan, MacKinnon attained notoriety by arguing in favor of censuring all form of sexual representation. MacKinnon's theses, articulated through a legal discourse, are refined and convincing, thus proving to be the most difficult to dethrone. Her theory continues to fit the Canadian prohibitionist paradigm of subordination and domination for which she is the main legal theorist; her definition of trafficking remains the focus for prohibitionists. It must be emphasized that the amalgamation of trafficking, sexual slavery, and prostitution leads to two opposing political/legal frameworks. Sex workers' organizations and their allies favor decriminalization of prostitution because of the harms that stigmatization, discrimination, and criminalization bring to sex workers' lives and work. Prohibitionists claim that decriminalization is an invitation to human traffickers. Human trafficking includes sweatshops, farming, and any other dishonest practices, but it is "sex trafficking" that has by far attracted the most attention (Lam and Gallant 2018; Bernstein 2017, 299; Engle Merry 2016, 115).

The Fallacies

The main problem with the prohibitionists' hardline approach is that it relies on fallacies, on "bad arguments that tend to persuade" (Cederblom and Paulsen 1996, 150). Central to these "bad arguments" is the often-erroneous definition of "trafficking" which must be clarified and distinguished from smuggling. This is also illegal but includes the element of volition which is absent in trafficking. Thus, a useful definition of trafficking avoids deliberately unsettling language and images and offers a nuanced approach which enhances our understanding of the situation of migrant sex workers. Thus, trafficking in persons is defined by three elements:

1. The Relocation of a person (activities linked to recruitment, reloca-tion, or crossing borders)
2. Constraint or deception (threats, use of force, fraud, abuse of authority or of a situation of vulnerability)
3. Exploitation of labour (the intention to exploit, once the person arrive at destination: forced labour, slavery and similar practices, debt bond-age, sexual exploitation). (Parent et al. 2013)

In order to have trafficking we need the three elements to be present—relocation, constraint, and exploitation. As I have indicated, trafficking in persons cannot be conflated with smuggling, which includes volition. I will use a quote from Engle Merry to demonstrate how easy it is to merge the victim and actor in a few sentences:

> [T]rafficking covers a very broad range of activities, and it is often quite varied in its forms of recruitment, the nature of the exploitation, and the extent to which a person has agreed to or accepted the labor—a decision typically made in the context of life circumstances and social and kinship expectations and obligations. It can only be understood within its social, political, and economic context. Since trafficking refers to a diverse set of practices shaped by local and national social structures, it is very hard to define it in a way that crosses national, local, and other social and cultural boundaries. (Engle Merry 2016, 116)

Her sentence—"the extent to which a person has agreed to or accepted the labor—a *decision* typically made in the context of life circumstances and social and kinship expectations and obligations"—this is smuggling—illegal, but not coerced. Smuggling is not trafficking, and the operative word here is *decision* which must be kept in mind when considering illegal migration. I will return to this discussion later.

The struggle for greater freedom and equality have influenced women all over the world, thus creating a desire to seek "a better future for themselves and their families, whereas others are looking for adventure and travel" (Lam and Gallant 2018, 295). However, the restrictions that some governments place upon migration complicate how women access that "better future." Introduced by anthropologist Laura Agustìn, a recognition of the cultural dimension demands that we consider the connection between women's agen-cy, or the lack of it, which varies greatly from country to country, when examining the issue of smuggling or illegal migration.

There could be many reasons why women migrate, but the main one is to find work (Toupin 2013; Swanson 2016; O'Connor 2017); indeed, "in homes and brothels around the world, migrant women are selling a unique commod-ity: care" (Gutierrez Garza 2019, 3). There seems to be a double standard regarding women and once again, agency and autonomy seems to be men's prerogative. Women are still "overwhelmingly [perceived] as pushed, obligated, coerced and forced when they leave home for the same reason as men: to get ahead through work" (Stella 2002, 11). O'Connor keeps the complexity of the argument alive when she writes, "[it] is contended that people currently being defined as trafficked persons are for the most part 'the ambitious and industrious poor who seek to improve their lives'" (2017, 9).

Clearly, this is a contentious issue, and often those who participate in the debate assume that the choice is "either/or"—the popular belief that "if you are not for me you're against me" when in fact there is a range of options along the continuum between these two points of view. Plus, the debate must remain open—it requires a genuine desire to dialogue, and both sides need to face their emotions regarding this question. The second fallacy is called the straw man, and consists of making one's position appear much stronger by making the other positions appear weaker than they are. It is during these debates that symbols gather their significance. The language used by prohibitionists during these debates brings images to mind. Extreme cases of violence and images of little girls situate the discussion within images that already have meaning, leaving little room for new interpretations. As argued by Maynard, "[a]lthough invoking slavery provides important emotional weight to those who wish to criminalize prostitution, its association with slavery results in an empirically inaccurate description of the sex industry as a whole" (Maynard 2018, 286). To appeal to emotions/disgust only exploits the situation; it is not about taking sides it is about creating a discursive space, collecting solid data, and developing a rigorous theoretical framework, and once again I must underline the work of Engle Merry:

> The major theoretical frameworks for conceptualizing trafficking focus on criminal justice, slavery, forced labor, and human rights. Each of these frameworks includes ways to count and control trafficking. The definitive conception of the problem will be determined by which mode is determining trafficking prevails. Since the way, a problem is defined points to the way it can be solved; the measurement system that prevails also determines what is done about it. These are the knowledge effects and governance effects of measuring trafficking. (Engle Merry 2016, 113)

What kind of data are we collecting if every migrant sex worker is counted as a trafficked person? I do not want to fall into the same trap and create a hard separation between trafficking in persons and smuggling, but at least we have a point of departure to further our discussion.

Another fallacy, one emphasized by prohibitionists, is the collective representation of sex workers, particularly those from the Global South, as victims. These supposedly defenseless women apparently are too weak to defend themselves, and are incapable of making decisions or life choices. Thus they need to be rescued. And while rescuing women may appear to be noble at first, under scrutiny it is often revealed as a lack of trust in women and in their capacity to judge their own situation and decide how to remedy it (Calhoun 2004). It is noteworthy that in 1984, during a conference in Amsterdam, Barry did not revise her theoretical position in the face of the subsequent denunciation of the colonization critique by professor Rudo Gaidzanwa of Zimbabwe, who criticized settlers who

> [. . .] Intentionally misrepresented customary law to even further disenfranchise black women by interpreting the customary law to mean that the black woman has not reached the age of majority, no matter what her age is chronologically. This effectively prevented black women from access to and ownership of land because they were considered minors. Under colonialism, for black women to be subject to the civil law which defined the white population, they had to become considered white in lifestyle, that is, in the economic middle class. (Barry 1984, 35)

These words, pronounced more than thirty years ago by Gaidzanwa, still resonate as non-Western women are often perceived as less capable of making decisions regarding their lives and are perceived to need saving. This point brings me to consider the argument articulated by Calhoun (2004) in "World of Emergencies." Always imagined as victims without any agency and treated as minors, women become a charity project. But acts of charity usually do not address structural inequality, inequity, and blatant injustices (Jones et al. 2018).

The forms of economic, gender, or structural inequality that foster trafficking and restrictive immigration laws are not considered in the Trafficking in Person Reports (2019).[5] The trafficking model "blames organized crime rather than economic disparities, violence in families, established patterns of servile labor, a lack of legal modes of movement, or a desire to travel" (Engle Merry 2016, 123). For many participants in the "prostitution as work debate," this point is definitive—rescuing women is not only sexist but also racist. Some studies of the sex industry rely on an analysis of colonialism that reveals the West's greediness in the Global South as sexual as it is economic. In most of these studies, racialized women, and women in poverty, are positioned as powerless beside men, white people, and the rich (Agustín 2007, 89; Engle Merry 2016). In fact, Stella contended that one of the consequences of the prostitution/trafficking link is the promotion of prohibitionist measures that endanger women because measures taken to counter trafficking are strategies of oppression and not protection. Arrests, fines, detention, and expulsion measures are anti-feminist, anti-migrant, and anti–sex work. Plus, anti-trafficking policies created to "rescue" women have historically been used as anti-immigration tools.

For migrant women in search of work, several filters are needed to overcome many taboos in several countries, such as those which prevent women from traveling alone, without the authority of a male figure like a father or husband, or prevent them from obtaining a passport or visa to travel. One must also cope with immigration policies, which are restrictive and practiced arbitrarily, often with racist motivations (Howell 2000), and at times with a complete closure of the borders. It is in this context of a gendered division of labor, and the international divide regarding both customs and legal structures, that trafficking operates.

As I have noted, sex workers are often perceived as victims without autonomy, decision-making capacity, or life goals. Sex workers come from all walks of life; they cover the entire class spectrum. Recognition means addressing women in the sex industry as social actors capable of reflection and analysis, owning their organizational and resistance strategies.

Finding work has left many women with no other choice except to leave their country, a decision that is difficult to execute. In addition to increasingly restrictive immigration politics, the demand for labor, especially in informal sectors, has increased. It is within that space created by restrictions and demands that human trafficking and illegal immigration take place. It is within that gap created by official policies that such illicit means evolved, and in examining this administrative paradox, Poulin (2003) and Toupin (2002a, 2002b, 2013) agree.

Once again, it becomes clear that a significant problem is the near impossibility for many women around the world to migrate legally and safely. Thus, one of the consequences is the use of illegal means to migrate, in which a third party organizes the illegal transportation. Or, as Engle Merry writes, it is a situation where organizers "abuse [the] condition of vulnerability" (2016, 120), and this is part of the definition of human trafficking. Did the woman take what is commonly called "calculated risks"? Trafficking (victim) and smuggling (actor) are not the same and prohibitionists refuse to at least discuss the difference. It is this victim/actor situation that makes the problem more difficult to study because only as a victim will a woman receive some attention. As an actor (smuggling) she will get arrested. If it was a "calculated risk," then this woman has certainly considered her situation, one that left her with few options but to take a chance and at this point she calls upon a smuggler—that is a clandestine, illegal, but willing transportation of an individual from one country to another, in return for material or financial compensation (Toupin 2013).

Why is it so difficult to accept the fact that women decide to migrate, despite the risk of the migration process? I agree it may be that these women were severely constrained, and thus could not make choices freely. As a result, I have stopped using the word "choice"—women who take such chances do not make choices, they make decisions; every single day, they must decide what will be their next step. It is essential to keep in mind that "moving across countries" may have been done illegally but it is not trafficking. Sex workers and their allies argue that for women trying to escape poverty and abuse, commercial sex is a good avenue to earn income and become self-sufficient. I wish for us to focus more on women's right to autonomy and safety and when we leave sex workers with no option but to travel illegally, we marginalize them even more and leave them unprotected. This situation is known, but still sex workers rarely work with the migrant justice movement in Canada—a reality that Lam and Gallant hope to change (2018, 295).

Massive unemployment in some countries, changing social contexts due to globalization, neo-liberalism, war, and recent terrorist attacks in France and London render people sensitive to issues of public security. A moral panic dictates that something must be done. Canadian prohibitionist Richard Poulin (2004), drawing on his statistical analysis, demands that "sexual slavery be stopped"; he claims that millions of innocent victims are being trafficked every year. As a legal anthropologist Engle Merry (2016) understands, attempting to quantify the complexity of the social world is misleading. To rely on numbers to interpret the world is attractive but numbers need to be explained. What are these numbers telling us? Too often quantitative data lack a strong analysis. And I must reiterate—trafficking or illegal migration? As argued by Jones et al. (2018), often non-governmental organizations in order to keep their funding must produce numbers of trafficking survivors without any documentation. Yet, this helps staff invest time in addressing women's needs if required. Numerical assessments such as indicators appeal to the desire for simple, accessible knowledge and a basic human tendency of seeing the world through hierarchies of reputation and status. Yet, the process of translating the buzzing confusion of social life into neat categories that can be tabulated risks distorting the complexity of social phenomena (Engle Merry 2016, 1) and prevents a valid estimation of needs. So instead of entering a battle of numbers I wish that we could fight for women's rights, migrant sex workers or not, and finally establish solidarity among all sex workers globally. Sex worker activists argue that what renders trafficking even more successful is the absence of women's rights and freedoms.

For researchers interested in the history of prostitution, trafficking in persons is not a new phenomenon. As seen at the beginning of this section, trafficking became part of the narrative at the end of the nineteenth century framed as white slavery, and it was raised again in the late 1980s at the international level, during the debate on pornography and sex tourism. The traffic in human beings entered the Canadian debate in the 1990s as part of what Agustìn (2007) and Jones et al. (2018) call the "rescue industry." Since then very few have taken the time to define this issue properly. No matter how different researchers define trafficking in persons, or do not define it, police, criminal justice professionals, and prohibitionists do not consider the vagueness of the definition problematic. If, as Jean-Michel Chaumont and

Anne-Laure Wilbrin (2007, 131) maintain, a worthy debate begins with a rigorous definition of the terms, then I must conclude that we are not ready to ponder the issue. If we are to have a debate, we must first define our concepts—the use of words like slavery, trafficking, organized crime, and street gangs lack the required rigor and result in exciting the public. Can we include smuggling? Can researchers such as Parent et al. (2013) convince prohibitionists to include the concept into their vocabulary? Only when we can agree on these terms can we begin a discussion. Debates on human trafficking are intense and hard to control. I have participated in a few of these discussions, including one at Concordia University in autumn 2017, and still it was impossible to get out of the victim narrative. The need for women to escape unstable conditions in their countries, cities, and families of origin by any means possible has created a situation that results in trafficking and illegal immigration.

The "prostitute" identity and the prostitution/trafficking/child slavery amalgamation have major consequences for the current debate on prostitution and sex workers' organizations. Plus, the amalgamation of women and children is also detrimental to women's agency (Sanders 2005, 41; Jones et al. 2018, 232). The desire to picture women as victims of circumstance prevents researchers from imagining that sex work can be an economic issue or an alternative form of work and ignores the complexity of migration (Lam and Gallant 2018). For sex worker organizations, there is absolutely no recognition possible, no legitimacy, if the organization is linked to deception and criminal activities. As demonstrated by Engle Merry, images of trafficking are characterized "by the image of a young girl, usually poor and brown, who has been kidnapped and passed from hand to hand until she ends up in a brothel [. . .] or has been sold by impoverished parents to a criminal network" (2016, 115). The image described above is the most damaging one, and it is one that prohibitionists exploit with impunity. The stereotypes must be debunked for sex workers to mobilize and attract allies.

While city officials are still struggling with what to do about the tension in certain neighborhoods, the face of sex work is rapidly changing, and this brings new challenges to law enforcement authorities (Swanson 2016), politicians, and, eventually, can have an effect on sex workers' organizations. In Montréal, the zero-tolerance policy may have changed the areas where commercial sex is negotiated, but it is not the only element responsible for the changes, and according to Redoutey (2005, 59), the other factor was certainly the Internet. New technologies have in many ways transformed the sex industry. The Internet has changed how entrepreneurs and sex workers conduct their business (Henry and Farvid 2017, 118). The sex industry in Montréal most definitely shifted because of the continued repression and has created a return of moral panic.[6] Fear among the general public reinforces the misrepresentation.

As for the Royal Canadian Mounted Police, the main issue is still trafficking, sex tourism, and matters of public safety. I suspect that any changes engendering an anxiety around sexuality add another level of uncertainty, which in turn renders the mandate sex workers' organizations—to assist and empower sex workers—a lot more difficult. So, while language has moved from white slavery to trafficking, the controversy surrounding trafficking seems to serve the same purpose described during the era of white slavery: to distract the public during periods of social change. Changes in sexual mores, intensified by the explosion of the Internet and other technologies (Maras 2017), often translate to fear concerning morals, and the fact that pop culture tends to be deliberately transgressive does not help matters (Young 2007). No one can deny the pervasive presence of sexual innuendo in popular culture and marketing since the Cultural Revolution of the 60s, and I suspect that the hyper-sexuality of popular culture makes the general population quite nervous.

MEDIA AND REPRESENTATION

Media technology attracts clients to a certain area by advertising bars, hotels, and escort agencies, but may also reduce the number street workers and more visible clientele by offering some services, such as cyber porn, that until recently were only available in "peep show" establishments. The Internet favors the exchange of information and helps to keep these exchanges even more anonymous. Although technology may have reduced the number of visible sex workers, it has created an entirely new level of uncertainty, since the advent of the Internet has made sex tourism and pornography even more accessible (Maginn and Steinmetz 2015). The latter can be a nightmare for parents despite all sorts of locking devices they can put on their children's computers. Access to cyber pornography and online exchanges with a sex worker may also affect the intimate relationship between partners and redefine the meaning of cheating if one member in the relationship wishes to use these services and the other does not. Lastly, hip-hop, which from the 1960s to 1988 used to be a political statement (Brym 2012, 17), has, since the early 90s, been almost completely transformed into gangster rap or soft-porn video clips (Hurt 2006).[7]

Moreover, as Jessica Swanson (2016) underlined, is the fact that all major television networks have included reports on prostitution and trafficking in their programming. American reality show such as NBC's "To Catch a Predator" and other fictional program such as "Law and Order" have also included sex workers as part of their storyline. Moreover, as Jones et al. (2018, 235) point out, newspapers and interviewers often look for stories of misery. Also, not helpful are articles such as the one in *Newsweek* magazine (2017) which states that "one of the fastest growing parts of the tech industry is sex trafficking." According to *Newsweek* 700 brothels or massage parlors are housing trafficked Asian women.[8]

The influence of these media is important when assessing "trafficking" and the sex industry in general. The constant blending of facts and infotainment (Deutschmann 2004) makes it difficult to undo the stereotypes, but my years of teaching a course titled Sex Work and Society may help in achieving this. Laurence Brisson Dubreuil, a journalist student working at one of Concordia's newspapers, *The Concordian*, has this to say:

> As a journalism student, I am very well aware of the impact the media has on the public, and how it ultimately shapes our society's political and legal structures. Still, I never recognized the extent to which the media plays a pivotal role in determining the environment in which sex workers live. Nelly Arcan was the only sex worker whose work I had read, as powerful and honest to her truth as it is—her work pervasively fixates on the antiquated Victorian moral perception of sex work which we learnt to critique. Engaging with sex work literature that actively challenged the whore stigma and the single narrative of victimization was sincerely riveting for me. Learning about the media's historical and present influence on the policing of sex workers was the most poignant portion of the course for me. From mainstream media's perpetuating misrepresentation of Indigenous women in the industry, to the harmful coverage portraying sex workers as victims of sex trafficking- time and again this class fueled my desire to inspire social change through the media.

This is not to say that sex trafficking does not exist, but Laurence in her insightful remarks underlines the fact that when we consider the contentious issue of sex work, it is important to avoid the issue of inflammatory language which prevents us from arriving at solutions.

NOTES

1. https://www.nswp.org/sites/nswp.org/files/research-for-sex-work-4-english.pdf.
2. S.T.A.R. http://web2.uwindsor.ca/courses/sociology/maticka/star/index.html.
3. Since 1995, city officials' main concern seemed to be security, hence, safety measures became paramount (Redoutey 2005; Hubbard 2004; Ryder 2004; Cameron 2004; Sanders 2004; Hubbard and Sanders 2003) and Montréal is not different from other major cities. In 1995, police and city officials began to tackle different issues intended to make Montréal safer. One aspect that fell under their gaze was street prostitution, and although the issue of prostitution is under federal jurisdiction, Montréal officials were under pressure to address it.

Initiated by New York Mayor Rudolf Giuliani, the zero-tolerance policy aims to rid cities of symbols of decay, signs that announce "dangerousness." (For the original theory see Kelling and Wilson 1982). For the Comité Montréalais sur la prostitution de rue et la prostitution juvénile (1996) and the creation the Pilot Project (1999), the main question that city officials and police needed to address was the safety aspect.

4. Communications scholar Gretchen Soderlund (2002) recalls that in 1909 in the United States *The Times*, which until then had given very little press coverage to the white slavery issue, found itself in an embarrassing situation when it printed a story that later on proved to be

lacking veracity. In fact, on May 20, 1910, readers were invited to partake in the impact "as the truth [. . .] was systematically revealed on the witness stand"—the sub-heading read "Some Surprises in Case—Girls Sold Not Children, as Supposed, but Women Beyond their Majority, Acting Voluntarily" (Soderlund 2002, 448). Nonetheless, accounts surrounding the issue continued and peaked between the years 1910 and 1913 (Keire 2001, 5). In June 1910, the US Congress passed the Mann's Act, which prohibited interstate transportation and importation of women directed toward the sex trade.

    5. https://www.state.gov/wp-content/uploads/2019/06/2019-Trafficking-in-Persons-Report.pdf.

    6. The term moral panic was coined by Cohen (1972) to describe a collective response, generated by unsettling social strain and incited and spread by interest groups, toward persons who are actively transformed into "folk devils." Through the use of highly emotive claims and fear-based appeals, a moral panic tends to orchestrate cultural consent that something must be done, and quickly, to deal with the alleged threat. The increase social control that typically follows from such consent ends up preserving and reasserting the very hegemonic values and interests that purportedly are being undermined by the folk devils. A moral panic, then, serves a distinct stabilizing function at a time of unsettling social strain (Deyoung 1998, 160, in Adler and Adler 2003).

    7. January 2006 (USA) Hip-Hop: Beyond Beats & Rhymes documentary Byron Hurt

    8. Lastly, the recent scandal involving Jeffrey Epstein who was convicted with one count of trafficking of a minor will certainly revive the debate.

Chapter Four

Stella's Forum XXX

Celebrating a Decade of Action and Designing Our Future

The Forum XXX witnessed Stella bursting out on the international scene. The Forum was a pure display of pride—a pride that drove sex workers in Montréal to connect and collectivize with more sex workers from around the world. This chapter recalls this celebration and illustrates perfectly the importance of emotions and the role these play in self-worth. This was a pivotal event as it was the fuel that fed the movement for the next ten years. We celebrated the movement, but for some it was more personal. We came together to celebrate ourselves. It was also a moment in Montréal that allowed for a visibility around the pride of the sex worker rights movement that counters popular discourse of victimization—this was the first time this happened on such a scale in Montréal. Though this happens in other actions, this is a good case study of it on a larger scale.

In 2005, Stella celebrated its tenth anniversary by inviting sex worker collective Durbar Mahila Samanwaya Committee (DMSC) from Kolkata, India, and Cabiria in France, who were both celebrating their first ten years, to organize a five-day forum in Montréal. This forum brought together 250 sex workers and close allies to Montréal from Canada, Switzerland, Thailand, Argentina, India, France, New Zealand, the United States, Australia, Sweden, South Africa, Taiwan, and Israel, to name a few. At this point, Stella's reputation with sex workers in the city had grown, and its members were ready to join the global political stage. Stella's educational tools at that time were widely known and shared across Canada: Guide XXX (Stella 1999a), a general guide for sex workers about rights, laws, and general working conditions; Guide Striptease (Stella 2003a) for dancers; and Dear Client

(Stella 2004) for clients. In 2004, the Bad Trick and Aggressors list had been transformed into a newsletter that outlined monthly activities. As part of their ten-year celebrations, Stella published a special *ConStellation* (2005b), recalling ten years of activism. This publication encouraged the team and new members to learn about its history. A few years had passed since the Pilot Project debacle and Stella's team, back on its feet, reconvened diverse committees and held regular meetings for sex workers on various topics. Stella's rendezvous for sex workers—the Forum XXX—came precisely thirty years after the creation of the International Committee for Prostitutes' Rights (ICPR) in 1975 (Mathieu 2001). The Forum was about celebration, empowerment, struggle, resilience, and designing a future with other sex workers; it marked a moment when Stella would join the global movement for sex workers' rights in more meaningful ways.

PREPARING STELLA'S TENTH ANNIVERSARY

The preparation for the Forum originated in 2002, when Stella's members decided to create a special celebration for its upcoming tenth anniversary. Along with Cabiria, DMSC, and various other community players in and outside of Montréal, they formed a committee to plan a celebration and find the funds to make it possible (Stella 2002, 17). By the end of 2003, the first draft of the project emerged—in Mensah's words:

> At the beginning, it looked like the project would be an international academic-style meeting, bringing together Canadian researchers whose work could be helpful to the sex workers' rights movement. Luckily, in 2003 and 2004, I asked for the opinions of various people who do different types of sex work, under various conditions and in different contexts, and it became clear that an academic tone for the event didn't really match the needs of this diverse community. The greatest desire that they brought up was to meet with other associations and to share our history and the history of the sex workers' movement as a worldwide movement. (Mensah 2006, 8)

This consultation with sex workers refocused the project on a by-and-for sex worker conference. The organizers endeavored to create a space that accounted for and minimized the barriers between sex workers—barriers that often stand in the way of mobilizing (Thiboutot 2006; Mensah 2006). A grant from Health Canada was obtained, and the event was on its way, and I was part of the executive team that planned and coordinated the event; therefore, the "we" and the "us" in this chapter include me.

In summer 2004, Mensah and Claire Thiboutot, then Stella's director, who were in Bangkok for the XV International HIV/AIDS Conference, began spreading the news about the upcoming sex workers' conference in

Montréal—Canada's third international conference focusing on sex work. The first was in 1985, in Toronto, Challenging Our Images: The Politics of Pornography and Prostitution, and the second in 1996, in Montréal, When Sex Works. The Forum XXX, with 80 percent of the registration spaces reserved for active and former sex workers (Stella 2006, 10), was the one that gathered the most sex workers. For us, the Forum was a source of pride among other things, because as noted by Mensah, it was very rare that financial resources were allocated to sex workers for anything other than exiting programs (2006, 9)

Empowerment/participation must begin with a feeling of some sense of pride and the desire to act together to change one's situation. As we were organizing the Forum XXX, we understood that, and planned the event, in part, to instill that pride, by bringing all sex workers together, creating solidarity among sex workers, and a strategy that made sense for a collectivity. Clamen writes, the Forum XXX intended to "drive efforts towards recognition of sex workers and feed sex workers' ability to survive as a movement [and pride] is one of the elements that drive the sex workers' right movement. Pride in sex workers' work, pride in sex workers' demands, and pride in sex workers' own selves" (Stella 2006, 53). What Clamen refers to as elements I refer to as emotion and the role of emotion is essential to understand the atmosphere that was present at the time. Pride, for most of us, means being able to come out and stand up for our work and our activism. It is tied in with empowerment and with the encouragement we give one another to go on, to build strength in our movement and in our individual lives. The ability to take pride in ourselves and in our decisions is not limited to sex workers; it can be extended to our supporters. One does not need to be a sex worker to participate in the struggle; anyone who believes in justice can fight with us. This fight becomes part of one's identity—moral identity (Taylor 1989), that is, the decisions we make on important matters.

The Forum XXX was organized around three large themes—Me and My Work, Sex Work and Society, and Sex Work and the Law—and these themes englobed all the ways that sex workers as individuals and as a collective fight for their rights in formal and informal ways. Our first task was to decide who would be invited and this created some tension. A forum includes debates, and from the outset, the discussion of who would be invited had been contentious. As the Forum committee struggled to determine who would be present at the Forum XXX they were guided by the objectives of the Forum XXX— to examine the past ten years of activism and strategize together how to move forward. To do this required a level of agreement on basic principles about sex work, about sex workers' rights, and about how to achieve that. Participation was limited to those who: 1) understood the diverse realities of sex work; 2) recognized sex work as a form of work; 3) is involved or would like to be involved in the struggle for and recognition of sex workers' rights; and

4) is involved or would like to be involved in the fight for the decriminalization of sex work. These criteria applied to both individuals and to associations and organizations founded by people who, in the past, worked in the
sex industry and currently offer services to sex workers, as well as allies. For
their birthday celebrations and deliberations, getting together with 250 people who shared this perspective was vital to move certain strategies forward.
A balance of needs and a focus on the goal was important in the context of
strategizing for the future. Defining criteria by "supporting decriminalization" turned out to be a contentious issue for the organizers. At this earlier
stage of the sex worker rights movement, there had not been a consensus on
the details of decriminalization and what implications it had for sex workers.
It was only in 2017 that the Canadian Alliance for Sex Work Law Reform
published its recommendations for law reform, Safety, Dignity, Equality, that
outlined the details of decriminalization on federal and provincial levels. One
participant at the Forum XXX, Clara, reflected on this:

> It is not decriminalization as such that produces disagreement but the un-
> known. What will come after? The state will not decriminalize unconditional-
> ly, and this leaves a lot to the unknown. Will sex work be legalized? This is a
> huge risk. What we need to do is discuss the issue and be prepared. There is a
> lot at stake.

As suggested by Frances Shaver (private conversation), and adding to Clara's insight, if prostitution were to be decriminalized, regulations would no
longer be under federal jurisdiction but rather municipal; cities may create
bylaws that could make sex workers life even more difficult. It is not about
"not doing," it is about the contingency of action. This is certainly important
when it comes to mobilization.

Ensuring a balance and diversity of sex workers also posed a challenge to
the organizers; stigma has the effect of dividing sex workers and isolating
sex workers from one another based on many factors, including their area of
work. The consequences of being out also served as a challenge for mobilizing sex workers from all sectors of the industry.

The Forum

For five days during the Forum XXX, sex workers exchanged information on
their strategies for survival and advocacy. Sex workers from all over the
world shared their power. Fighting the victim representation, Elena Eva Reynaga, from Argentina's Asociación de Mujeres Meretrices de Argentina
(AMMAR), claimed the right to speak for herself as a sex worker:

> I am not the secretary of AMMAR because I say what others want me to say,
> but because I say what sex workers want to say. That, you don't learn in

school. Even if someone is totally supportive, she or he can't truly explain
police violation, bad treatment from society [. . .] if they have not experienced
it. [. . .] That is why it is so important that the ones who have the knowledge
and the theory remember that they can't do anything without us, we who have
the practice and the life experience [. . .]. (Stella 2006, 67–68)

Rama Debnath introduced the DMSC that represents 65,000 sex workers,
men, women, and transgendered persons, including their children. The organization has been an active partner in the execution and management of the
sexually transmitted infections and HIV Intervention Program. Debnath attributed their success to the fact that the DMSC has built organizations with
sex workers to "make the community self-reliant and visible" (2006, 29).
The goal of their fight is unambiguous: safety of their children and decriminalization of adult sex work. One DMSC accomplishment is worth noticing
since it sliced across the popular labeling. The group challenged the stigma
and discrimination and demanded to be seen not as victims but as active
agents who have the capacity to change their lives. The most visible manifes-
tations of this have been the takeover by sex workers' organizations of the
Sonagachi Project in 1999 from a government research institute, and the
formation of a sex workers' cooperative bank (Stella 2006, 28). To fight
inequality inside the industry, the DMSC organized and mobilized sex workers from brothels and the street, working toward a shared identity and shared
aspirations centered on rights. The following excerpt from Debnath illustrates what so many activists say about sex work being work like other
work—a place where inequality, oppression, and exploitation is possible.

We have challenged and changed existing power relations within the sex trade
that stigmatize, oppress and exploit sex workers. We have successfully challenged and stopped old practices of bonded sex work. We have challenged and
neutralized the power of the pimp-landlady-madam-moneylender-police-thug
nexus that oppressed and exploited us. We have, through our struggle, usurped
the power of stakeholders as arbiters in disputes and as those who decide the
fate of sex workers. (Stella 2006, 30–31)

Lastly, it is important to underline the fact that the DMSC instituted systems
and procedures within the industry to prevent trafficking of underage girls
and unwilling women into sex work, particularly through the formation of
Durbar Self-Regulatory Boards. Moreover, they are quite visible when it
comes to denouncing "police atrocities and other forms of violence against
sex workers, and [. . .] violations of citizen's rights by state and government."
The DMSC had been active since 1995. They seek a world where all communities "enjoy equal respect, rights, and dignity [. . .] where there is no discrimination based on race, class, creed, religion, caste, gender, occupation or

disease status and all global citizens live in peace and harmony (Stella 2006, 30).

Sex workers from Thailand also took the stage to express their solidarity and excitement about meeting sex workers from across the pond. "Hi, my name is Ping Pong, real name Table Tennis. I come from Empower in Thailand. I am happy to be here visiting my family in Canada." This was how this activist from Thailand introduced herself. Ping Pong represented Empower, a community of sex workers in Thailand. Empower is experienced as a community "because it gives us strength, we share a particular sex worker culture, we are all away from our home communities, and we are looked down on by mainstream society. Our community is rich and varied. Empower looks and sounds different every day" (Stella 2006, 51).

Ping Pong explained that Empower changes every day because most of its members are women in transit; they migrate or immigrate to find work, therefore the group offers a place away from home. The group works hard to join women that society tries to divide. According to Ping Pong, Empower has been successful at blurring the lines that keep sex workers apart. Indeed, during the conference she emphasized Empower's collective identity: "we are good at combining our strengths, skills, and experiences; we are good at coming together. We are not so great at dividing ourselves up. Sex workers are Empower; Empower is sex workers, we can't feel the difference. The power we have is the power we share" (Stella 2006, 51).

In addition to the rich solidarity and education that Empower's participation brought to the Forum XXX, Empower's presence in Canada challenged prohibitionist interpretations of sex workers in Thailand espoused as only being a place of oppression and human trafficking. The conflation of sex work and human trafficking was not coherent when hearing directly from the women in Thailand's sex industry, an argument supported by various scholars (Toupin 2002a; Agustìn 2002, 2007; Engle Merry 2016). Women self-organize and resist oppression. Empower, still very much in existence, was already twenty years old at the time of the Forum XXX.

Also present at the Forum was Liad Kantorowicz, a sex worker rights activist from Israel. In 2004, she started a pilot outreach project that made access to health services by migrant sex workers possible. The project was in cooperation with the Israeli non-government organization (NGO) Physicians for Human Rights, and the Health Department's Clinic for the Control of STIs (Stella 2006, 49). The symbols are tenacious, and Kantorowicz experienced the same situation denounced by Agustìn (2002, 2007). As she said:

> Working with mainly Israeli-born middle-class activists from other organizations, I have found tremendous amounts of underlying racism and patronization. For example, a common belief among "professional feminists" is that the basis of the migrant sex workers' "inferior decision-making capabilities"

which led them to work in prostitution was their background, coming from an inferior and backward culture that has no awareness of women's rights. (Stella 2006, 48)

Just as French sex workers (Mathieu 2001) and Margo St-James (1988) said before her, Kantorowicz reiterated that "the public image of and public policy pertaining to sex workers has been almost entirely shaped by outside forces, such as policy-makers and prohibitionists, many of whom have never met a sex worker in their lives" (Stella 2006, 49). This situation guided Kantorowicz's question "what needs to be done in order to promote the visibility and the legitimacy of the existence of sex workers?" Her answer is to attack the stereotype and to educate, and Kantorowicz exemplified these endeavors that have been the cornerstone of the movement. Her project came to be about education: her own, the volunteers, and "professional feminists" about migrant sex workers' lives, cultures, and issues (Stella 2006, 48). Other sex workers like the Debbys Don't Do It For Free, a sex worker artist troupe from Australia, provided a much important creative element to the public conference of the Forum XXX, where they used art for advocacy and demonstrated the creativity necessary for the survival of movements like the sex worker rights movement, something Stella has always tried to incorporate into their activism.

Counter Effect

Stella's publication *eXXXpressions: Forum XXX Proceedings* (Stella 2006) is a testimony to sex workers' many years of activism. For women from India, Thailand, Israel, New Zealand and elsewhere, the demands were distinct to regions but similar in their content: decriminalize sex work and recognize our work as a legitimate revenue-generating activity. Sex workers' claims and celebration, however, were attacked viciously and contested by Montréal's prohibitionist faction. In her attempt to shut down the Forum XXX, prohibitionist Micheline Carrier appealed to Stella's funder, Health Canada, to retract their financial support (2005). She wrote:

> Obviously, the cause of "sex work" mobilizes more Canadian and Québécois institutions than the sexual exploitation of children, violence against women or the traffic of women for prostitution. Besides the Public Health Agency of Canada's major support, [. . .] the group Stella seems to maintain tight bonds with the University of Québec in Montréal (UQÀM). Forum XXX benefited from the "logistics" support, especially concerning the request for funds from this University. (Carrier 2005, 2)

Carrier insinuated, as other prohibitionists such as Richard Poulin (2005) and Yolande Geadah (2003) did before her, that sex workers organizations are puppets for malicious third parties referred to as "pimps" or used the language to insinuate sex workers' link to organized crime or shady dealings with institutions. Canadian prohibitionists were joined by Marianne Eriksson, then a delegate at the European Parliament, who ignored the important role of sex workers at the center of HIV movements and accused human rights organizations receiving HIV funding to be using HIV as a Trojan horse to finance and promote the legalization or decriminalization of prostitution, which is an endeavor that is controlled by organized crime. After talking with the commission's civil servants, it appeared to Eriksson,

> [. . .] that the nature and politics of the organizations are not controlled during the expert groups' constitution. What is very surprising is that there is no represented organizations' control. When we think of the way organized crime manifests itself, it is possible that the Commission, which takes the common legislation's initiative is advised by criminal organizations' representatives. (Carrier 2005, 3)

Making use of the Internet, newspapers, and flyering through the opening public conference of the Forum XXX, prohibitionists voiced their discontent throughout the entire duration of the Forum. As the prohibitionists did in the aftermath of the Pilot Project debacle, they challenged Stella's integrity and the sex workers involved. The aggressive tactics from prohibitionists to shut down the event and sex workers' visibility was very concerning for Montréal sex workers.

One of the goals of the Forum was to exchange ideas on how to mobilize sex workers, how to get them involved in collective organizing (Stella 2006, 25). Mobilization under duress was the reality for Stella since its inception. Mobilization was and remains the most difficult task for discredited groups (Demazière and Pignoni 1999; Martinovic and Verkuyten 2014; Blankenship et al. 2017, 165); however, the task is even more difficult for stigmatized and criminalized groups such as sex workers. As a group, sex workers often lack what Blankenship et al. (2017 165) call "a positive and cohesive collective identity," making mobilization difficult. The Forum was the remedy to fight the constant onslaught by prohibitionists, yet this constant opposition during the Forum did not make things stress free. To have everyone under the same roof for five days was fantastic and challenging and occurred despite the unrelenting assault by prohibitionists to discredit the event and the sex workers who took part in it. One week before our public discussion at l'UQÀM, a group called Concertation des luttes contre l'exploitation sexuelle (CLÉS),[1] the Struggles Against Sexual Exploitation, initiated an action that was a direct attack against sex workers in the city. To this day, the CLÉS has been feeding all stereotypes related to sex work. The group is steadfastly promoting the conflation of human trafficking and sex work.

The Forum XXX was a huge success—Montréal sex workers made connections with sex workers across the globe and Stella was able to learn from other sex worker organizations. The large event gave Stella and its members a chance to think and raised some challenges. One of those challenges was around accessibility; most sex workers are sex workers, and they are not activists, so some of the language used during discussions was not familiar to all. Another challenge was balancing the needs of sex workers from such a variety of working milieus and ensuring that the needs of the most marginalized sex workers were at the center. Creating cohesion and a feeling of unity in turn encourages mobilization, making it essential that a collective must pay attention to its members' emotions (Walker and Palacios 2016, 180). Moments of anger, sadness, and disappointment, such as at times the perception that one is not being listened to—all of these feelings and emotions are present when organizing in community. To balance people's emotion is not easy and discussions about activism are less relevant to sex workers trying to survive and those working in poverty.

The Forum XXX was not only educational but carried another important dimension—celebrating Stella and the entire movement. For a group like Stella, who is constantly struggling against criminalization, social/institutional/legal discrimination, and delegitimization, celebration and pro-active organizing is vital to the health of the organization. The Forum offered memorable moments and displays of solidarity. At the end of the meeting, sex workers from around the world were visible at the press conference, and that was a moment of extraordinary universal solidarity. Further, the Forum XXX itself was one of a kind event in Canada, and all forms of sex work and working conditions from around the world were represented at the Forum XXX. Again, in Clara's words during an interview:

> I loved the Forum! The Forum, I believe, was a huge, huge success and had a huge impact. It gave a window of opportunity, a window into the possibility of what this movement could look like [. . .]. [The Forum was about] learning how to build a community [. . .] those who were ready to learn, who were open-minded and with an open heart, came to learn what is empowerment, what is mobilization.

Clara's argument is valid. In fact, accounts by women from India, Argentina, New Zealand, and Thailand leave no doubt: the work frame is relevant to sex workers. In addition, human rights issues are central to the work of sex worker rights organizations: a master frame. At the Forum, sex workers from across the globe framed their demand as the right to work. Again, in the words of Elena Eva Reynaga from Argentina:

> We are asking for the recognition of sex work as real work, we are asking to be considered workers, the same as any other worker in our country and for these reasons, we have to have rights. And with those rights we also recognize our responsibility and obligation. (Stella 2006, 67)

According to Alain Touraine (2000), conceptualizing the person as an actor implies that that person acts toward a goal that she sets for herself and that she can communicate that goal to others. Therefore, my analysis point of departure is an individual who acts—who interacts—within opportunities and limits (Melucci 1995). Sex workers can transform the structures as they are themselves being transformed by them. Paraphrasing Touraine, "we as individuals searched for an environment that gave us the means to become the actor of our own history" (2000, 56). Stella's founding members created that environment ten years ago. Now it was time for Stella to tackle, to lead a bigger project, and concerning this goal, Clara had this to say:

> That Forum was about strategies [. . .] we did leave the Forum with many action paths, and these were the most important things. We needed to learn about community, what are the issues? We experience, like other social movements and marginalized groups, lateral violence and infighting, so we need to think about how to remedy this. It is a strategy for the movement, and this is what we talked about at the Forum and [debated after].

Side Effects

The Forum was a great achievement, but it tired the staff at Stella who, for a week during the Forum, suspended outreach activities, all other work and political committees, and spent all the organizational resources making sure the many media calls received responses, sex workers were mobilized for the event, and that the Forum XXX went off without a hitch! However, the context of criminalization, backlash, disgust, and contempt for sex workers was not put on hold during the week of the Forum and in fact was intensified by the added visibility that the Forum XXX brought to sex workers during that week. Federal HIV funding for *all* communities was also being questioned by more conservative members of government around this time which meant that the Stella staff of eighteen at the time of the Forum XXX would soon be minimized, leaving a small team to manage and enact the strategies that came out of the Forum. Precarious funding can mean that it is difficult for social movements to be proactive on certain issues. The attention that the Forum XXX brought to Stella was unexpected and overwhelming for the organization and meant that new strategies needed to be created to sustain the new advocacy commitments that Stella made to the international sex worker rights community and its local members. Clara says, "Stella was not on the map before the Forum, perhaps a few people knew of the *ConStellation* magazine, but nobody knew the strength or the beauty of the organization."

One of the tensions could be described as one between service provision and advocacy. This tension was not new (Stella 1996) but needed to be managed differently after the Forum. This tension is one that is felt by sex worker rights groups across the globe: funding is often dedicated to service delivery but not human rights advocacy. As a result, advocacy efforts are often volunteer, but this of course also comes with tensions in the community about resource distribution and who gets funded to fight for sex workers' rights. As Stella also served as a place of employment for sex workers, who would be funded was an even more poignant preoccupation! The Forum XXX relied on the work of volunteers. Angel says,

> [. . .] regardless of funding, there was nothing to stop our staff and the director from creating a volunteer database, empowering our constituents, and teaching them to mobilize themselves for them to become a viable resource for Stella and included in Stella's fight for sex workers' rights. We do not need loads of funding to do this. [. . .] Volunteers are the lifeblood of a non-profit organization.

It is impossible to deny the existence of limitations/structures. These are insidious, but they are there and hence the pitfall—the paradox—of community organization. Funding from Health Canada helped Stella to organize, to mobilize sex workers. However, with growth also comes necessary reflection and the internal mechanisms need to be present to support these reflections. Indeed, citing Foucault and Bourdieu, King (2006, 874) maintains that at times, becoming an actor in Touraine's sense has been overestimated. Can an activist think outside the social norms and be genuinely creative? Acknowledging the fact that within oppressive situations there is always the possibility of resistance, King asks, "Can this resistance be creative rather than reactive?" (King 2006, 874). According to her, yes if one confronts internalized knowledge through re-evaluation counseling, a course of action that includes listening, co-counseling, and sharing. "Unresolved emotions impact on the way we think and act in the world," she writes, and the practice of emotional reflexivity is essential to becoming an actor. Without it, activists are in danger of reproducing the injustices that they are trying to right.

When it comes to organizations, emotions are often linked to what some activists have called the institutionalization effect, a phenomenon that may perhaps convey the seeds of inequality that in turn engender emotions. Institutionalization, the tendency to develop bureaucratic structures, has become an issue among activists. Organizations like Stella are often required to become more institutionalized to receive funding, adapt strategy to an institutionalized world, and generally to account for growth and the need for efficacy. To become an actor is at times a formidable endeavor and here we can appreciate Bourdieu's cultural capital theory and how helpful it is to make sense of the persistent feeling of inequality among some of our members. As Duperré (2002) observed, social structures have become internalized and so entrenched that they seem natural and eventually some of our most vulnerable members come to realize that social issues, such as class and inequality, are not "out there" but apparent within the group (King 2006, 883). The best intentions do not prevent individuals from operating within social structures that they themselves have contributed to producing and reproducing. Because this reproduction is not always conscious, it can contribute to the reproduction of oppressive systems (Tilly 1999). Stella's staff and its members are constantly engaged with these concerns and it requires a level of self-reflexivity and the internal processes to support this. Thus, to become an actor and, most importantly, to create an environment where one can become an actor, leaders and organizers need to become and remain conscious of class and social status (life chances) and their accompanying culture.

Sex workers need to feel listened to, accepted, and have their voices heard, hence the importance of being recognized first and foremost within their own groups. Having one's ideas and actions rejected or perceived as being rejected—not recognized—may cause shame, and when this happens within a group which is supposedly united in the pursuit of justice it is worse (Amit-Talai 1996, 102). Activists must pay attention to the role of structure and how these structures are impacted when supported by health promotion programs. It is ironic to watch the state pouring its resources into health programs, while at the same time doing nothing about the structural issues and legal issues which compromise the safety of sex workers and their capacity to care for their health. Indeed, it is rare that marginalized organizations, such as Stella, benefit from the full support of the funders, and it would take a lot more resources to organize meetings with neighborhood groups. Stella does not have the resources to deal with the overall structural obstacles such as safety issues, lack of adequate housing, and poor nutrition for street sex workers who live in precarious conditions.

Collective consciousness is an important element of group analysis because, as stated by Sztompka (1994, 288), structural conditions (criminalization) and strains may be conducive to collective actions but not sufficient for their actualization. The legal, medical (Lerum 1998), and prohibitionist discourses that label sex workers as "immoral, sick and deviant," and are often internalized by sex workers, may be transcended through participation in a collective which reinforces a positive identity (Melucci 1988; Demazière and Pignoni 1999). The environment, however, must be conducive to this transformation. During the emergent phase of Stella, founding members understood these challenges: some circumstances are too demanding to be involved in activism; it is not the person but her situation. The founding members understood, just as Demazière and Pignoni (1999, 42) did about the unemployed, that sex workers' struggle is not an individual problem but a social issue. Sex workers' autonomy is limited by norms that construct the sex industry as intrinsically violent and exploitive.

It was during the summer of its thirteenth anniversary that Stella held its next birthday event at Montréal's mythical bar the Cléopâtre and members came in large numbers. It was a moment of true celebration attended by some founding members, as well as old and new members. The place was packed, and I remember the music, dancing, the laughter, and the flamboyant spectacles that were offered that evening. Sex workers may be many things, but they are not boring! The same year, in December 2008, Stella celebrated the holidays, and its locale was filled with members. Stella was changing as all organizations should.

The Forum was restorative; it was the perfect place to heal that sentiment of "social inferiority" observed by Demazière and Pignoni (1999, 41). The Forum XXX highlighted so many great examples of what a collective can do. Its successes inspired some members and gave them ideas for strategies and provided them the opportunity to learn about what was occurring elsewhere. Listening to sex workers from different countries it was evident that their sentiment of self-respect was evident—their strength was palpable.

The Forum XXX: The Affirmation of Self and Social Identity

Sex workers must constantly struggle against a construction of identity that comes from the "outside." They are often labeled by the public as vectors of disease or as victims, or by authorities as criminals; thus, sex workers must fight these dominant perceptions and attitudes and sex worker rights organizations must work to move sex workers beyond the whore symbol. The struggle is to change an entire cultural environment. Culture, that is, symbols and their meaning, is probably the most important element for understanding people's resistance to sex workers' demands to decriminalize prostitution and their reluctance to participate in protests for sex workers' rights. Meaning comes out of usage and employing Mead's definition, the object becomes a significant symbol when it arouses the same attitude in the user as in the person hearing it (Côté 2015, 67). When people refer to sex workers as "whores" and "prostitutes," when women who are not following social rules are referred to as "sluts," each of these words become symbols, and they often provoke shame and embarrassment for sex workers and disgust for many outside of the sex industry.

Among all the buzz about identity, Zygmunt Bauman's voice stands out and gives us something to work with when he wrote, "[it is the] not belonging, the social exclusion that renders discussions about identities relevant" (Bauman 2004, 12–20). Indeed, until one is met with a refusal such as lack of protection against violence, as sex workers often are, or inconsistencies, such as rights that seem to be granted to members of some groups but not to sex workers, identity may not be a huge concern.

No matter how liberal the 60s were, or how omnipresent sexual innuendos are today, sex workers are still viewed as deviating from traditional norms and values, and in doing so, their claims continue to attract, offend, and disgust a large part of the population. People gather around certain symbols while rejecting others; therefore, sex workers have had to engage in a massive public relations project as part of their fight to protect their human rights. As noted in the introduction, the whore character, constructed in the late 1800s, has been an enduring symbol of social decay, sexual deviance, and psychological immaturity. To this day, sex workers and their allies struggle to alter this perception. Their fight has been geared toward the recognition of their revenue-generating activity and their transformation from pariahs to citizens with legal and social rights. Sex workers want to be declared as citizens—full members of the social—and this struggle is about the legitimacy of their claims that sexual services are legitimate work. As anthropologist Paola Tabet (1987) argues in "Du don au tarif" (From a Gift to a Fee), depending on the society, women may receive gifts and lodging in exchange for sex, but they cannot specifically ask for a fee.

Give Me the Words and I Will Re-Write Myself

Our world is "in profound respects [. . .], quite distinct from that inhabited by human beings in previous periods of history" (Giddens 1991, 4–5). Indeed, contemporary life requires that we become a "modern subject" (Marchand et al. 1998, 958) and develop a self-identity which according to Giddens is the capacity to say "I," to be able to narrate oneself (1991, 53). Too many sex workers must sustain a narrative parallel to the one that is made public or with hidden passages, even to her. But who "I am" remains a story unfolding (Freeman 1993) and sex worker organizations such as Stella allow for biographies to be re-written and actors to be born. As I mentioned in the introduction, the expression sex work gives meaning to this revenue-generating activity and its accompanying rituals.

It has been argued that participation in collective action cannot be separated from identity (Melucci 1996), at least as an entry point for collective action. I would add here that the initial participation is often triggered by an emotion, a desire or attraction—a visceral feeling of recognition. Self is transformed, biographies are re-written. The Forum XXX and the visible discussion around sex work as work mobilized more sex workers who view their work as labor and it provided a possibility for sex workers to re-write their selves and social identities as workers—sex workers. It is mostly in private that sex workers can imagine themselves as different from victims, pariahs and deviants, the immature, or the sick. Re-written intersubjectively, collectively with others, her biography has more potential for diversity and can now be completed. As a member explains:

> Before coming to Stella [. . .] I did not fit anywhere; however, once at Stella, I was accepted [without having to change anything]. Even those who were totally flipped were making comments but were still accepting me. To work at Stella, was a revelation for me, me as a person, my feminine side which I had

rejected since my adolescence. I remember while in therapy for drug addiction, [the therapist] would say to me "hey, what about your femininity?" Why are they talking to me about [my femininity]? What is the connection? They had no right to talk to me about that. But when I arrived at Stella, I accepted myself as a woman a mature woman and this only since I am at Stella [. . .].

For stigmatized and marginalized women, a sense of belonging is important. Being recognized as morally equal, someone capable of making life decisions is essential and it must begin at the group level. Another participant, Joyce, mentioned the feeling of belonging: "Once at Stella I felt like I belonged. I was with others; I was with sex workers." For me it was the expression sex worker that was meaningful: "I am a retired sex worker, I can say this now." Stella is also about a cause; participation becomes part of one's moral identity (Taylor 1989), a choice we make to participate, to fight for a cause. It becomes about self and transformation of self through collective action. A member has this to say:

In the 1980s [. . .] because I was pointed out, identified as [different], I thought: I'll question these rules imposed on me. "Did I hurt someone? I started to live with my own rules—my own norms. The social pressure that I felt when I made other choices that did not fit with the majority. The fact that I had to continually justify my choices is what guided me to become an activist. It made me think because I was living this [marginalization]. I had to position myself and reflect on why people react like that? What is social control? I was thinking about this, in fact, I was 12–13 years old then.

Dominique: I'm with Stella for three reasons. The first and most important is for the cause. I find it inconceivable that women are criminalized for an activity which is safe for society, so that should not be criminalized. In addition, it is a choice no matter why we do it. I am also convinced that it is possible to practice the work of sex in security and with dignity in conditions that women should be able to choose. It is important for me to work in an environment that meets my values and allows me to believe that I participate in the development of my community. The second reason that motivates me to continue to be involved in Stella as an employee and a volunteer is the team spirit and solidarity that exists within the team. I have the impression to be part of a group that shares the same values as me. And finally, when possible I can earn an income while campaigning.

Culture and engaging in action go together. Symbols—beliefs and values—trigger emotions that cause people to join the struggle or be repelled by the issue. Isabelle, and more so Dominique, illustrates the link between self, symbols, and participation in collective action. In her presentation at the Forum, Liad Kantorowicz recalls how she "came out" as a sex worker and for the first time the expression sex work was used in her language. Gradually, being a sex worker meant something to her and to others, which is the first step toward altering self-identity.

In May of 2002, Kantorowicz first agreed to out herself publicly through an interview with Israeli national newspaper *Haaretz*.

> The article stirred up lots of public attention, as this was the first time that a sex worker was outing herself and referring to sex work as a source of income rather than a source of oppression. It was also the first time that the term "sex worker" was used in Hebrew, the first time that the concept of sex workers' rights was discussed, and the first time that a sex worker who does not see herself as a victim was discussing it. Since then, I learned that I don't need others to write about sex work [. . .]. I first started by writing a weekly column on sex work and feminism. [. . .] I also started getting interviewed for TV, a process that required me to come out of the closet completely—not just by name but also in that I would from then onwards be recognized by my face. (Stella 2006, 48)

As for Ping Pong, self is linked to her community and recognition comes from her generalized other.

> I could be as smart, powerful or well-connected as I like, but unless the other women in Empower call me [by my name] "Pi Ping Pong," it is impossible for me to be a leader in Empower. It is a role and a title that my community gives me. [. . .] It does mean that I have the heart and knowledge to be a leader in my community. It does mean that when I speak out in public, I am respected for having firsthand knowledge of my subject. However, [it is important to] remember that [our] individual experience is not relevant to everyone or important in every situation. At Empower we respect and use everyone's experiences together; no one has more value than another. (Stella 2006, 51)

For Rama Debnath from Durbar Mahila Samanwaya Committee, participation in a collective relates to both the self and esteem. They have created an environment where self can be re-written:

> We have created selfhood and self-esteem among sex workers and generated the discourse that sex work is an occupation and not a moral condition, and therefore sex workers are workers in the sex industry and not merely "fallen" or "aberrant" women, men or transgendered people who are entitled to a set of rights (odheekar). [. . .] We have created environments and institutions where our children can learn, play and grow. We run two residential homes for children to provide them with educational opportunities usually denied them by "mainstream" society, which stigmatizes our children along with us. (Stella 2006, 29)

For many women and their families, the opportunity to gather cultural capital is denied from the very beginning. Sex workers of the Durbar Mahila Samanwaya Committee are not victims but actors and they delivered a powerful message at the Forum. These are moments that fuel a movement.

Contemporary conflicts arise in areas of cultural reproduction (Habermas 1981, 33; Melucci 1996, 9; Joas 1997, 208). Individuals "claim their autonomy in making sense of their lives" (Melucci 1996, 8); they place the struggle around meanings and symbols. The demand of sex workers—the decriminalization of their revenue-generating activity—is situated at the juncture of legal and cultural terrains. I place the emphasis on the latter, for law, which is under federal jurisdiction, follows culture (Gaudreault-DesBiens 2001; Jochelson and Kramar 2011). As van der Poel (1995) before me, I wish to argue that the belief that sex workers lack volition and agency creates uncertainty; my contention remains that it is this exact image of sex workers as victims that is not only at the foundation, but is legally enshrined in Canada's sex work laws, as introduced through the Protection of Communities and Exploited Person's Act (PCEPA). The law, according to prohibitionists' argument, is there to protect the "prostituted" woman against herself.

Although more research needs to be conducted to deepen our knowledge concerning culture, self, and participation in a community organization, observing Stella and the Forum XXX was a great opportunity to observe a stigmatized group of people exchange experiences, which is in and of itself an empowering process. In hindsight, it was telling to observe women from all over the world stand up and disclose their individuality as sex workers and recognize themselves as part of a group. If, as Jenn Clamen, co-author of *eXXXpressions*, affirmed, "pride is one of the elements that drives the sex workers' right movement" (Stella 2006, 53), then I wish to add the role of emotions, such as pride, to the culture/praxis link. As argued by Javelin (2003), Ost (2004), King (2006), Tonkens (2012), and Walker and Palacios (2016), emotions are important for understanding collective action.

Self-reflexivity is as essential to the researcher as it is to all members in order to understand one's participation in a collective and to pay attention to its emotional temperature. Stella must be recognized as a sex workers' group by the city, by the state, and by other groups. We can trace symbols and images of sex workers through public policy and advocacy: the Pilot Project debacle in 2002, the Forum XXX in 2005 and the introduction of PCEPA all center on these symbols. I concur with Honneth: "there are always opportunities for people to create a counter-culture of respect in compensation for absent forms of social recognition" (in Peterson and Willig 2002, 271). People create zones of resistance—Stella is that zone of resistance.

One of the major roles of community organizations' paid staff is to train members to represent themselves (Lamoureux et al. 1989, 25). According to Lamoureux et al. (1989, 26) and Shragge (2003), there is a tendency in Québec's community organizations to neglect this important function and to assume leadership. For sex workers' organizations, whose first mandate is to attend to sex workers' needs—and who try to prioritize sex workers who work in public spaces and suffer the harshest brunt of enforcement, surveillance, and public disdain—that may be a gargantuan task. Special attention must be given to the internal, intimate life of the group. As King (2006, 877) maintains, directors, employees, and members must be self-reflexive and try to challenge their beliefs. For King, this is the only way to become a subject in Touraine's sense. To this I add that it is the only way to empower oneself and others. However, constantly running after grants and meeting deadlines, all the while dealing with prohibitionists and different authorities, leaves one very little time to do what Lamoureux et al. (1989) and Shragge (2003) consider the primary task, which is to empower women to speak for themselves.[2] Melucci (1995, 1996) and Honneth (1996), as with the symbolic interactionists before them, recognize the role that (significant) others play in the creation of (self) identity. Collective actors can identify themselves when they have learned to distinguish themselves from their environment. The collective becomes aware of its external environment—the action field—the bearer of opportunity and constraints identified by the actor (Melucci 1995, 47). It is within this relational dimension that criminalized groups, such as Stella, exhaust themselves. Non-recognition, even limited, is repressive (Melucci 1995); in its extreme form it is social death (Honneth 1996). Self-identity created through social relationships is maintained through difference and separation but always infers some degree of equality and reciprocity (Melucci 1995, 48). The Forum XXX aimed to bring us together and for a brief moment we were almost sheltered.

NOTES

1. http://www.lacles.org/.
2. Regardless, one must be careful not to fall into the trap of meritocracy and make sure members who are refused jobs understand why. "To be better off" is a matter of life chances, serendipity, personality and capacity; it is not a matter of being worthy of something better.

Chapter Five

Transformation of the Landscape for Sex Worker Organizing in Canada

> There will always be haters, and the best thing that sex workers and allies can do in the face of that is just work harder every day to gain more visibility and claim more space that is rightfully theirs.
> —Jenn Clamen (2019, in an interview with the author)

Leading up to founding Stella, in 1992, its founding members identified sex workers' social and legal status as key contributors to discrimination and violence. It was clear by the end of their first meeting that a sex worker rights group needed a holistic approach, which included addressing the criminal status and socio-economic environment of sex workers. The conditions under which sex workers were working increased their vulnerability to HIV and hindered their capacity to exercise their right to security. That same year the Association québecoise des travailleuses et travailleurs du sexe (AQTTS) cited decriminalization as a goal for sex worker rights movements. Stella and AQTTS' missions fell squarely within the mandates of larger national and global movements for sex workers' rights. Sex workers have been formally organizing in North America since the late 1970s. Part of that organizing consists of combatting the impacts of criminalization, stigma, and discrimination, and other structural factors that are key contributors to violence against sex workers. Decriminalization of all elements of sex work is part of that mandate; decriminalization is understood not as a magic bullet, but as a necessary condition in a larger struggle to counter violence and improve standing for sex workers.

This chapter brings us into the current context for sex work advocacy, the discourses, frameworks, and legislative context that defines part of that context. It outlines the evolution of the sex worker rights movement in Montréal and Canada, highlighting the tireless work of sex workers who continue to struggle at the front lines for respect and protection of their human rights. To walk us through this discussion, I interviewed Jenn Clamen, activist for sex workers' rights, long-time staff at Stella, and the national coordinator of the Canadian Alliance for Sex Work Law Reform, an alliance of more than twenty-eight sex worker rights and allied groups across Canada fighting for sex work law reform.

THE BEDFORD DECISION: CHANGING THE LANDSCAPE FOR SEX WORKER ORGANIZING

Francine: Jenn, the title of this chapter is based on one of your presentations, and while preparing for our conversation I associated the transformation of the landscape to the Bedford decision, was I mistaken?

Jenn: I agree, in November 2010, an Ontario judge forever changed the landscape of sex worker activism in Canada by ruling that prostitution law contributes to the violence experienced by sex workers and she ruled in favor of striking down three major prostitution laws—this recognition was both a surprise and a relief for many sex workers, and was a huge step in the appropriate framing of violence against sex workers as a human rights and justice issue. Criminalization of any part of sex work contributes to vulnerabilities and harms that sex workers experience, including violence. The sex workers who bear the brunt of prostitution law, in terms of violence, police brutality, and constant arrest and criminalization, are the most marginalized sex workers—Indigenous, black, trans, migrant, and drug using sex workers. Under the current legal framework, sex workers face extreme forms of discrimination and violence. In order to understand this framing and the use of the courts, and the Bedford case itself, one needs to understand the context for sex workers in Canada.

F: Before going any further can you please elaborate on what principles are at the base of sex worker rights organizing? And what does sex worker rights organizing mean?

J: There are shared principles across sex worker organizations, regions, and the globe—how these principles are prioritized may differ. The principle at the heart of the sex worker rights movement is sex worker leadership: placing sex workers at the center of decision making and policies and practices that impact sex workers' lives. In some regions people call this empowerment—I prefer the French term for this which is "reprise de pouvoir." It's a good way of describing how sex workers attempt to position themselves vis-à-vis power and institutions, and the need for sex workers to shift power relations. Sex workers are so often viewed as weak or victims and described by some as not having any consciousness around their actions. But sex workers are brilliant, skilled, and thoughtful humans who can responsibly hold power and take action when spaces of power are given to them. Another value or principle of sex worker rights organizing is the recognition of sex work as a form of labor—and valued labor. This is often misunderstood by the general public—they assume because we understand sex work as work that it translates as "everyone is really happy and bouncy in their work." Rather, when we talk about sex work as work, we recognize that it is an income-generating activity, or practiced for the exchange of goods or services, and it is done so in a context where work is something that people do to make money to live, to support their families, to pay for school, clothes, drugs, and a whole slew of other things. We do not judge the type of labor being done here but rather recognize that people do all sorts of labor to generate income. In this sense, the value of this labor is underscored by the struggle for better working conditions and an end to informal working conditions where exploitation can flourish. A third principle that outlines many of the actions of the sex worker rights movement is the recognition that as long as any part of sex work remains criminalized, law enforcement will serve as an antagonistic force in the lives of sex workers. The call for decriminalization is to alleviate some of that antagonism. It can by no means eliminate the antagonism—even in a context where there are no sex work–specific criminal or immigration laws, sex workers who are in constant conflict with the police will still be overpoliced and surveiled. Police use a variety of laws beyond criminal and immigration law—including municipal bylaws and drug laws—to target sex workers, in particular sex workers who occupy public space—Indigenous sex workers, migrant sex workers, racialized sex workers, black sex workers, drug-using sex workers. So, decriminalization is a first and necessary step to protecting the rights of sex workers, but by no means the only step.

F: Can you tell us a bit about the Bedford case and how it came to be?

J: Debates on prostitution, or what is seen as a "prostitution problem," are not new to government—various inquiries into prostitution law have been instituted over the past thirty years, in which sex workers have testified in differing numbers. The most recent parliamentary discussion was in 2002, which addressed the horrifying and at the time ignored fact that more than sixty sex workers were murdered and had gone missing from Vancouver's Down Town East Side (DES) since the 1980s. These parliamentary subcommittees have proven to be futile since they have been happening since 1985.

There were actually two constitutional challenges launched in 2007. The media and the public reported mainly on the Bedford since this case for decriminalization made its way to the Supreme Court. But a second constitutional challenge launched by sex workers also made it to the Supreme Court and resulted in a very exciting win that could impact future constitutional challenges not just for sex workers but for all groups.

Bedford was initiated by Terri-Jean Bedford, Amy Lebovitch, and Valerie Scott, three sex workers—one of them currently active—at the Ontario Superior Court of Justice in 2007. They were seeking the removal of three section(s) of the most frequently enforced prostitution offenses:

- s210 (Bawdy-house)—which made it an offense for sex workers to work indoors or any other private place;
- s212 (1)(j) (living on the avails)—which made it an offense for sex workers to work with other people; and
- 213 (1)(c) communicating in a public place for the purposes of prostitution—which made it an offense for sex workers to work on the street or any other public place.

The plaintiffs in Bedford argued that their constitutional rights to liberty, security (s.7), and freedom of expression (s.2)—as enshrined in the Canadian Charter of Human Rights and Freedoms—were contravened by prostitution offenses. More specifically, they argued that these criminal provisions deprive sex workers of their s.7 rights to liberty, by exposing them to the risk of imprisonment; to their s.7 right to security, by creating legal prohibitions on the necessary conditions required for sex work to be conducted in a safe and secure setting; and finally, that their s.2 right to freedom of expression was contravened by the communicating law. Sex workers had long been arguing that the criminal laws around sex work made it difficult to put safety measures in place. At this time, Canadian criminal laws did not criminalize prostitution itself but rather the activities essential for sex workers to work safely were criminalized, such as working with other people and therefore not in isolation, communicating clearly with clients, and working in indoor work spaces.

The second Charter challenge—*SWUAV v. Canada* (2010)—originated by the Sex Workers of the Downtown Eastside United Against Violence (SWUAV) in British Columbia made similar arguments by claiming that the vast majority of prostitution laws (not just the three being challenged in Bedford), violate their s.7, s.2(b), and s.2(d) rights by forcing them to work in dangerous conditions. They also added s.15 equality argument that indicates street sex workers are being disproportionately targeted by the law. The plaintiffs were a group of forty sex workers, predominantly Indigenous and working on the streets of the Downtown Eastside, who were extremely well placed to challenge the laws after the fiasco of unrecognized brutal violence against sex workers in the DES for over twenty years. Another member of the group was a sex worker named Sheri Kiselbach who had more than thirty years of experience in all parts of the industry. This case was blocked due to an issue of legal standing, which brought into question who has the right to bring forward a legal challenge and on behalf of whom. The courts argued that SWAUV, as a group, was not affected by prostitution laws despite the fact that its individual members may be impacted, and they argued that Sheri, because she was not currently working, had no standing. But the reason the individual sex workers created this collective was to protect their identities and barricade them from the onslaughts of media and public attention. Such a media presence would be difficult for the sex workers in SWUAV, who were known to police and living and working in very precarious conditions. And of course, the reason that Sheri was no longer working was because of the dangerous conditions on the DES that had already seen the loss of lives of over sixty women. The case was no longer about prostitution laws but rather about who can access and make demands in the court. The amazing news that very few people talk about here is that SWUAV won at the Supreme Court level! On September 21, 2012, the Supreme Court Judgment (SCC) decided that SWUAV and Sheri Kiselbach had public interest standing and the right to challenge sections of the Criminal Code that criminalize and harm sex workers. This decision creates a legal example that others can build on to improve access to justice for marginalized individuals and communities.

The Bedford case was about whether or not our Canadian Charter would allow for criminal provisions that contribute to the risk of violence and death faced by sex workers. A quote from the memorandum says, "It is about our responsibility for the harms we cause when we seek to criminalize conduct that some find distasteful. It is about whether or not we believe that sex workers are people deserving the same rights and dignity as the rest of the public" (Plaintiffs' Memorandum Bedford v. Canada 2012).

On December 20, 2013, the SCC agreed—and ruled that all three laws were unconstitutional and must be struck down. For most sex worker rights movements both nationally and globally, sex workers' arguments for decriminalization are not limited to safety and security—meaning, there is recognition of sex work as valuable work and of sex workers' autonomy and self-determination. But Bedford was, indeed, focused on the harm of prostitution laws and presented evidence for decriminalization pertaining to safety, security, and harm.

Sex workers won the Bedford case because there was ample Canadian and international evidence demonstrating that criminalization of any aspect of the sex industry causes harm to sex workers. There is no dearth of evidence of these harms. Between 1980 and 2000, more than sixty women were murdered or went missing from the Downtown Eastside of Vancouver in the province of British Columbia. Several women who had escaped and survived violence inflicted by the same perpetrator attempted to report this to police, to no avail. This is only a fraction of the crisis of Missing and Murdered Indigenous Women in Canada that continues to receive little attention. It also speaks to the epidemic of violence against sex workers in Canada—particularly black, Indigenous, and sex workers on the street. John Lowman, long-standing Canadian researcher commissioned by the Department of Justice for many of the parliamentary investigations, illustrates this violence repeatedly in his various studies. His 1989 report concluded that female sex workers who work on the street are sixty to seventy-two times more likely to be murdered than non-street sex working women. As a comparison point, Statistics Canada also estimated that between 1991 and 2004, 171 female sex workers were murdered, 45 percent of which were unsolved homicides. These levels of violence speak to the crisis entrenched and amplified by criminalization in Canada.

Bedford changed the landscape for organizing in a variety of ways; not only had sex workers been validated before the highest court in Canada, but the harms of criminalization became part of popular discourse. This framing was not new, but it has continued to frame much of the activism in Canada moving forward and has impacted on the way that policy debates are interpreted.

Benefits and Pitfalls of the Harm Framework in Our Organizing

F: The Bedford case required the collaboration of sex workers and lawyers. In my courses—Collective Action and Social Movements—I always refer to Sheldrick (2004) to debate the benefits and the dangers of addressing the legal system. My contention is that interfacing with institutions like the legal system changes how we organize. Did it in fact change how sex workers organize?

J: One of the reasons that Bedford was so game changing for the sex worker rights movement in Canada was that it not only changed the way sex work was being discussed publicly, but it meant that sex workers were now engaging more frequently and more directly with the institutions that had the power to make decriminalization happen. Sex workers had, of course, been directly interfacing with Parliament before this time, but not necessarily en masse and not necessarily gaining the public attention and media that the Bedford case was able to gain. The ways that sex workers fought for decriminalization had primarily, until this point, been visible on the streets during protests, in public education campaigns, and personal testimonies shared through different media sources, to name a few. But to change written law, we need to engage directly with the courts and Parliament and engaging with Parliament to date had proven futile. This also meant that the learning curve was steep: learning to work with lawyers and translate sex workers' demands into legalese, demystifying the court process, learning about human rights legislation, and learning about the minutiae of court detail—and consequently about patience—and how arguments made their way through the court. Of course, it also meant that so many of the realities for sex workers were not being ad-dressed—Bedford arguments were limited to Charter arguments and dis-cussions of harm permeated the media and public discussion as a result. The visibility of Bedford was also due to the prominence of the Charter, which while implemented in 1982 only gained traction and begins to be systematically used by communities over the past few decades to claim human rights violations.

At Stella we responded to this learning curve by equipping sex workers with knowledge! We held discussion days and created info sheets that explained in more accessible terms the court case and its potential impli-cations, and the process of law reform through the courts. We also mobi-lized sex workers to come to Ottawa to witness and learn about the Supreme Court case, and organized protests and visibility through media around the country. So, we didn't stop organizing the way we had before, but we had to learn a lot of new information and engage with the institu-tions in ways that we had not before.

The language and the framing of the arguments in Bedford were couched within human rights and a framework of harm, and that has influenced what parts of sex workers' realities come into focus. One of the central messages that is overlooked in a harm framework is the value of sex work. Another is around economic empowerment for communities who continue to live in poverty, which is of course also tied to the value of sex work. Another is around the right to work, or the right to privacy. Many different arguments can be made about the negative impacts of criminal-izing any part of sex work. Framing the discussion of sex work within the "harm" that Bedford established now has consequences for how we talk about sex work publicly and how we are able to fight for our rights. It has consequences on which sex workers' challenges get recognition and trac-tion, and who gets recognition, in the end.

The Bedford case also created a perfect context to create a national move-ment for law reform; we started mobilizing a year before the Supreme Court case. Bedford garnered the attention of activists worldwide and also people with resources, like funding. Because of Stella's history in the global sex worker rights movement as well as our strong infrastructure, Stella was approached after the Bedford case by people at the Open Society Foundation who wanted to support our efforts in building a national movement around law reform, in particular. It was this support that gave us the freedom and space to mobilize sex worker rights groups across the country into an alliance where we were able to create cohesive messaging and develop a common vision of decriminalization. This was vital for the policy work we do across the country to this day. It also provided a space for sex worker rights communities across the country to share skills and knowledge around policy development. This kind of support for sex workers' human rights advocacy, as opposed to service provision, is difficult to attain and difficult to sustain. In 2012, we birthed the Canadian Alliance for Sex Work Law Reform, a national alliance of more than twenty-eight groups led by and for sex workers, and a few choice allied groups. Its sole mission is to interface with law and policy makers. We invested time and resources in advocacy with law makers on Parliament Hill, creating documentation about the harms of the new laws, building up the capacity of sex workers to do advocacy with law makers, and making visible our collective call for decriminalization. Although separately, our groups are busy providing front-line service provision, personal care, education, outreach, and much other work, together we only tackle law and policy reform. Having the singular goal of law reform as an alliance contributed to a focused campaign for law reform, which can be limiting but important as one part of a complex tapestry of advocacy taking part across the country. The mobilization that the alliance has allowed for has created a stronger movement across the country. We still have a ways to go, however.

F: Again, when I teach I keep telling my students that I find mobilization to be one of the most difficult tasks of activism. There are so many causes to choose from; since we are all so busy, how do you manage to find the right frame of mind to mobilize our troops? How do you create the best emotional state of mind that leads to the desire to fight?

J: Mobilizing in communities of sex workers is, indeed, very challenging. Criminalization, isolation, poverty, structural violence, stigma, and discrimination all create real barriers for sex workers to fight for their own rights and to organize collectives to make their needs visible. Despite this, sex workers from all areas of the industry manage to do so, in different ways. The fight for sex workers' rights is not limited to sex workers—sex workers are Indigenous, LGBTQ2S+, black, migrant, people who use drugs, people who are homeless, people who experience violence, people who belong to trade unions, I could go on. All of these social movements are connected, and we need to work in interrelated ways while simultaneously making space for each individual movement. Solidarity, movement building, and highlighting the connections of our movements is key to real social change. There is no best emotional state required to be a part of movements—rage, sadness, anger, fear, and all the emotions that people experience in their lives are part of what drives our necessity for change. We can't ask people not to show up with all of this—we need to encourage it and make space for it. The frustrations and rage are often internalized in social movements and it creates a lot of infighting, and that infighting can disrupt in difficult ways. Of course, it can, in other contexts, flourish with other movements and other efforts too, which is also important. Everyone, every sex worker and every organization, espouses different values at the heart of their activism. At Stella, the value of heart and openness and willingness to learn is fundamental to the success of the collective—because most people arrive to a social movement with their individual experience, and we need to teach what it means to be a part of a collective, how to account for others' realities, and how to raise each other up.

One of the biggest challenges in community is mobilization and balancing the needs of such diverse communities who, for the most part, only have traded sex for money or goods in common. So many factors of race, class, and the fact that informal labor in street economies is ignored make creating cohesive community challenging. It comes with time, and attention to balance, and a lot of education within our community. But it absolutely creates tensions and feelings of exclusion from all ends. For this there is no quick solution, it just means having difficult conversations and taking the time to understand others' realities.

F: So, what was the best frame—the right call—that mobilized the win at the Supreme Court?

J: Central to understanding the movement for law reform in Canada is about examining the concepts and language that drive our movement—how we talk about, represent, and push for recognition of sex workers. The language we use has meaning, and it shapes and influences how people engage with us. The messages and strategies of sex worker rights activism shift over time, and the Bedford case and what happened afterward most definitely created historical shifts in sex worker organizing. The frame that helped the public, and the courts, understand what is at stake for sex workers was a human rights framework—one that talked about harm and the right to safety. But that doesn't mean it is the "best" frame—it's just the one that is digestible and one that the public and the courts were willing to accept. They are less able to accept that sex work is valuable. When we talk about the "value" of sex work we are talking about the various reasons people do sex work, not necessarily arguing that "sex work is positive"—indeed while it can be positive, whether someone likes their work is not what underscores the movement for human rights. What can get lost in frameworks of "harm" is value.

The economic value of sex work gets lost. Sex work has economic value for people who choose informal labor markets because either they lack a visa or permanent status or a status that allows them to seek work in formal labor markets, or simply they need additional revenue to provide for themselves and their family, and to fulfill their aspirations. This economic value extends to some trans women who cannot gain employment elsewhere because of discrimination

The self-affirming value of sex work gets lost; for example, trans women find sex work can be affirming in their transition or their gender identity. What also gets lost is that there is nothing inherently wrong with doing sex work. It is not a "last resort" for some people and even for those for whom it is that doesn't mean it's a "bad" or "bottom of the barrel" stop/ resort. Sex workers should not be made to feel ashamed for doing sex work. What also gets lost is our struggle to transform ideas of sex and sexuality, where suggesting that sex should always and only be a unique, sacred act and only occur in certain contexts, and in certain ways, and between certain people are contested.

Also, what about the right to work? Occupational rights are not a protected ground for discrimination in Canada, and there is a deep reluctance to look at sex work and the rights that come with work (when we speak about work we are often speaking about harm and protecting from harm at work). What about the right to choose occupations? Labor choice is an internationally protected right and many of our community members decide to do sex work because of a limited range of options when in poverty or otherwise.

A focus on the harms of the laws is limiting and we are unable to give as much space as is needed around the harm of structural factors that make life so difficult for people selling or trading sex, as well as the institutions that promote those structural factors, particularly for street sex workers, Indigenous, and migrant sex workers. Even in a decriminalized system, so many of our sex working comrades will be living the difficulties of poverty, homelessness, systemic, structural, and institutionalized violence, overpolicing, and under protection. The challenge with focusing our legal strategies on harm means we don't get to talk about everything we need to talk about—the application of other laws, the criminalization of drugs, HIV non-disclosure,[1] for instance.

But the harm framework has, of course, also given us strength and propelled our movement. I am not suggesting that the legal strategies were incorrect—in fact, organizing around law reform has allowed us to create a strong and focused national movement for law reform that we have not seen in Canada for forty years.

The harm framework has allowed us to focus on fundamental human rights—the right to life, liberty, and security of the person, and to highlight human rights violations that sex workers are experiencing. It has allowed an incredible showing of solidarity and learning among sex workers. It has allowed for movement building and strategy sharing with movements of black, HIV+, LGBTQ2S+, and Two Spirited communities, drug-using communities, and migrant communities, to name a few. It has allowed sex workers to be recognized by the Supreme Court of Canada—this is pretty bigtime! It has allowed recognition of agency—the recognition that sex workers have the ability to make choices and be discerning and be active players in mitigating harm in sex workers' lives. Additionally, legal arguments around harm—s.7 arguments to the right to life, liberty, and security—if done properly, allow us to talk about the connections among diverse groups of sex workers. It is an argument about preserving integrity and well-being, and this matters to everyone. It honors and makes visible this connection across sex workers.

Lastly, it has allowed us to build capacity around one small element of sex worker organizing (law reform), but we have been able to create a strong movement that actually puts sex workers at the center of law reform efforts. Sex workers are meeting with Parliament and the Minster of Justice, teaching ourselves and learning how to put together legal documents, and building capacity so that members of our community can take part in advocacy days where they are face to face with the people making the laws that govern our lives. This organizing in the face of such adversity and disdain has been extremely motivating and empowering for our communities. And we will continue to fight and build power in our communities as we move forward.

While earlier movements in the 80s and 90s were characterized also by bodily autonomy, health, pride, and labor, the 2000s saw a shift in discourse toward harm and human rights. The Bedford case brought the discussion of harms from criminal law to the forefront, and this argument was popular likely in part because it was easier for people to digest, and it allowed the public to still victimize sex workers, this time as victims of human rights violations.

F: Of course, while we were organizing the prohibitionists were doing the same. What language/argument and emotion allowed them to convince the state to reverse the Supreme Court decision and the creation of the Protection of Communities and Exploited Persons Act (PCEPA)?

J: Just to be clear, they didn't "reverse" the decision—the courts put a one-year stay on the decision and gave Parliament one year to respond. They responded with something that completely defied the principles and ethos of Bedford, and they did so based on their party politics of "prostitution as exploitation," one that is very much supported by a strong lobby of prohibitionists. The Conservative Party—with a strong backing from prohibitionists within and outside of the party—legislated prostitution in a way that wasn't new—criminalization—but also now positioned sex workers not as a nuisance but as victims. This dichotomy is as old as the industry itself, and as dichotomies go, often gives the same result. In this case, criminalization of any part of the sex industry results in harmful conditions for sex workers, regardless of whether sex workers are directly criminalized (which sex workers still are in the current regime).

F: The battle always seems to be around evidence—the prohibitionists had theirs obviously, and we have ours. What do you think tipped the balance in their favor?

J: There is not necessarily any solid, methodologically sound evidence to support prohibition and criminalization. In fact, in Bedford there were over 25,000 pages of evidence supporting the Supreme Court decision to strike down the laws. Some prohibitionist evidence was rejected! In particular, at the beginning of the case in 2007 at the Ontario Superior Court level, the stage the evidence is submitted, Himel discredited the work of Melissa Farley and Janice Raymond, two widely known prohibitionists who argue for the eradication of sex work. She noted that Farley contradicted her own evidence and admitted that her opinion of prostitution as a form of rape was established prior to her research. Raymond's ideological opinion—that prostitutes are receptacles and prostitution is a form of sexual exploitation—was also not deemed to be based in evidence. Equally, she discounted Farley's research for drawing false conclusions around abolishing the sex industry because violence exists. While it is true that sex workers experience violence, Statistics Canada cites 29 percent of direct care nurses also experience violence every year. To conclude that violence in the sex industry is inevitable and hence we must abolish it is a conceptual leap that would seem absurd if we apply it to direct care nurses. The fact that there is a risk of violence in any line of work does not mean we prohibit it completely. We ensure that workers have access to laws, regulations, and other government protections that safeguard them from the specific harm they are experiencing. We also know that risks of violence in any work can be mitigated—the way that sex workers mitigate this violence, and how the laws prevent us from doing so, are described in detail in the government research reports.

F: How do we get out of this "We say they say" tug of war?

J: That's a great question and I am confident that anyone you speak to would have a different answer. As far as I am concerned, for me it's clear who should be crafting sex work laws—people who do sex work or people who recognize sex work as a valid means of income generation. For those who experience sex work not as a form of income generation, but as a form of abuse or violence, or those who are seeking to abolish sex work, there is no reason for them to be at the table. The Canadian Alliance for Sex Work Law Reform proposes a model of law reform that would protect sex workers and not increase harm or violate sex workers' human rights. This means acknowledging crimes against sex workers when they happen, and not including sex work as a crime against a person or defining it as exploitation. There is a whole slew of other laws that are currently not used when sex workers—and others—experience violence or assault. In the absence of criminal laws against sex workers, existing criminal laws of general application can be applied to address violence and exploitation in the industry. If people care about the safety of sex workers, they would support decriminalization.

F: As I said at the beginning of this book, I was shocked at the state decision to oppose the legal decision—a decision that could have enhanced sex workers' safety. Criminalizing sex work endangers women— it forces workers to go even deeper underground or to cut corners while negotiating a service. I cannot help but comment on the ridiculousness of taking women's livelihood away to protect them, or even worst turn them into a criminal. Again, all I see in the PCEPA is the remnant of the "whore symbol." What are your thoughts on this?

J: The Conservative government decided to implement a set of criminal provisions that disregarded the decision and the spirit of Bedford. The courts and Parliament are two separate and distinct entities, but they are supposed to respect each other's decisions. There are few checks and balances to ensure this happens, however. The reason this is important is because we need to understand the limits of these judicial and parliamentary systems to strategize appropriately about law reform efforts. We cannot rely on either system or one institution to respond holistically to sex workers' needs, and our activism must account for public education, service improvement, individual intervention, and a whole slew of other interventions needed for law reform to be effective. Law reform is a small piece of a very large puzzle that has created systemic discrimination, violence, and human rights violations against sex workers. It's also an important process to understand because it demonstrates the power of political institutions and of government—the Conservative party, despite what the Supreme Court of Canada ruled, did not take direction from the evidence nor the Supreme Court decision. That's a problem, when politicians can outright disregard a human right ruling because it doesn't fall in line with their party ethos. (As an aside, many Conservative MPs tell us in private meetings that they support sex workers and decriminalization but "their hands are tied"—so to speak—because of their party's position. This hypocrisy is very common.)

With regard to the PCEPA and what you are calling the "whore symbol," I agree that despite PCEPA positioning itself to view sex workers as victims, the "whore symbol" as the other side of the victim-whore dichotomy reproduces very similar police, institutional, and social responses to sex workers. Sex workers—and women more generally—have been straddling these imposed labels and dichotomies for centuries. When women don't act like they are expected to act, when they are not repentant for their actions, they are punished for it. When sex workers don't identify as victims, they are treated as "whores," and they are punished as "criminals." PCEPA legally entrenched the idea that NO woman can ever decide to do sex work and that ALL sex workers are victims. So not only are those who decide to do sex work invisibilized in legislation, but when sex workers continue to experience the harms of criminalization—as they do under PCEPA—those experiences are also invisibilized and denied. Supporters of PCEPA and the lawyers who wrote it argue that sex workers are immune to being criminalized under the current legal regime. Not only is this an outright lie, since there are still provisions that criminalize selling sexual services in specific locations, but only a superficial understanding of how sex workers operate would lead one to this conclusion and analysis. Also, the fact that PCEPA criminalizes every element of sex work means that sex workers—despite any supposed immunity—are still operating in the context of criminality, which means they are still avoiding detection by law enforcement, which is exactly what Bedford deemed to be harmful for sex workers' safety. But even more to the point is that we know this is a lie because many sex workers in our communities are still rotating in and out of prison and getting arrested under several charges.

F: I have one more question relating to the Bedford case. I wonder if academics and their research had at times undermined sex workers' voice. What is your take on this?

J: In the case of Bedford, the research evidence was absolutely vital. Sex workers won the Bedford case because the courts were provided with Canadian and international evidence demonstrating that criminalizing any aspect of the sex industry causes harm to sex workers. In a case such as this, social science evidence plays a pivotal role, and the trial judge's assessment of the evidence is crucial. Her evaluation of the admissibility and validity of evidence alerts us to the importance of reflecting on the nature of evidence and recognizing that not everything that is framed as truth stands up to scrutiny. Policy and laws should be evidence and be informed by people who do—or will—directly experience the impact of a given law. Prioritizing evidence research means we need to be discerning consumers of research: examining the research methodology used; where the sample comes from; who is included; who is excluded; the rigor of the research; whether it follows recognized ethics protocol; and who funded the research. It also imperative that the research is applicable to the actual context to which it is compared. For example, the context in Germany and the Netherlands where some aspects of the sex industry are legalized is irrelevant in evaluating decriminalization, such as we see in New Zealand. These are two distinct legal regimes and cannot be conflated. Another example is repeatedly citing research that asserts, "the average age of entry into sex work in Canada is between 12–14 years old"; this random statistic does not help us understand where these numbers come from and whether these studies exclude adult sex workers from their sample.

One needs to look at an entire body of evidence in its totality and the patterns that emerge. That is precisely what Justice Himel did in Bedford. In her 2010 decision, she reviewed over thirty years of research on the impact of prostitution laws on sex workers; she analyzed the methodology used, the conclusions, and the context for each research. She accorded more objectivity to research commissioned by the government itself, and less credibility to academic expert witnesses she ruled as biased by their own ideology. She also discredited research from expert witnesses who focused on issues "incidental" to the case, such as human trafficking, sex tourism, and child prostitution, which she ruled as not relevant to assessing the violations of the plaintiffs' Charter rights to safety and security.

If your question refers to a larger inquiry of how academics approach sex work and whether they center sex workers' experiences, and the role of sex workers in creating social science evidence, we could definitely speak about how sex workers are often the objects of research, despite their capacity to produce stories.

F: Yes, Jenn it was my question.

J: Early sex worker rights activists did not rely on research as a method for changing policy, though academics were publishing a lot. They told their stories, their stories *were* the evidence. We cannot rely solely on social science evidence to tell sex worker stories, and people need to expand the way they understand evidence. Sex workers are collecting and telling stories all the time, but these methods are often ignored in favor of more "accepted" research that comes from the academy.

F: I think that we both agree that decriminalization is not a panacea only the first step, right? Can you talk about it?

J: Absolutely. What decriminalization means and the way it is practiced is highly misunderstood by the public and by policy makers. Further, sex workers within sex worker movements may disagree on the details unless their own definitions are elaborated and explained. Often it means no sex work–specific criminal laws to regulate sex work, and the removal of police from the lives of sex workers, which means systematically removing the tools that police use to overpolice communities. Sex work–specific criminal laws are one set of these tools, but by no means the only one, which is why decriminalization needs to move beyond criminal law reform. The twenty-eight member groups of the Canadian Alliance for Sex Work Law Reform undertook a one-year consultation process with their members to articulate decriminalization. We developed a series of recommendations that highlight what a holistic plan for decriminalization would look like, and recognize that decriminalization is about more than removal of criminal laws around sex work. Within the recommendations *Safety, Dignity, Equality*, the alliance reiterates: "The criminalization of sex work results in a constant police presence, social and racial profiling, harassment, surveillance, arrest and detention—all of which contribute to isolation and vulnerability to violence. Some members of our communities face police harassment regardless of their participation in sex work, particularly Indigenous women and youth, people who are im/migrants (particularly racialized women), and trans people (especially trans women). The criminalization of the sale or exchange of sexual services exacerbates their stigmatization and marginalization. Decriminalization is a first necessary step in realizing sex workers' rights and safety, as it eliminates the dangers caused by working in a criminalized context. But decriminalization by itself is not sufficient to realize sex workers' rights and safety, which requires approaching law reform holistically. This means not only repealing federal criminal laws specific to sex work, but also examining the use of criminal laws of general application and the use of provincial/territorial laws including employment standards, occupational health and safety, and youth protections."

SEX WORK AND TRAFFICKING:
THE UNDYING CONFLATION

F: The sex work debate was and, as I am writing these lines, remains entangled with the prohibitionist discourse—sex work, in all its forms, is perceived as intrinsically violent without a single redeeming quality. In September 2017, sitting in a conference at Concordia on violence and prostitution with Cherry Smiley, co-founder of Indigenous Women Against the Sex Industry; Trisha Baptie, founder of formerly Exploited Voices Now Educating (EVE); and Sherene Razack, a UCLA professor, it was clear that dialogue was not possible. I heard racism, painful accusations, and Frances Shaver's fifty years of research reduced to an opinion— I could not even elevate the discussion to an exchange of ideas. All I could hear was defensive comments and accusations in an emotional atmosphere that was heavy with anger. I can understand these feelings from a woman who had a terrible experience in sex work, but from a researcher, it was difficult to accept. I remember that you did not want me to participate, but I needed to be there. I needed to witness the fact that the prohibitionist's position has not changed from the 70s, that MacKinnon's influence is as strong as it was in the 80s, and that the conflation of sex work, victimhood, and trafficking is as strong as ever. It was difficult at the time, but I am very happy to have done it. I do recognize the other side as actors, and this is something that makes me proud. I am ready to listen, I tried to start a dialogue, but it was impossible. I still do not understand why prohibitionists refuse to put women's safety first.

The trafficking issue introduced another level of ambiguity into an already contentious and complicated debate on the legitimacy of sex workers rights claims. In one of my conversations with Christine Bruckert, she situated the return of the trafficking issue in 2002, and I contend that it became the nemesis of Canadian sex workers' organizations. It had been somewhat dormant but came back with a vengeance. Still, today, when I bring sex work in my classes for sure one of the first comments will be about trafficking. Every year, if I am not mistaken, Stella must face the same crisis before and during every Montréal F1 Grand Prix. Newspapers such as the *Journal de Montréal* and Montréal prohibitionists the CLÉS send a special communiqué to denounce the F1 event as the perfect occasion for the exploitation of women and girls. In 2017, Montréal mayor Denis Coderre promised monies for prohibitionists to investigate the trafficking of women and girls. I gave two interviews this summer about the F1, and the public still links the F1 with trafficking. How does Stella deal with this year after year? What should be our strategy at this point? How do we mobilize if the perception is still that we are linked to criminal activities? How people interpret the situation is once again so important and the role of emotion is significant.

J: The trafficking panic is not new—sex workers and academics have been countering fears of the "white slave trade" for decades in action and writing. The more current incarnation of anti-trafficking campaigns has been an extension of trafficking to mean not only all forms of sex work, but all relationships that include an exploitative element, whether or not it's related to the exchange of sexual services for money or goods. Human trafficking is a phrase now used to refer to everything from porn, to abusive relationships, to Indigenous traveling across regions, to all experiences within the sex industry. Funding, resources, and obscene amounts of financial investments have gone into efforts to curb an elusive definition of human trafficking and, over time, organizations have also amended their mandates in order to access this funding and support, despite the fact that their work sometimes rarely, if ever, brings them into contact with people experiencing human trafficking. Sex workers do experience exploitation—it is because of this exploitation that sex workers began to organize and form social justice movements over fifty years ago. But human trafficking is very different from sex work and undoing this conflation is vital to addressing the problems in the sex industry and to addressing human trafficking. Sex workers—as experts in the sex industry with contacts in the sex industry—are vital in the fight against human trafficking.

Sporting events are moments where anti-human trafficking discourse is highly contagious, despite the lack of evidence to support a link between sporting events and human trafficking. In fact, numerous reports across the world have conducted studies as to whether or not human trafficking and exploitation increase during sporting events and all of them have turned up results to indicate it does not. In Montréal during the Grand

Prix prohibitionist organizations are high on attack, and their anti-client and other anti–sex work campaigns have since been funded and partnered by the RCMP. This has also resulted in police conducting numerous raids and setting up fake appointments with sex workers. Thus, one cannot take for granted that police are a symbol of protection for all members of a society because these uninvited visits from police are experienced as a violation. These visits or raids carried out by RCMP and local police are often coupled with the Canada Border Services Agency and agents arriving with mandates to detain and deport sex workers. Very often these operations yield interviews with sex workers and third parties in the 300s and claim to have "saved" one or two sex workers. Our work during these moments is to ensure that sex workers know their rights in terms of police powers, and that they are well equipped with information about immigration rights, workers' rights, and human rights. We are also on high alert for sex workers who call Stella during this time. On national levels we try to raise awareness of the harms of anti–human trafficking campaigns and the need to distinguish sex work from human trafficking.

One of the most frustrating consequences of these prohibitionist movements is the fact that they ignore, discredit, and spread false information about what sex workers who are fighting for their rights actually do. Sex workers who fight for their rights are often labeled as "pimps" or accused of being "happy hookers." This negates the entire reason the sex worker rights movement exists: to fight for the human rights of sex workers, which includes countering the exploitation that so many sex workers experience in a criminalized context. The stories that prohibitionists are using to claim that sex work is violence are the stories from sex workers in our community. They are the stories of violence that sex workers are trying to eliminate, rather than eliminating the sex work itself.

F: I would like to go back to mobilization for a moment. I did address this in chapter 4—the Forum XXX—but can you talk about post-Forum mobilization? How do you mobilize women who as we know are so different in needs, lifestyles, and socio-economic classes, without leaving some feeling even more alone? Here I have in mind migrant and indigenous women.

J: As I mention earlier, mobilizing people across such diverse realities is most definitely a challenge, and it's not something that the sex worker rights movement has perfected any more than other movements. It involves a dedication to ensuring that sex workers are at the center, and that communities have humility and a willingness to grow together. The success of mobilization depends on what you are mobilizing for: there are various sex worker discussions, activities, and actions throughout the year that seek to bring a diverse group of sex workers together. At other times we want to create space for sex workers that don't often get space and hold activities for particular groups of sex workers, like Indigenous sex workers or trans sex workers. The important things to consider when mobilizing sex workers is to keep in mind what the barriers are to mobilizing: people not wanting or able to be visible at an action or a meeting; meetings organized in ways that are not culturally appropriate; activities and actions organized in ways that don't count for different abilities, comprehension, language, culture; actions that focus too much on one sex work reality and not another; and most importantly people who are living and working in poverty, experiencing homelessness, discrimination, stigma, violence. These are all barriers to getting people active in social movements. We need to create a multitude of ways for people to be involved that do not just mean physically showing up, because that is not a possibility for everyone. The challenges need to be named and addressed.

F: Talking about challenge, how do you work under constant duress, that is, dealing with the constant aggression from prohibitionists?

J: Most people don't speak too publicly about the constant aggression from prohibitionists. Prohibitionist discredit sex workers at every turn: they diminish the significance of sex workers' claims for human rights protections by calling sex workers the "1 percent" or the "10 percent," or whether they refer to sex workers as a "prostitution or pimp lobby." Most of us are not sure which sex workers prohibitionists are referring to because they claim to want to save sex workers but ignore sex workers' very public calls for safer working conditions. As I mentioned earlier, sex worker rights activists are knee deep in the fight against exploitative working conditions, violence, and abuse. Prohibitionists attempt to delegitimize the struggle for sex workers' rights by calling it a "happy hooker" or "choice" movement, which diminishes the people involved who are living in poverty, being profiled both socially and racially by police, the sex workers who continue to experience abusive working conditions because criminalization creates a context where abuse can flourish. Sex workers fight exploitation, sex workers fight violence—this is their struggle, not the struggle of prohibitionists. For prohibitionists, the only response to exploitation is to abolish the sex industry; no one suggests this for other industries. One of my favorite campaigns at Stella was a recent one that attempts to reclaim the core messages and principles of the sex worker rights movements that are so often coopted by prohibitions: Contre l'exploitation, Contre la prohibition (translation: Against Exploitation,

Against Prohibition). This phrase recognizes the core of the sex worker rights movement as fighting for sex workers' rights and against exploitation, without supporting repression and prohibition as a response.

F: Jenn I think that not being able to discuss issues because prohibitionists are always surveying us is a real setback. I find it very difficult to be constantly under surveillance. I want the readers to understand how difficult it is to write, to argue under duress. I had this nagging feeling while writing my dissertation, and I still feel the same way—prohibitionists just waiting to twist my words.

J: I agree. The reason the sex worker rights movement was created was to counter violence, injustice, and human rights violations and gain recognition for sex workers. When sex workers are public about this, they are either scrutinized for the way they tell these stories, or their stories are coopted to promote eradication of the industry. We need to be able to create an environment where sex workers can tell their stories and are heard—if sex workers say they need better working conditions, eradicating the industry is not the response. Sex workers also want to talk about bad clients and shitty work days, but these stories are used to demonize clients and justify police repression. Sex work, like other work, is not like any other job unto itself, but workers across work sites have similar work stresses. Sex workers are held to some standard of "work satisfaction" that workers in other industries are not. There will always be haters, and the best thing that sex workers and allies can do in the face of that is just work harder every day to gain more visibility and claim more space that is rightfully theirs. Sex workers should not have to sell personal stories to gain this recognition.

F: Has our activism shifted over time and if it did why?

J: I have only been doing this activism since 2001 so I have not witnessed all of the shifts nor do I have a complete analysis. But in the eighteen years that I have been present there has most definitely have been significant shifts. There are also cycles: issues and priorities change depending on the social and political environment. One of the shifts we talked about earlier was around Bedford and the framing of human rights and harm. Another shift was around pride, which is something sex workers have a hard time taking up in public lest they be mistaken for "happy hookers" and a small minority. People don't like seeing pride in communities unless they are repentant, they prefer victims. But I know sex workers who use drugs, work on the street, work indoors, live in poverty, single mothers—all of whom have deep pride in themselves, in their work, and in the way they live. This isn't about some awkward notion of "happiness," it's about a sense of integrity and dignity. It's important to have pride in oneself, and for people to determine what gives them pride. We also exchanged earlier about "value" and how the value of sex work enters and exits into the advocacy stage. Context is key to understanding how tactics, messaging, and strategy shifts over time for any social movement.

FRAMING SEX WORK AS WORK AND CHOICE

F: I have been giving a lot of thought to one of our claims that sex work is legitimate employment—it worked for me, but again talking to Chris Burkert it does not seem to catch the public. Recently, I was reading a text by Judith Butler *The Frames of War: When Is Life Grievable?* who, referring to the anthropologist Talal Asad, wrote a passage that she claims deserves our attention: "[Asad] is saying something important about the politics of moral responsiveness; namely, that what we feel is in part conditioned by how we interpret the world around us; that how we interpret what we feel actually can and does alter the feeling itself" (Butler 2009, 41). Prohibitionists are quite successful with their interpretation of prostitution and any form of sex work—women are sex slaves. I say quite successful because it seems to resonate with the public in general. What moves us, Butler argues, is not always clear—"[I]f we accept that affect is structured by interpretative schemes that we do not fully understand, can this help us understand why it is [. . .] that some people might feel disgusted by the exchange of sexual services for a fee, some not at all?" I am still ambivalent about the claim that sex work is work but not as a retired sex worker, as an activist I am not sure any more. Do you think that we could/should rethink our claim that sex work is work? Like it or not we need to convince people that have the power to make this revenue-generating activity legitimate or at least safer.

J: Saying "sex work is work" is not a claim, it's a lived reality and a practice and it's a shift of how people understand work, and perhaps sex. Work is a very classist notion and so much informal labor gets excluded from popular conceptions of work, particularly street economies. Babysitting for some teenagers is a job. In other families, children taking care of each other are understood as duty and there is no money exchanged for this service. Work as a "choice" is also a pretty privileged notion— everyone and anyone living in capitalist society needs money to survive. People busk on the street to raise money. People work in corporate offices for the same reason. Job satisfaction is a different story and a discussion that is imposed more on sex workers than many other kinds of jobs. When we talk about sex work, we talk about "decisions," not some flighty notion of "free choice." People make the decision to sell sex within a range of decisions that they have to make every day. Sometimes those decisions can involve more foresight, sometimes they are day to day. But talking about "choice" is a manipulative tactic that ignores the reality for so many women—particularly women who live in poverty, black women, Indigenous women, and migrant women, women who are often working contract jobs, mothers, students, and so many more. People can return to Marxist theory here, and of course one could argue that Marx was very much opposed to "a system of" prostitution, but one could argue the opposite if they have a deeper understanding of the power dynamics actually present in a sex work exchange. Whether or not sex workers have free choice is a conversation reserved for middle-class feminists, and not one these same feminists are having about other types of work. Most sex workers—most people—do not have the luxury of this type of pontification where they debate if the decisions they make in their lifetime are "free" and "liberated" of the constraints of society.

F: Again, relating to our claim sex work as work I have a question regarding choice because I try to get away from it by using decision—too many women have no real choice. What they have is extremely limited; however, what they do every day is making decisions and this for me is autonomy. Women work with what they have at their disposal, and prohibitionists do not seem to understand this. My research keeps bringing me back to this concept of choice—because it is a concept. So, yes, I think that women's agency is often exaggerated, and as I mentioned in chapter 3, the choices available to women are often overestimated, but the fact remains that the world has changed a great deal, and so have women. Do you think that prohibitionists and Stella can find some common ground? Can we fight oppression together? Can we fight trafficking and for human rights together?

J: As long as some feminists use the reach of patriarchal tools like law enforcement to remedy violence against sex workers, I do not think we have common ground. I also do not believe that prohibitionists can accept women where they are at—they impose an ideology on women who are in an inherently problematic place as long as they are doing sex work. At Stella, and in other sex worker rights organizations, we do not care if women are coming or going from the sex industry; getting people in or out of the sex industry is not part of our mission. Our goals are to support people in whatever they want support with—sex work is a good decision for some people and a bad decision for others, and for most it's just a decision. But as long as prohibitionists have an opinion about that decision there is no way they can respond to people's needs effectively. This is, of course, in a context where it is simply an ideology that is at odds. In reality, prohibitionists are much viler than that, and not only do they actively discredit sex workers who don't seek to abolish the industry, but some also seek to discredit Stella and sex worker rights organizations that support sex workers—they discredit the sex workers who fight for their rights, these are the "bad" kind of sex worker for them and those that are undeserving of support. However, there are times where prohibitionist-leaning organizations are actually just really removed from the ground and don't see how their prohibitionist policy is harmful. They sometimes approach Stella with requests on how to respond to sex workers' needs and this can be an opportunity for education.

MONTRÉAL AND STREET SEX WORK

F: There is a very interesting paper by Krüsi et al. 2016, "'They Won't Change It Back in Their Heads that We're Trash': The Intersection of Sex Work-Related Stigma and Evolving Policing Strategies Reporting on Police Harassment in Vancouver." In chapter 3 I recalled the Pilot Project debacle and the emotional impact it had on Stella and sex workers. Almost twenty years after this traumatic event what is the situation now in Montréal? According to a retired inspector the situation in Montréal has not improved for street sex work. Are sex workers once again left to fend for themselves? Are they stigmatized and not seen as worthy of protection as Krüsi et al.'s research argues? Can I go as far as to say they are being abandoned by the state? This is the emotion behind it—one of abandonment and yes, betrayal. Some women are left behind, unworthy of the same protection as another citizen. What is your observation on the situation? And what do people need to understand?

J: At the time of this writing, the country is in an overdose crisis and many people who work and live in public spaces are living and working in conditions that are very difficult, in addition to homelessness and poverty. Street sex workers are not visible on the street the way they were when the Pilot Project was happening, since that time a lot of police repression has not only moved sex work around the city, but it has moved it indoors and into crackhouses. I can't speak to what M. Leclerc's barometer of "improvement" is, but there has not been a significant shift in the ways that people who occupy public space are receiving services, financing, housing, or food in the city of Montréal. In this sense the basic needs of some communities, particularly Indigenous and drug-using communities in Montréal, have most definitely been abandoned by the state.

INTERNATIONAL DAY TO END
VIOLENCE AGAINST SEX WORKERS

F: Can you tell us about this important day—it is such an emotional, meaningful yearly event.

J: The International Day to End Violence Against Sex Workers was initiated by Annie Sprinkle in the United States in 2003, in part as a response to the more than forty-eight women that were killed by one individual who claimed he did so because he knew he wouldn't get caught and no one would be looking for them. Sex workers were framed as his perfect victims, in this sense. Although fighting institutional, physical, state, individual, intimate partner, and other forms of violence against sex workers is an every day, every moment task, it's important that there is one moment globally, like December 17, where sex workers and allies can be visible in this struggle. Sex workers are targets for violence because the world is taught that sex workers should expect violence in their lives, that doing sex work is violence. So, when people enact violence on sex workers, they do so and know they can with impunity and they feel justified in this. Whether this means ripping away someone's children, denying them housing and important life-saving materials, physically violating sex workers, or arresting sex workers—all of these actions are condoned by deeming sex work as problematic, as exploitative, and as something that needs to be eradicated. As Stella said in their 2002 paper, there is a fine line between eradicating sex work and eradicating sex workers.

Technology and the Re-Birth of a Moral Panic

F: In chapter 3 I describe how the public fed with the media think many sex workers work online, that sex work is getting out of control because of the Internet, and it is getting close to a moral panic. Can you say something about that?

J: The Internet—and technology more broadly—has most definitely shifted the way that people can do sex work. People who work on the street, indoors, independently, or for agencies use technology to advertise, find and communicate with clients, and all other sorts of ways to gain visibility for money making. The Internet has also made knowledge and information more accessible to the entire world! That means the sex industry as well. The Internet did not give birth to the sex industry, but it gives it visibility in the same way that other things gain visibility. What it has given sex workers, however, is a lot of different ways to communicate in safety. It has also helped to break isolation for sex workers who work alone. It has mobilized sex workers into action, into community, into writing and a whole slew of other ways. It has helped to form stronger movements across regions and across the globe. The moral panic was there before the Internet, and it's there now. This safety, of course, is now at risk with new policies that are coming not only from Canada but from the US that are impacting gravely on how sex workers are able to be visible and work.

F: Before going further I have kept prostitution but eliminated "prostitute" in quotation marks as a term I find offensive. During the harm-reduction conference in Montréal you did use prostitution and gave us your rationale behind it. I have been criticized for using it by one of my first Canadian reviewers can you please say something about this?

J: As with all language that is derived from stereotypical, negative, damaging ideologies, the word prostitute is acceptable depending on who is using it. As you mention earlier in your book, the term sex worker was a strategic decision by Carol Leigh and one that allowed a new social movement to form based on respect and dignity for people who sell or trade sex. It's not a euphemism, but a descriptor of labor, and one that is mobilizing for people to come together under that banner. I use the word prostitute because I think it's powerful. Some people, similarly, find the word "whore" powerful. I think it's important to use language intentionally and responsibly, because words have social, cultural, and historical meaning. So, if we use words like "prostitute" or "fag" or other words that hold meaning to describe ourselves, I think it's most responsible to do so in a context where you can explain why you are doing that, because the educative component is necessary, and language should do more than just have shock value.

F: Thank you Jenn, I also like to use language to initiate a discussion/dialogue not just to shock people and this brings me to the topic of the so-called pimp. Recently you wrote the foreword of Getting Past the "Pimp" (Bruckert and Parent 2018), a book that I consider important in many aspects, particularly for demystifying the so-called pimp and the sex industry in general. Can you say something about the book and why you accepted to participate in its creation?

J: Chris Bruckert hired me as the research coordinator for the Management Project that was the research on which the book is based. It was a natural step for me to be a part of the book that came out of the project. The foreword I wrote is based on a lot of the discussions that Chris and I had throughout the years the project was undertaken. It provided an important context for people reading the book, explaining why research on third parties in the sex industry is so vital and critical to understanding sex work regulation and policy as well as the context of hatred, stigma, and discrimination that sex workers and third parties are laboring in. I always told Chris that I think the research was ahead of its time, and I still believe that in the sense that the public is not ready to dismantle notions of "pimping" and "third party" involvement in sex work. It's too complicated for the majority of the public to understand that other people are involved in the sex work exchange besides the people providing or receiving sexual services; they are not accustomed to thinking of sex as a commerce in this way, and they are easily offended by it. People also have very limited understandings of what third parties do; they assume and designate a certain imaginative level of control to third parties that may not exist in the sex work exchange but is rather more descriptive of abusive relationships. This can be complicated because sometimes abusive relationships overlap with sex work. The research and the book unpack this to a certain extent, and it's a really important contribution to understanding the labor of sex work. In doing this research, we also uncovered old research from the 50s and earlier that also looks at the ways third party labor in the sex industry is organized. This may be old research, but it's still innovative and will be until people start to recognize third parties as vital parties in the sex work interaction.

Stella and the Fédération des Femmes du Québec (FFQ)

F: Jenn can you talk about our relationship with the FFQ?

J: Stella joined the FFQ in the year 2002 and has been a member since then. Directors of Stella sat on the FFQ board of directors in the past, and again joined the board in 2016. Relationships and discussions about sex work within the FFQ have been fructuous, very difficult, and stagnant over the past twenty years. Some would argue that the recent resolution passed in October 2018 has changed that, and if we look broadly at the discussions of sex work within the FFQ over the past twenty years, that is likely true. The FFQ is made up a huge diversity of feminist organizations—some that support sex workers' rights, some that are silent on sex workers' rights, and others that are furiously in opposition to sex workers' rights and to Stella. Staying a member of the FFQ has been strategic on Stella's part—to ensure sex workers' visibility within feminist movements but also to act as a watchdog of sorts to ensure that the FFQ did not err completely on the side of prohibition (abolition). Stella has had to fight hard to be at the table with other feminists in Québec, to be recognized as feminists, and to be recognized in the fight for gender equality.

When Stella was first created, its members naturally approached different members of feminist movements in hopes of support for their work, which included countering violence against sex workers and fighting for our economic and social autonomy. Stella was met with a lot of resistance from so-called feminist groups and Stella's participation was contested. Although you did address this topic in your second and third chapter, I would like to add and clarify a few things regarding our relationship with the FFQ.

In 2000, a dialogue on recognition of sex workers within the FFQ began. This was triggered by Stella's participation in the Marche mondiale des femmes, and a provincial tour that Françoise David, then president of the FFQ, was doing around prostitution, with the goal of developing and adopting a resolution on the language to use around sex work or prostitution, when the FFQ would speak publicly. Not only were members of the FFQ having difficulty taking a position around the rights of sex workers, but they were also debating about how to talk about sex work itself. Members of the FFQ have been debating back and forth about sex work for twenty years; typically debates center on what to call it, whether or not to support the calls for decriminalization or prohibition (abolition), and generally to talk about how feminists feel about sex work. Despite that the FFQ membership had not taken a position to recognize the harms of criminalizing any part of sex work, there have been smaller gains over time. More recently, in October 2018, the FFQ passed a resolution that recognized sex workers' agency—this resolution has been misunderstood to mean the FFQ supports "choice" or "sex work as work," neither of which is true. The resolution simply recognizes that sex workers are capable of decision making, in a wide range of contexts. It also suggests that the FFQ must fight for sex workers to have a context in which they are able to make decisions, which taps into the structural factors that make sex workers' lives dangerous or difficult. Of course, at Stella we would have hoped for a resolution that called for the removal of unwanted police encounters from sex workers' lives through decriminalization, as a first step. But recognizing that sex workers are thinking beings is okay, and the very least of what sex workers in Montréal deserve from feminist movements.

F: Last summer we met in Toronto to celebrate the work of Frances Shaver and we had a few meetings including a private one by invitation only. What came out of it for you?

J: The meeting was important for various reasons—social movements are strong because they are made up of a diversity of people who have a diversity of interests and skills to offer. Researchers have historically been very good allies to social movements because they produce information that can be used by social movements, if produced respectfully and in ways that honor community knowledge. Sex work research has been centered over the past twenty-five to thirty years in particular because of discussions in Parliament, and regardless of how important it is to place knowledge of the community at the center of these discussions, researchers simply have the ear of parliamentary members more than sex workers do. So, researchers and sex workers need to work together. There are also sex workers based in academics who can bring a completely different set of knowledge, of course. I would say that Fran Shaver is the godmother of sex work research in Canada—she was doing it before anyone was saying "sex work" in the academy. She laid the groundwork for a lot of the sex worker research that followed, and she has the credibility that parliamentarians are seeking, and we need to capitalize on that with her. She is also just retired, and it is important to honor the people that support community and to celebrate them when we can, which is also why that meeting in Toronto was important. One of the things that came out of that meeting in Toronto for me was a reminder of the collaborations we need to foster between sex worker rights communities and academics. Since Bedford there has been a bit of a lull, a silence, and lack of close collaboration with sex workers and researchers and we need to get that back on track. The realities and what happens on the ground in the sex worker rights movement and in sex workers' realities need to inform research, and research needs to serve the purposes of those communities. There is no point of research that is not research for social change, in my view. The Toronto meeting was a good moment to get Canadian researchers up to date with what is most needed right now for advocacy—what kinds of research and evidence do we need to document in our fight for sex workers' rights? Researchers are an important part of how social movements can be stronger.

At Stella, we take research requests and participation of sex workers in research very seriously. We have a research committee where we assess the research proposals that come our way—whether from students doing their undergrad, Ph.D., or professors—to determine if they meet our requirements of community-based research. In 2003, we established guidelines for Stella's research committee to ensure that sex workers were at the heart of the research production and process. This set of guidelines has prioritized respect for sex workers in research and can simultaneously teach researchers what good, ethical research practice looks like when working with over-researched and marginalized communities. Although the process may be frustrating at times for researchers who are reluctant to change their methods to be more inclusive, it has resulted in stronger and more meaningful relationships with researchers and our community.

NOTE

1. For the criminalization of HIV non-disclosure in Canada see Swiffen and French 2018.

Chapter Six

Final Reflections: The Trouble with Sex in Sex Work

At the beginning of my reflection I maintained that three concerns were responsible for the Protection of Communities and Exploited Persons Act (PCEPA): trafficking, sexuality, and sex work as labor. In this final chapter I wish to address the last two. And in order to build my case I must first explain how an image, a symbol, becomes a stereotype, and for this I will refer to Durkheim's concept of collective representations, which are forms of knowledge born during rituals (Schmaus 1994).

Collective representations (CR) transmit ideas and values to a particular group about themselves, such as the middle class described in the introduction. CRs are "symbols and myths about a group," they give meaning to their everyday rituals and practices (Mallory and Cormack 2018, 5–12). There is a sense of identity attached to CR; members recognize each other by the language they use, their diction, education, and religion, just to give a few examples. "Categories presuppose the existence of boundaries, or lines of division that enable the 'lumping' or 'grouping' of practices, actors, and spaces into recognizable groups" (Mayrl and Sarak 2016). The sex worker category has become "real" through the birth of middle-class and bourgeois symbols of sexuality and femininity. The sex worker is incompatible with the middle-class notion of the mother/wife and thus *she* became the *other*—the unchaste. Or as a Durkheimian would say, a collective representation of all that is threatening of the stable bourgeois social order. The following chapter is about sexuality, its place in sex work, and examining the fear or malaise which this elicits in the general public. I argue that it is this fear, often linked to the fear of trafficking, which drives the prohibition movement.

Perhaps no better example of the fear of sexuality can be found than in the following website discussion offered by an extremely conservative media outlet which nevertheless appears to have its own adherence. Let us briefly examine their main ideas.

> The Love and Fidelity Network believes that the flourishing of society de-
> pends on healthy family lives and stable marriages to provide the next genera-
> tion with sound moral instruction and character development [. . .]. These
> values are often either forgotten or attacked at today's universities, where
> casual, "anything goes" attitudes about sexuality and relationships reign. It is
> crucial that young men and women in college—our next generation of parents
> and leaders—learn the realities of the sexual culture around them and how
> they can embrace a healthier and more responsible way of living out their
> sexuality and preparing for their own future marriages and families. (The Love
> and Fidelity Network 2017)

As I have indicated, the position elaborated above is clearly very conservative and therefore may not express the views of the majority of the population. Nevertheless, the fact that the Love and Fidelity Network exists at all is
a manifestation of a deep-seated fear of sexuality which must find an object
to justify such fear. Clearly the whore stigma is ideally suited for this purpose, and while this may not be the only target of the wrath of the Love and
Fidelity Network, it is certainly a collective representation which would be at
the forefront of the right-wing collective conscience.

   In 2002, amid the trafficking rhetoric in Montréal, Stella's board members and employees intensified the internal discussion about human rights,
and the general perception that sex workers are incapable of making sense of
their own lives. Stella was systematically confronted with the prohibitionist
portrayal of sex workers as symbols of patriarchal oppression and as quintes-
sential victims. Stella instead argued that these stereotypes contribute to the
schism within women's movements, and denounced the impertinence of certain feminists who accuse sex workers of being responsible for all wrongs
committed toward women. This is an accusation which was often leveled
against Stella. A challenge facing Stella revolved around notions of sexuality
and the part they play in sex workers' struggle for recognition. So once
again, I must take the reader back in time when during the white slavery
discourse and the ensuing agitation, something else entered the construct of a
middle class: "sexology" (Hall 2004, 37). Indeed, the 1880s marked the
beginning of interest in the sexuality of children (Foucault 1976, 142), working-class girls, and women in general (Foucault 1976, 211; Walkowitz 1980;
Hall 2004), giving rise to the Social Purity Movement.

   Foucault (1976) and Walkowitz (1980) both demonstrate how in the
1800s, public authorities seemed to be increasingly preoccupied with the
behavior of members of the working class and those living in poverty—their
sexual habits, and their lifestyles. Later, Howell (1999) states how race became a concern for public authorities—the fear of "pollution" a concern with

race. It was the sexual habits of the working class, or the residuum as they were often referred to that, according to Walkowitz, contributed to the emergence of the moral reform campaigns in England. This crusade was "oriented to a male audience [and] more hostile to working-class culture" (Walkowitz 1980, 246). Although never openly stated, the assumption was that the working-class male's sexuality was uncontrollable (Jochelson and Kramar 2011) and that working-class woman needed the money (Hall 2004, 39). Their alleged mutual weaknesses made them prone to "immoral" behavior, which collided with middle-class values; hence, the creation of different laws aimed at protecting certain sensibilities.

In "Hauling Down the Double Standard," Hall (2004, 37) underlines the emergence of gendered forms of sexuality. *Scientia sexualis* perceived women's sexuality differently from that of males. Female sexuality was deemed superior to male sexuality, hence, worthy of leading the way to higher moral realms. The new and supposedly "higher" form of sexuality was to be enjoyed in deep communal, monogamous relationships, and the "pure" woman came to symbolize this ideal. However, while this ideal of monogamy was being introduced, industrialization was triggering still more social changes, and two of these changes are important to constructing the "prostitute" as a threat to the sacredness of sexuality. According to Corbin (1990), in order to find work, working-class men had to leave their neighborhoods or villages, resulting in delayed marriages (Gilfoyle 1999, 35); and second, "the blossoming of male's sexuality" in the bourgeois milieu was paired with the cult of purity among bourgeois women, making them inaccessible (Wilkerson 2012; Corbin 1990, 194). As a result, men began to patronize "prostitutes" in exceptional numbers" (Gilfoyle 1999, 35). Intersecting with middle-class ideals of the "higher development of sexual life" were economic transformations of sexual desire, which in turn led to the distinction between "types of women": the idyllic woman, the one who elevated her newfound sexuality to higher realms, and the whore who required money to survive. As Corbin reports, "[p]leasure in sexual intercourse could not in such circumstances be sought with [wives], who were dedicated to motherhood" (1990, 194)—sexuality was now closely linked to the notion of maternity as a duty.

Sexual desire has long been perceived by many religious authorities and moral entrepreneurs as the most dangerous of forces, one that needs to be controlled. Undisciplined sexuality in general and prostitution were a threat to the rise of the middle-class family. "A 'fit' family, it was reasoned, produced 'fit' citizens of a healthy nation able to compete with other nations" (Knowles 1996, 38; Berkowitz 2015, 2–3). The health of the family was therefore viewed as the key to collective wealth. For the Ladies Association, matters regarding the sanctity of marriage, gender differences, and their accompanying roles were at the heart of the Social Purity Movement. The home ideal offered shelter from the harsh realities and deceptions of the business world. Gradually, the differentiation between public and private established itself and slowly specific sex roles emerged inside the family home. Ultimately, the home was where the woman stayed pure—it was her place of salvation.

No matter how the 1960s shook up North American rules about sexuality, not much has changed for a large segment of the population (Halperin 2017). Some may argue that social class has disappeared, but I disagree, and the remnant of the bourgeois middle class and its accompanying distinct standards for sexual behavior are still in existence. Although the following quote from Marian Burchardt refers to his research in South Africa, it substantiates my position.

> Social class is central for understanding the relationships between religion and sexual ideologies and practices of intimacy and dating. Social class status not only prefigures the entire set of choices regarding conjugal life and practices linked to sexual health, these influences are also reinforced by and expressed through an evangelical idiom of life and sexuality as *gifts from God*. [. . .] My point of departure is what can be construed as the conceptual triangle of social class, religion, and sexuality and the ways in which they are mutually shaped. (Burchardt 2014, 128; emphasis in original)

There are many ways to express sexuality, and some make people uncomfortable for they are contrary to the marriage vows (Moore 1994, 15–19). For example, the idea that bondage can be a fantasy and become a source of desire is offensive to prohibitionists such as MacKinnon and Barry and yet for many it does create desire. Sex workers transact all sorts of demands; some make people uncomfortable, such as domination and some types of role playing. This uneasiness and, yes, at times, disgust prevents a genuine dialogue between prohibitionists and sex workers, which brings us to the heart of Stella's demand for the legitimization of their revenue-generating activity.

> Yes, we question these [prohibitionist] approaches to sexuality through the prism of violence against women that lays beneath a "natural" a universal vision of the brutal, unstoppable male sexuality. As for female sexuality, we refuse the sanctimonious and misogynistic postulate that it is basically impossible to conceive that sexual services could be sold, bought and commercialized. As if selling sexual services always meant alienation of what is most precious and intimate for a woman. We denounce the unique and universal discourse which defined sexuality as a link to the highest form of consensual rapport, intimacy and identity. (Stella 2002, 3)

Once again, the passage challenges middle-class recommendations, which state that sexuality is a higher form of expression and should not be used outside of the intimate relationship and certainly not be involved in a monetary transaction. The assertion might be dated, but it is one that remains unchallenged by many, including Canadian and Montréal prohibitionists. The fear of being marked with the stigma keeps some women from transgressing the rules that govern their behavior and prevents sex workers from acknowledging their work. But more importantly, the stigma exposes women to violence and reinforces the idea that sex workers are deserving of violence. By positioning sex workers outside of the legal structure, they are denied fundamental human rights, and the stigma becomes a license to violate. The whore symbol evokes, in many women within the sex industry and in the general population, the same contempt. The word, as it is used, recalls the image of shame, immorality, and illegitimacy, as being unworthy of protection and consideration. Therefore, I, as Parazelli (2000) did before me, refer to this as a form of symbolic violence. The whore stigma is still alive and remains one of the main barriers to mobilization and recognition.

The whore transgresses the rules of sexuality—she is "the radical and different 'Other': morally depraved, crazy, mentally deficient, sexually abnormal, legally deviant or criminal, medically a vector of contagion, infantilized, socially traumatized by violence and poverty, and a threat to public order" (Stella 2002, 4).

Assigned an identity—the whore identity—a sex worker cannot be anything other than the antithesis of the feminine symbol, the good woman, and the mother. Although the word "whore" is not generally used, except by sex workers reclaiming the insult, the word "prostitute" remains common (Henry and Farvid 2017, 114). In 2002, directly confronting Geadah's argument that conceptualizes women in the sex industry as the exploited, as victims, as children to be saved (Le Devoir 2002), Stella entered the politics of signification at its core.

Sex workers challenge the bedrock of the nation—the family and its symbols. By doing so, sex workers are left without legitimate recourse. While recognizing that we live in times when there are increasing demands for law and order, I agree with Colette Parent that the increased forms of restriction are really directed at women's sexuality; the target is women's sexual freedom. Indeed, once everything has been decanted, what we are left with is women's sexuality (Parent 2001, 176).

Foucault in the *History of Sexuality* posits that the relationship between symbol and symbolized is not only a reference point or a description, it is also productive, it creates knowledge. The result: a constant, historically changing deployment of discourses on sexuality. The expansive growth of this discourse is part of an ever-expanding management of sexuality. However, this explosion of discourses is not a unitary strategy across the social environment. These discursive creations do not "control" through prohibition, but through definition, imposing a grid of definitions on the possibilities of the body—what is normal. These definitions penetrate the body and sexuality is power's point of entry. The "prostitute" became this category and is defined as dangerous and immoral. To stray from proper sexuality was to become that unchaste, abnormal character named "prostitute." The whore makes visible these hidden "perversions" which, as Foucault (1978, 19) points out, bourgeois morality demands must be confessed and repented. It is those "sick" transactions that must remain criminalized; women must be protected from these male "perversions." To prohibitionists, commercial sex is sexual violence, which brings us to the cornerstone of criminal law: the concept of harm.

The Concept of Harm

> [F]eminists have uncovered a vast amount of sexual abuse of women by men.
> Rape, battery, sexual harassment, sexual abuse of children, prostitution, and
> pornography, seen for the first time in their true scope and interconnectedness,
> form of distinctive pattern: the power of men over women in society. (MacK-
> innon 1987, 5)

Since 1979, harm and the sex industry has been tackled by seasoned feminists such as Kathleen Barry and later Andrea Dworkin (1974, 1981), and law professor Catharine Mackinnon (1987, 1989, 2005). The inability to distinguish prostitution from violence is one of the most stubborn and socially rigid arguments that sex worker rights groups have had to face. Articulated through legal discourse, MacKinnon's arguments are refined and convincing, proving to be the most difficult to challenge, and one blatant result is the Protection of Communities and Exploited Persons Act (PCEPA) that was ushered into Canadian law in 2014.

In 1985, Catharine MacKinnon and Andrea Dworkin co-authored the *Pornography Ordinance* (Brigman 1985), a new statutory definition of pornography. Even though in the United States the ordinance was rejected, MacKinnon and Dworkin's argument played a major role in Canada's jurisprudence (Gauvreault-DesBiens 2001). In fact, on February 27, 1992, the Supreme Court of Canada handed down its decision in *R. v Butler*,[1] a decision based on MacKinnon and Dworkin's argument. Although their argument addresses pornography, it had an immense influence on the prohibitionists' position on sex work in general and on the Canadian debate in particular. Their position fits the radical feminist paradigm of women's subordination and domination for which MacKinnon is the main legal theorist.

In 1979, MacKinnon published *Sexual Harassment of Working Women*, which marked the beginning of her campaign against what she considers women's exploitation: pornography and prostitution. A self-declared post-Marxist, MacKinnon distances herself from liberal feminism, which demands equality of rights (MacKinnon 1987, 9). This demand, she claims, is not enough. She writes: "A theory of sexuality becomes feminist methodologically, meaning feminist in the post-Marxist sense, to the extent it treats sexuality as a social construct of male power: defined by men, forced on women, and constitutive of the meaning of gender" (1989, 128).

MacKinnon has a very narrow definition of power, she approaches power as something that belongs to someone, and that cannot be negotiated. If I take a Foucauldian approach, power is experienced between two people and it is situated within that relation. Moreover, power relations can change any minute especially around sexuality and these relations require more extensive explanations. Once again, prohibitionists such as MacKinnon have the tendency to imagine women as a homogenous group and she fails to recognize the nuances among women and differential power among women. Further, MacKinnon seems to mix power with subjugation; however, these are two different issues.

According to MacKinnon, the feminist movement has not changed women's social and legal status: men still dominate women through sex (MacKinnon 1987, 2; 1989, 127; 2005). Sexuality permeates social life and women must constantly deal with sex and defend themselves against it. Except on rare occasions, sex is not sexy; it is violence, and it is objectification. Pornography sexualizes rape and presents battery, prostitution, and child sexual abuse as a form of amusement. It turns dominance and submission into a game and makes hierarchy sexy (MacKinnon 1989, 138). MacKinnon's theories of sexuality and gender address one of prostitution's main issues—consent. MacKinnon's argument is that sex, aside from rare occasions, cannot be consensual. Sex is endured; sex is imposed on women (MacKinnon 1987, 15; 1989, 135). Consent is given between equals, and women, under men's laws, are not equal; hence, the impossibility of women to have consensual sex and for those who argue that it is possible, MacKinnon has this to say:

> The price of this equal access to sex, which means equal access to those with less power without regard to gender, the price of this so-called abstract equality is loyalty to and defense of the substantive system that delivers up all women as a class to all men. Women who defend this system are, in effect, procuring women for men. (MacKinnon 1987, 14)

In *Women's Lives, Men's Law* (Albertini and Blake 2005), MacKinnon claimed that women are not protected by civil rights. For Catharine MacKinnon, sex workers' rights groups err by placing the issues of prostitution and civil rights side by side. Sometimes, as Stuart Cunningham (2016) reports, it pays to address the court with the highly contested linkage between sex work and dignity in his research on sex work and stigma. The passage in Cunningham's text is important enough to quote in its longer version:

> In justifying the award for loss of dignity, the Tribunal [New Zealand] referred to the Canadian Supreme Court case of *Law v Canada* where Justice Iacobucci stated that human dignity "means that an individual or group feels self-respect

and self-worth," that it is "concerned with empowerment" and that it "is harmed when individuals and groups are marginalized, ignored, or devalued." So, in the [Aaron] Montgomery case, the Tribunal situates the "loss of dignity" not in the sex worker's involvement in commercial sex per se but in the harmful experiences that occurred while she was selling sex. The focus shifts from a concern with how sex workers' actions impact on their dignity, [. . .] to how their dignity is affected by their treatment at the hands of others. If the Tribunal had adopted the view that the complainant's human dignity was already diminished by her involvement in commercial sex, as the other courts chose to do, then this precludes a complete recognition of the harm caused by [brothel owner] Mr Montgomery's actions. After all, how can a subject whose dignity is already diminished by selling sex maintain a sufficient sense of self-worth such that sexual harassment or other wrongs can be recognised? And how can a subject that is already stigmatised as degraded and undignified be any further marginalised, ignored or devalued? The Tribunal in the Montgomery case resists any stigmatising discourse and constructs a humanised sex working subject, concertedly asserting the rightful place of sex workers as equal human beings who "have the same human rights as other workers." (Cunningham 2016, 61)

There is one category of harm that should remain indisputable, that is, a sex act obtained by force, threat, or deception. If sex work can always be associated with violence of this sort then it can be said that in that instance sex work is prejudicial. Although an in-depth discussion on the concept of harm would take us well beyond the scope of the present work, it is important to underline once again the fact that prejudice is not that easily defined when it comes to commercial sex. What constitutes harm must be clarified and I would argue that Cunningham in the above citation makes a powerful point. However briefly, a central issue can be discussed, and that is the argument around objectification presented by Martha Nussbaum (1995).

A Kantian analysis is central to MacKinnon's and Dworkin's argument (Nussbaum 1995). According to Kant, sexual desire is a powerful force that prompts people to treat each other as "tools for the satisfaction of one's own desire" (266). Instrumentality, denial of autonomy, and denial of subjectivity, which were Kant's concerns, are according to MacKinnon intrinsic to pornography and prostitution. Thus, it is not difficult for Nussbaum to imagine that for the two prohibitionists, instrumentality could lead to the four other conditions, which are inertness, fungibility, ownership, and violability. At variance with MacKinnon's thesis, Nussbaum argues that context is important, and objectification is not always problematic. One can objectify his sexual partner, and as a matter of fact, under certain circumstances, it can be a "wonderful feature of sexual life" (Nadine Sunstein in Nussbaum 1995, 250). What is damaging, and there she agrees with MacKinnon and Dworkin, is to treat someone primarily or merely as an instrument (1995, 265), and that is exactly what a medium such as *Playboy* does (283). However, her critique of prostitution does not reach the same conclusion and highlights those prohibitionists' allegations about sex work and sex worker rights groups are unfounded.

Since 1973, inspired by diverse movements such as the gay and feminist movements, contemporary sex workers have organized collectives, participated in acts of resistance, and articulated claims. The most important one is the recognition of commercial sex as work. Over fifty years of struggle have led to some successes. For example, in recent years, governments of the Netherlands, New Zealand, Britain, and Germany have granted sex work some form of recognition. However, Colette Parent (2001, 169) has noted that in North America the recognition of commercial sex as work is far from being a *fait accompli*. Although COYOTE has been able to alter public opinion to some extent, the quest is, thirty years later, still viewed by many as "immoral" (Parent 2001, 170).

Sex is also important for the social sphere (Phoenix and Oerton 2005), and as sexual experiences become detached from stable sexual partnerships (Jordan 2004, 37), the fear arises that the exchange of sex for money will threaten not only the integrity of self but also that of the social. Individuals may be free to experience sex as never before, but that freedom transgresses "the rules of engagement" (Phoenix and Oerton 2005, 20) and threatens to dismember society. In this highly individualistic life and in a time when individuals must strive for freedom (Rose 1998, 79), sex may very well be the glue that makes people "stick together" (Phoenix and Oerton 2005, 20). Thus, sex workers transgress the codes of sexual intimacy and disturb "the rules of engagement" that (should) keep people together. Sex workers' rights groups have challenged some of the most enduring Western symbols (Bartley 1998, 45; Parent 2001). However, family, sexuality, love, and intimacy are not matters of implicit agreement, as structural functionalists argue, but are the outcome of hegemonic discourses (Hewitt 1989, 73). Attached to these symbols are beliefs, and one of the most enduring ones is that sex workers are essentially different from other women, that is, the whore identity. Prohibitionists deny sex workers recognition and treat sex workers who fight for their rights as a separate class of sex workers. As King did (2006), I wish to argue that in order for researchers to penetrate the divergence, the emotional and self-reflexive dimension must be addressed, and this begins with genuine dialogue.

Sexuality is not an easy topic for feminists. In the 1970s, questions pertaining to sexual freedom and reproduction were at the forefront of the feminist movement. The discussions have shifted over the years, but these issues give rise to intense debates and create schisms within the movement—slogans such as "hands off my body" and "my body my choice" meant totally different things to some feminists than they did to the first US sex workers group COYOTE. Colette Parent (2001) highlights that the role of the Social

Purity Movement in sex work research has been overlooked, and PCEPA clearly demonstrates that the whore stigma is very much alive. The exchange of sexual services for remuneration remains a difficult reality for some, and I suspect that many of us, academics and sex workers included, have underestimated the unease or fear that comes with this exchange. The symbols and emotions attached to sexuality by religion, medicine, and middle-class/bourgeois attitudes are vital to understanding the successes or challenges of the sex workers' rights movement.

Everyday Life and the Burden of Choices

> Until you get women to have an economic power base [. . .] where [they are] able to walk out of an uncomfortable situation [Until] people see themselves as having their own power base, it becomes imaginable that you could turn somebody [or something] down and still survive.
>
> —Susan Sarandon[2]

Charles Taylor in *Sources of the Self* (1989) claims that the life of the contemporary person is dissociated from Aristotle's double concept—the contemplative and the politicized citizen—and replaced by a new consideration for everyday life. Now dignity, our value as a human being, is found inside our daily activities, such as making a living, that is, "going to work" and becoming self-sufficient. One can be conscious of this fact, but the chance to become self-sufficient depends on one's age, and cultural, social, and economic capital. As far as I can recall being financially independent was always important to me. As an adolescent in the 60s, I remember that having my own money made me independent of my parents. At that time of course, my social capital was relatively low, but I had my personality and a strong drive to become independent. Was this a choice, conscious and well thought out? Probably not, but making "choices" is part of becoming self-sufficient. In fact, making choices is expected of all of us, regardless of our financial or emotional capacity to do so (Giddens 1991, 5). It is with this notion of choice that recognition takes its full meaning; for some women, choices about their means to become self-sufficient are criminalized and shamed, that is, not recognized. The term choice is itself contentious because for far too many women, options are limited; therefore, as mentioned in chapter 3 I have replaced the concept of choice with the notion of decision and following Jenn Clamen's lead; I conclude the present work with ideas that will steer the debate away from the sex in sex work and in the direction of labor.

Any discussion of sex work is likely to be polarizing and even incendiary because it elicits such profound and visceral reactions. Even women who are considered to be "feminists" and "activists" have difficulty reaching a consensus on this issue, since it appears to demand a reconciliation of opposites.

One group of activists—the prohibitionist faction—calls for the criminalization of clients and ideally the complete abolition of the sex service industry. Their argument assumes that sex workers are "victims" who must be "saved," rather than rational agents capable of making economic decisions. My argument, in contrast, follows Jenn Clamen's position and pursues the belief that sex workers, like the rest of us, do possess some degree of agency. But most importantly I want to focus on the work aspect; sex work is about earning a living and should be understood as a labor issue. Hence, I wish to move away from moral arguments, and the force/voluntary dichotomy and move into the domain of labor. But the work frame does not seem to work, to attract people to the fight, so I will join Clamen and ask, "what about the right to work? Why are occupational rights not a protected ground for discrimination in Canada? Why is there a deep reluctance to look at sex work and the rights that come with work?"

Since 1973, sex workers have demanded the recognition of sexual services as work (Leigh 2004). Because work is linked to social integration, self-worth, self-esteem, and dignity (Forrester 2000), preventing someone from working could be perceived as irresponsible. Therefore, sex workers must not be infantilized and denied the right to engage in work but allowed a legitimate revenue generating activity that is necessary for their survival and closely linked to citizenship.

Again, the labor issue brings me back to the agency discussion and how to best earn a living. So, while I am sitting here cogitating on what should be my next sentence, thousands of women struggle to pay the rent, feed their children, pay school tuition, and whatever else they need to live a decent life. And my contention and my sense of outrage remains the same today: when the state successfully challenged the Supreme Court decision, they prevented sex workers from earning a living and do so under state protection. I do not want to argue from a moral position because my position right now is safety first. I understand how important women's autonomy is, but as Anne Wilson writes in *Fix: A Tale of An Addicted City* (2002), to attain that independence one needs to stay alive! And live without fear of arrest and violence.

As this present work concludes, I am thinking about the very beginning of COYOTE (1973) and Stella (1992) and how founding members of these two groups insisted on improved working conditions. Returning to chapter 2 and following my interview with Jenn Clamen, I feel confident in my claim that the first and most important demand by sex workers remains their working conditions. With the adoption of PCEPA the Canadian government responded, as Clamen said, with "something that completely defied the principles and ethos of Bedford, and they did so based on their party politics of 'prostitution as exploitation,' a position that is very much supported by a strong lobby of prohibitionists." With the PCEPA and its focus on morals and the demonization of men, the state has eliminated any space to examine labor laws in general.

Individuals are born into a cultural environment which is shot through with symbols and shared meanings. This environment depends for its continuation on our acceptance of prevailing norms and the symbols we use to reify them. The word "whore" brings out feelings such as anger, pity, disgust, or admiration and pride that predispose persons to act or react in various ways. The symbol is indeed an enduring one, making sex workers' major claim— sexual services as legitimate employment—a difficult "sell." Social symbols such as intimacy, love, and sexuality may play a more important role in the sex workers' debate then previously implied. Thus, it is not farfetched to perceive the current controversy over sex work as a debate over the meaning of family, sexuality, and gender roles. Clamen is quite right when she mentions that sex workers are "challenging the codes" of sexual conduct. The perception is that sex workers are upsetting the meaning of sexuality, its function—to express love. Reacting to the prohibitionists' constant onslaught has forced many of us to develop counter-arguments relating to sexuality, the right to be different, and to reaffirm our enjoyment of the job. It is on this terrain that many of us have spent time defending our position; according to Heather Berg (2014), we spend too much of our time in that kind of argument. Although I do not identify as a Marxist I do battle with exploitive work arrangements; hence, my attraction to the work of Marxist scholars Heather Berg (2014) and Holly Lewis (2016).

Bypassing the sexual debate completely, Heather Berg argues that "[c]ommercial sex exchange is not exploitative because of anything unique to sex; it is exploitative because it is labor under capitalism" (2014, 694). The same argument is made later by Holly Lewis concerning human trafficking: "[. . .]—sexual or not—is a problem of political economy, that is the distribution of wealth, not a question of evil or patriarchy" (2016, 101). Both authors are demanding that our focus should be on labor issues and even if Berg claims that for many women sex work is a better way to earn a living, the fact remains that it is still labor under capitalism. Berg claims that work is exploitive; in contrast, I say it is potentially exploitive.

In "Working for Love, Loving for Work: Discourses of Labor in Feminist Sex-Work Activism" (2014), Berg presents an evaluation of sex workers who defend their position vis-à-vis prohibitionists "but often do so by constructing versions of agency that are dependent on social privilege, reinforcing the dominant notion of intimate labor as unmediated performance of the self and ignoring the violence inherent in wage work" (Berg 2014, 720). I do not need to peruse Berg's references to know that many of us have somewhat overestimated our freedom, our choices, especially when we have entered the business at a young age. Of course, this brings me to controversial conversations around the "glamour of sex work," how "natural it feels to be in the industry," and other narratives, but to make work, any kind of work, glamorous, Berg states that it can discourage workers "from making demands for improved labor conditions" (706). Stella is not taking the bait and as Clamen said, "[understanding] sex work as work does not translate as everyone is really happy and bouncy in their work" (See *Getting Past 'The Pimp'* [2018] and Durisin et al. [2018] for labor issue discussion).

Sex work is in many ways just like any other job and some workers do have a lot more control; this depends on their capacity to walk away from situations they find unacceptable. I would say that economic capital is the most important dimension here—the capacity to say no. When prohibitionists insist on describing sex workers as victims, or as minors without the legal right to make decisions on their own, they sustain a moral argument versus one that could lead to changes in the economic structure. Catharine MacKinnon, a self-declared Marxist, should pay more attention to all forms of labor—her powerful influential voice should be there to guide all women, not just the ones who agree with her. Women's safety and autonomy should be paramount.

Even though the distinction between free and forced prostitution has been acknowledged and debated at great length by Doezema (1998), the voices advocating for sex workers' rights are still challenged, and working conditions ignored. In Canada, public policy has become fixated on the notion of the sex worker as a victim as exemplified by the adoption of the PCEPA in 2014. The outrage surrounding trafficking and child prostitution diminishes concern for sex workers' rights by diverting the issue and bringing up other imagery and cultural meaning. The worst division, however, is the voluntary/guilty and the forced/innocent dichotomy that incorporates the belief that women who transgress sexual norms deserve to be punished (Doezema 1998, 42). This forced versus voluntary split reinforces the argument that prostitution is not work and that choosing to make it such is suspect, and only innocence (virtue) and helplessness deserve to be protected (43). As I mentioned in chapter 3, the innocence of the victim seems to be of primary importance. Doezema also argues that focusing on forced prostitution means that governments are not challenged about the poor treatment of voluntary "prostitutes." For instance, sex workers are protected solely if they are victims, but have no human rights if they are sex workers of their own volition. In other words, the victim is not responsible for sexual wrongdoing, but the whore deserves what she gets.

Comparing prostitution to other forms of work, Martha Nussbaum (1998) maintained that instead of criminalizing women in prostitution, states and organizations should work on improving sex workers' working conditions. Nussbaum acknowledges the fact that prostitution is problematic because it is often practiced by women with restricted choices, but adds that the freedom to choose our work is a luxury that non-affluent people do not possess, so despite the concerns that Nussbaum has regarding the exchange of money for sex, she concludes that:

> The correct response to this problem seems to be to work to enhance economic autonomy and the personal dignity of members of that class, not to rule off limits an option that may be the only livelihood for many poor women and to further stigmatize women who already make their living this way. (Nussbaum 1998, 723)

We all work; some do so to make a living; some, as in the case of the independently wealthy, do so for other reasons. Some jobs are defamed, and some are regarded as prestigious. Arguably, "feminine" jobs, for the most part, are not regarded as prestigious—necessary yes, respected no. Highly stigmatized and in many places criminalized, sex work is too often practiced in dangerous surroundings without the protection of state agencies. Since for many women sexual services are the best way to earn a decent living, it may be time to move away from the merry-go-round of force, choices, and morals and let people decide their best path to attain self-sufficiency. On this subject this is what an escort has to say:

> Within a capitalist economy we all must choose how we will labor in order to survive. For some they choose to take the traditional route that our capitalist society has provided them by slowly and painstakingly working their way up the ladder. So one might start as a sandwich maker at Subway, slowly move up to assistant manager and maybe if they take a management course eventually run the chain. For others they choose to take a more innovative route and enter into the sex industry. Now the sex industry isn't all easy and filled with rose petals (partially as a result of its criminalization and its resulting stigma), but with a lot of hard work one can make enough to graduate from university debt free and live quite comfortably in comparison to their peers living on loans and bursaries. Others might enter into the industry and save up enough to start a business, pay for a messy divorce while caring simultaneously for the roof over their children's heads. Some might enjoy the freedom of a flexible schedule while others actually need that flexibility of not having to report to a boss since they may have to negotiate dealing with a mental illness or chronic pain. Whatever the case might be the majority of individuals working within the sex/entertainment industry have made an autonomous, strategic decision to exercise they're agency and enter into the field. Some might enter for a short time to fulfill a monetary goal, while others find a career that fulfills them and allows them the opportunity at upward mobility they thought they'd never have. (Miss B 2019, in an interview with the author)

To date, what most prohibitionists have done appears like the parlor room socialists of the nineteenth century—formulating prescriptions for the good life that seem to be out of touch with many women's reality. Again in Miss B's words,

Many street based workers are out on our streets, because they don't have the ability to labor indoors. Either because of funds or because many of the websites they used for advertising were taken down post fosta/sesta, systematically forcing them back onto the streets or into the hands of a local pimp. Whatever the reason might be they are deserving of the same dignity and respect as any other individual. We all labor however we can for whatever reason we choose too. Life puts us in different circumstances, but at least these individuals are trying to make a living to pay for whatever they need however they can.

And when questioned about her victim status this is what a former sex worker had to say:

Yes, absolutely I am a victim of life circumstances my environment, being unqualified, being too old, inexperienced—having kids. Sex work adopted out of despair? Totally! It flows better, [the victim role] sounds better than being a prostitute or stripper. I am in the sex industry. Bad enough we must do it—I was not born for this, but it was my best option in order to feed five mouths! (Miss M 2018, in an interview with the author)

Some who chose to be in the industry must deal with racism and having to work harder to earn their money:

A class I took a few years ago really allowed me to reconcile with the internalized sense of shame that I had felt from being a sex worker myself. It confirmed the ideas that were in my head revolving around the fact that white privilege is prominent within the sex work industry. As a mixed-race woman of colour dancing in a strip club, I had always noticed that a white woman would make more than me, and my black and Hispanic colleagues. I thought that maybe I was crazy for thinking that way, and for seeing that I was either completely ignored or completely fetishized. The two extremes that women of colour often tend to face in the sex industry. The fact that women of colour need to work ten times harder than a white woman to make the same amount of money, or even less. It highlights the idea that women of colour and women who have suffered the aftermaths of colonialism use sex work as a means of survival, and even steady income. And that victimizing women of colour in the sex industry is not the solution to the issues that they face. (Kaya 2018, in an interview with the author)

I support the decriminalization of prostitution and its peripheral activities and even though sex work is not for everyone, and as my interviewee makes clear, it was clearly not her first choice, I conceptualize sexual services as legitimate work.

When it comes down to it, we all exercise our bodily autonomy to labor how we see fit. Entering into the sex industry isn't for everyone, but for those who enjoy it or feel like it is providing them with what they need at this time. (Miss B 2019)

Give women choices; give them the means to attain *their own* goals. And although recognizing the downside of the industry Kaya recognizes the upside:

> Such as being able to spend more time devoted to school, having a higher wage, and not getting mentally drained for no pay at a retail job. It really makes us wonder who is more exploited: a person working in retail for twelve dollars an hour while dealing with constant abuse from customers, or a person taking charge of their sexual autonomy, escaping the normative ways of earning income, and making potentially ten times the amount of someone working a minimum wage job? All in all, the course I took really did a good job and removing the victim narrative that many people associate to sex work, and bring out the empowerment aspect of it.

Following Kaya's comment I must wonder how different other places of employment are when it comes to race and social class.

As Sewell (1992) claims, people have "a capacity for agency for desiring, for forming intentions, and for acting creatively is inherent in all humans" (1992, 19). Women are a lot more resourceful than is usually imagined and this became clear to me during the Forum XXX. Many of our beliefs are based on our Western definition of comfort and success. Hewell states,

> [. . .] agency is formed by a specific range of cultural schemas and resources available in a person's particular social milieu. The specific forms that agency will take consequently vary enormously and are culturally and historically determined. But a capacity for agency is as much a given for humans as the capacity for respiration. That all humans actually exercise agency. (Sewell 1992, 21)

As introduced in the historical retrospective, the "whore symbol," constructed in the late 1800s, has been an enduring symbol of social decay and sexual deviance, as well as psychological immaturity. Sex workers' rights groups' fights have been geared toward the recognition of their revenue-generating activity and their transformation from pariahs to citizens with legal and social rights. Sex workers want "to be affirmed as full participants in humanity" (Dubet and Thaler 2004, 561), and this struggle is about the legitimacy of their claim that the sale of sexual services is legitimate work. As Paola Tabet (1987) argued, depending on the society, women may receive gifts and lodging in exchange for sex, but they cannot specifically ask for a fee. Sex workers violate norms and values and in doing so their claims attract and/or offend. People gather around certain symbols while rejecting others—such is the situation with the expression sex workers and sex work. It became clear in November 2017 during a panel titled "Speaking Publically about Violence against Indigenous Women" in the Sociology/Anthropology Department at Concordia involving prohibitionists that dialogue is still impossible in Canada. As I mentioned during my interview with Jenn Clamen, I tried to open the discussion, to acknowledge the hurt and the fear experienced by both sides of the debate, but to no avail. The conference at Concordia was emotionally charged as I sustained heavy accusations regarding sex workers' organizations ignoring trafficking victims and in part being responsible for the death of Indigenous women.

In its final report, the Canadian Solicitation Subcommittee ignored the claims of sex workers and their allies and stated that the government could not endorse "the commodification and invasive exploitation of a woman's body" (House of Commons 2006, 90). Therefore, after Canadian sex workers' victory—the Bedford decision—on December 20, 2013, prohibitionists mobilized and demanded the decriminalization of "prostituted women," coupled with tougher sanctions against clients or pimps and they won via the PCEPA born as Bill C-36, which amended the Criminal Code after the Bedford decision. The PCEPA makes "prostitution between adults a de facto illegal activity for the first time in Canada's history" (Casavant and Valiquet 2014). Prohibitionists do not consider decriminalization as a solution and believe it reinforces women's subordination. The only way to reach political equality and full recognition of women's rights, according to Kat Banyard (2016), is through the abolition of prostitution. According to Banyard, there is no redeeming quality in sex work; there is no such a thing as "'a safe place' for people to be abused in" (2016, 208). One is always a victim notwithstanding the social or economic capital of women. Working in the sex industry always jeopardizes one's physical and emotional integrity—it is always a form of violence (Smith 2014, 8).

In 1995, Radhiha Coormaraswany of the UN, responsible for a special committee on violence against women, concluded that the only common denominator shared by all prostitution rights movements was of an economic nature, recognizing prostitution as an income-generating activity. Besides this common language, prostitution remains a difficult phenomenon to conceptualize since it is a construction constantly produced and reproduced by social and sexual relationships. The concept of sex work allows the debate to get away from the legal discourse, the public health discourse, and the issue of social order. Further, it situates sex workers in the domain of work, where they should be protected, and away from the domain of medicine where they should be rescued and rehabilitated. Framing sexual services as work allows us to "fight the social construction that sees us as a class of outcasts, to stop moralizing or perceiving women who exercise these professions as sick. Sex work is not, in fact, an identity, a social defect, moral, legal, psychological or even necessarily the central aspect of the practitioners' lives" (Stella 2002, 7).

As I have noted, symbols, and our relationship to them, have important consequences for sex workers and for sex workers' rights groups. For the most part, our shared understanding of the meaning of culturally specific symbols motivates us to engage in the behavior and actions that are expected of us. Yet, an important activity of sex workers' groups is to constantly challenge the validity of accepted cultural symbols. For law enforcement officials, who for the most part subscribe to these enduring symbols of decadence and victimization, the solicitation law is still perceived as the only way to control prostitution, protect "prostitutes," curb their addictions, and possibly convince them to leave the trade. The term whore has become a significant symbol and until the emergence of sex workers' groups, the whore signified the fallen woman, to be feared or pitied. Part of the struggle for sex workers' groups is to decide what to do with the word. Carol Leigh, in her book *Unrepentant Whore* (2004), certainly uses it to claim her right to be a whore. This kind of decision is linked with mobilization strategies.

FINAL WORDS

Stella was formed on the advice of public health researchers studying the needs of downtown street prostitutes in terms of HIV/STI prevention (Stella 1998, 1). Although Stella was created as a project within an HIV program, local sex workers were involved every step of the way. Stella was and remains by-and-for sex workers. In Montréal, Stella endeavors to be unique and innovative. Stella also wants to create links and alliances with other health resources and community and social services. Stella is part of an international community, one that never asked its members to stop sex work and always respected sex workers' choices. Stella, whose main battles relate to issues of freedom, safety, and human rights, denounces strategies such as targeting "johns." In fact, Stella has a publication called "Dear Client" that addresses clients in the industry, as a way of creating safer working conditions *with* clients and because the laws force sex workers and their clients to move further underground, which increases the risk of violence. On this issue Stella joins the international sex workers' movement. Since 1975, sex workers have indeed claimed that their criminal status pushes them underground. Just as COYOTE and French sex workers did before them, Stella reframes their issue as one of safety and security. Consistent with the principle of framing, Stella, as with other sex workers' groups, became a claim-maker and offers a new way of looking at the causes of violence against sex workers. Violence is not intrinsic to sex work; violence is in part due to the criminalization of prostitution and the maintenance of symbols.

What constitutes violence and its source remains another area of contention between sex workers and prohibitionists. Both discuss violence, but cannot agree on the source, or the cause of violence often attached to sex work. Sex workers and prohibitionists remain deeply divided on this issue.

For the latter, violence is intrinsic to sex work. Regarding commercial sex as work, prohibitionists' position is clear. They condemn the contemporary discourse that articulates prostitution as work (Legault-Roy 2014).

I will not deny that some women do not belong in the sex industry and should be helped to leave, but the prohibitionists' position opens the door to the following question: what is detrimental to women? Is it sex work or the stigma attached to the nature of the work; in other words, the lack of social recognition and its criminalized status? What is hurtful for us is the constant disavowing of our agency and to be perceived as lacking in judgment—of not knowing when and how exploitation occurs—the so-called "false consciousness." The prohibitionist denouncing of the role of sex workers' organizations remains a violent act toward sex workers—attempts to remove the services, the support, and the community that sex workers have is no less than an attempt at eradicating members of our community.

Pornography and prostitution are not benign subjects and can be used by people to cause harm, but not more than can most words and images (Sumner 2004, 141). No one can deny that the expansion of sexual economic exchanges has permitted certain countries to profit from the sex trade (Gilfoyle 1999); it has also facilitated the growth of sex workers' organizations. Worldwide, sex workers' rights groups are finding ways to bring their realities onto the global stage by organizing themselves and mobilizing around their needs. When I began this reflection twenty years ago, I claimed that taking money from the government meant more paperwork than activism and I held that argument until recently (Beers and Tremblay 2014). The success of Stella demonstrates that, at times, more paperwork might be worth the risk. Winning at the Supreme Court level changed my position regarding the collaboration of state funding and activism. Entering the discursive universe that was until recently the reserve of the political, academic, and medical professions, sex workers are transforming themselves into actors. By standing up to experts who claim to know what sex workers need, they have taken their rightful place. Sex workers have earned the right to decide when and how to resist exploitation; women working in the sex trade are rewriting their biographies.

As I stated at the beginning of this work, it was my anger that led me to write this book. The idea that some lives are "grievable," as Judith Butler expresses it, and therefore worthy of protection, while others are disposable has always been profoundly disturbing to me. Here I have focused my attention on sex workers, but my research also applies to the lives of other marginalized groups, such as Indigenous people, people living in homelessness, and people with mental health challenges, those who are often ignored, pitied, or reviled, but who are seldom seen as fully human. Our government must recognize the worth of all people, acknowledge its responsibility to provide us with equal protection under the law, and act accordingly. This work has been, first and foremost, a call for such action.

NOTES

1. The accused owned a shop selling and renting "hard core" videotapes and magazines as well as sexual paraphernalia. He was charged with various counts of selling obscene material, possessing obscene material for the purpose of distribution or sale, and exposing obscene material to public view, contrary to s. 159 (now s. 163) of the Criminal Code: https://scc-csc. lexum.com/scc-csc/scc-csc/en/item/844/index.do.

2. https://www.theguardian.com/film/2017/nov/26/susan-sarandon-i-thought-hillary-was-very-dangerous-if-shed-won-wed-be-at-war, accessed September 13, 2018.

Documents Consulted

Code	Date	Source Type	Description/Title
1993M-A	1993	Minutes	Exploration de la faisabilité d'une intervention en prevention du VIH/sida et autres MTS pour les femmes prostituées de Montréal-Centre: Première reunion des intervenants—29 septembre 1993; 14h30—16h30; Unité de santé publique—Hôpital general de Montréal
1993M-B		Minutes	Compte-rendu de la Deuxième reunion des intervenants—Pour une intervention en prevention du VIH/sida et autres MTS pour les femmes prostituées de Montréal-Centre; Vendredi, 5 novembre 1993; 9h30—11h30; Unité de santé publique—Hôpital general de Montréal
1993M-C		Minutes	Compte-rendu de la Troisième reunion des intervenants—Pour une intervention en prevention du VIH/sida et autres MTS pour les femmes prostituées de Montréal-Centre; Lundi, 20 décembre 1993; 9h30—11h30; Unité de santé publique—Hôpital general de Montréal
1994R-A	1994	Report	Le Project Stella—Une Intervention Destinée Aux Femmes Pratiquant La Prostitution Dans Les Rues De Montréal-Centre; présenté au Programme D'Action Communautaire Sur Le SIDA (PACS) Santé Canada; par le ProJect D'Intervention Auprès Des Mineur(e)s Prostitué(e)s (PIaMP); Montréal, le 15 mai 1994
1994M-A		Minutes	Compte-rendu de la Quatrième reunion des intervenants; Pour une intervention en prevention du VIH/SIDA et autres MTS pour les

Code	Date	Source Type	Description/Title
			femmes prostituées de Montréal-Centre; Jeudi, le 27 janvier 1994, 13h30—15h30; Unité de santé publique—Hôpital general de Montréal
1994M-B		Minutes	Compte-rendu de la Quatrième reunion des intervenants; Pour une intervention en prevention du VIH/SIDA et autres MTS pour les femmes prostituées de Montréal-Centre; Mercredi, le 23 février 1994, 14h30—16h30; Centre Ozanam—94 est rue Sainte-Catherine, Montréal
1994M-C		Minutes	Compte-rendu de la Quatrième reunion des intervenants; Pour une intervention en prevention du VIH/SIDA et autres MTS pour les femmes prostituées de Montréal-Centre; Mercredi, le 20 avril 1994, 14h30—16h30; Centre Ozanam—94 est rue Sainte-Catherine, Montréal
1994M-D		Minutes	Compte-rendu de la rencontre au poste de police 33; Vendredi le 6 mai 1994, 10:00 à 11:00; 105, Ontario est, Montréal
1994M-E		Minutes	Compte-rendu de la rencontre avec le conseiller municipal du district St-Jacques; Lundi le 9 mai 1994, 10:00 à 11:00; 2145 rue Visitation, Montréal
1994M-F		Minutes	Compte-rendu de la Quatrième reunion des intervenants; Pour une intervention en prevention du VIH/SIDA et autres MTS pour les femmes prostituées de Montréal-Centre; Vendredi, le 13 mai 1994, 13h30—15h30; Centre Ozanam—94 est rue Sainte-Catherine, Montréal
1994M-G		Minutes	Compte-rendu de la Huitième reunion du comité aviseur; PROJECT STELLA; Mercredi, le 15 juin 1994, 13h30 à 15h00; CLSC Centre-Ville, 1250 Sanguinet, Montréal
1994M-H		Minutes	Compte-rendu de la Neuvième reunion du comité aviseur; PROJECT STELLA; Vendredi, le 9 septembre 1994, 14h30 à 16h00; Unité de santé publique Hôpital général de Montréal; 1616 boul. René-Lévesque ouest, 3e étage, Montréal
1994M-I		Minutes	Project Stella Minutes; Tuesday, October 25, 1994 at CLSC Centre—3:00 pm
1994M-J		Minutes	Project Stella; Compte rendu de la reunion du comité aviseur; Mardi, 29 novembre 1994,

Code	Date	Source Type	Description/Title
			15h—17h; CLSC centre-ville, 1250 Sanguinet, Montréal
1994M-K		Minutes	Project Stella; Procés verbal de la reunion du comité consultative; 22 decembre, 1994
1994L-A		Letter	To: Santé et Bien-Etre Social Canada, Programme d'Action Communautaire sur le Sida (PACS); Montréal, le 13 mai 1994 From: Projet d'Intervention auprès des Mieur-e-s Prostitué-e-s
1994L-B		Letter	To: OrkiaLefebre; Conseillère en planification et recherché; Régie Régionale de la santé et des services sociaux de Montréal-Centre; 3723, rue Saint-Denis, Montréal, Québec; November 24, 1994
1994R-B		Report	ANNEXE 1; Compte rendu des groupe de discussion en milieu carcéral
1994R-C		Report	ANNEXE 2; Comptes rendus des rencontres du comité aviseur
1995M-D	1995	Minutes	Stella—Compte Rendu De La Reunion Du 24 mai 1995; tenue a STELLA 1422 ST-Laurent #2
1995M-E		Minutes	Stella—Compte Rendu De La Reunion Du 9 août 1995; tenue au CLSC centre-ville
1995R-A		Report	Stella—Rapport du comité de la programmation sur le déroulement de Stella déput de l'été 1995
1995M-F		Minutes	Stella—Compte Rendu De La Reunion Du 6 septembre 1995; tenue au CLSC centre-ville
1995M-G		Minutes	réunion du comite aviseur; 19 octobre 1995
1995M-H		Minutes	Stella—Compte Rendu De La Reunion Du 20 décembre 1995; tenue au CLSC centre-ville
1995R-B		Report	Rapport Des Verificateurs—Aux Membres du Conseil d'Administration; Project d'Intervention Auprès Mineurs Prositués P.I.A.M.P.; "Project Stella"; Montréal, QC.
1995M-I		Minutes	Compte-rendu de la rencontre du 23 février 1995 entre les représentants du comité interquartiers sur la prostitution et les intervenants
1995M-J		Minutes	Comité Interquartiers Sur La Prostitution; Compte-rendu de la réunion du sous-comité sur lees revendications tenue au 2022 rue de la Visitation, le 25 mai 1995
1996R-A	1996	Report	La Prostitution De Rue À Montreal—L'urgence d'une nouvelle approche

Code	Date	Source Type	Description/Title
1996L-A		Letter	Table Interquartiers Sur La Prostitution; Montréal, le 1er février 1996
1996L-B		Letter	Tandem Montréal; Plateau-Mont-Royal—Centre-Sud; 31 julliet 1996
1996M-A		Minutes	Stella—Compte-rendu de la réunion du conseil d'administration; CLSC Centre-ville; 1250, rue Sanguinet; Mardi, le 20 février 1996; 9h30 à 12h30
1996M-B		Minutes	Procès Verbal—Conseil d'administration de Stella; 22 avril 1996; 10h000 à 12h00
1996R-B		Report	Stella—Annual Report of Activities; April 1995—March 1996
1996M-C		Minutes	Comptu-Rendu De La Journée de Réflexion "STELLA" Tenue Le 10 mai 1996
1996M-D		Minutes	Procès Verbal—Conseil d'administration de Stella; 16 septembre 1996; 18h15 à 20h10
1996M-E		Minutes	Stella—Réunion du C.A.; tenue le 18 décembre, 1996
1996M-F		Minutes	Stella—Compte Rendu De La Reunion Du 15 janvier 1996; tenue au CLSC centre-ville
1996M-G		Minutes	Stella—Réunion du C.A.; tenue le 20 novembre 1996
1996M-H		Minutes	Stella.l'amie de Maimie; Compte rendu du comité des finances—17 julliet 1996
1996R-C		Report	Stella—Bilan Des Activités; Juillet—Septembre 1996; Journé de retraite du Conseil d'administration—Vendredi, le 8 novembre 1996
1996M-I		Minutes	Stella—Réunion du C.A.; tenue le 23 octobre 1996
1996M-J		Minutes	Procès Verbal—Conseil d'administration de Stella; 11 juin 1996; 18h15 à 20h10
1996M-K		Minutes	Procès Verbal—Assemblé Géneral Annuella—Stella; 17 juin 1996, 18h00; CLSC Des Faubourg—1250 Sanguinet, Mtl
1996M-L		Minutes	Procès Verbal—Conseil d'administration de Stella; 25 juin 1996; 18h15 à 20h10
1997M-A	1997	Minutes	Procès Verbal De La Reunion Du Conseil D'Administration De Stella, L'Amie De Maimie; Tenue le 22 octobre 1997
1997R-A		Annual Report	Stella—April 1, 1996–March 31, 1997

Code	Date	Source Type	Description/Title
1997M-B		Minutes	Procès Verbal—Assemblé Générale—Stella; mercerdi le 18 juin 1997, 18h00
1997N-A		Newsletter	Constellation—A Newsletter by and for Sex Workers
1997M-C		Minutes	Proces Verbal De La Reunion Du Conseil D'Administration De Stella, L'Amie De Maimie; Tenue le172 décembre 1997
1997R-B		Report	Rapport De Mission D'Examen—Aux Membres du Conseil d'Administration; Stella, L'Amie de Maimie; Montréal, QC.
1997M-D		Minutes	Stella—Compte-rendu de la réunion du 22 janvier 1996
1997Z-A		Misc.	Stella—L'Histoire De Stella
1997R-C		Report	Règlements Généraux—Stella; Julliet 1997
1997Z-B		Misc.	Participants, Stella
1997R-D		Report	Stella—Action Plan 1997
1997L-A		Letter	Renouvellement de la "Stratégie québecoise de lutte contre sida—Phase 4" Subventions pour les projets de prévention de la transmission du VIH et des MTS; Prolongation de la subvention 1997–1998
1997L-B		Letter	Letter to Monique Tessier, Chef de services; Adaption social; Régie Régionale de la santé et des services sociaux—Montréal-Centre; October 22, 1997
1997L-C		Letter	Letter to M. Carl Juneau, Acting Director of Charities Division; September 8, 1997
1997L-D		Letter	Letter to Mme. Claire Blais, agent de planification; subject: Funding for Stella from April 1, 1998 to September 30, 1998
1997R-E		Annual Report	Stella—Rapport D'Évaluation; Volet I: La participation des travailleuse et ex-travailleuses du sexe dans la structure de Stella et le soutien apporté à cette participation; Le 1er julliet au 30 juin 1997
1997M-E		Minutes	Procès Verbal—Conseil d'administration de Stella; 20 janvier 1997; 18h15 à 20h30
1997M-F		Minutes	Procès Verbal—Conseil d'administration de Stella; 17 Février 1997
1997M-G		Minutes	Stella—Réunion du C.A.; tenue le 17 mars 1997
1997M-H		Minutes	Stella—Compte-rendu de la réunion du conseil d'administration; tenue le 23 avril 1997

Code	Date	Source Type	Description/Title
1997M-I		Minutes	Procès Verbal De La Reunion Du Conseil D'Administration De Stella, L'Amie De Maimie; Tenue le 16 septembre 1997
1997M-J		Minutes	Procès Verbal De La Reunion Du Conseil D'Administration De Stella, L'Amie De Maimie; Tenue le 12 Novembre 1997
1997R-F		Report	Stella—A Resource for Sex Workers—Progress Report—Submitted by Karen Herland, Coordinator—October 1997
1998M-A	1998	Minutes	Procès Verbal De La Réunion Du Conseil D'administration De Stella, L'amie de Maimie; tenue le 22 janvier 1998
1998M-B		Minutes	Procès Verbal De L'Assemblée Générale Spéciale De Stella, L'amie de Maimie; tenue le 22 janvier 1998
1998M-C		Minutes	Procès Verbal De La Réunion Du Conseil D'administration De Stella, L'amie de Maimie; tenue le 6 février 1998
1998L-A		Letter	Letter from "Régie Régionale de la Santé et des Services Sociaux de Montréal-Centre" to Madame Karen Herland, a coordinator of Stella; Subject of letter: Subventions pour les projects de prévention de la transmission du VIH et des MTS 1998—Demande de prolongation pour le projet no 6: "Stella"
1998M-D		Minutes	Procès Verbal De La Reunion Du Conseil D'Administration De Stella, L'Amie De Maimie; Tenue le 13 mars 1998
1998R-A		Financial Report	Stella, L'aime de Maimie—États financiers au 31 mars 1998
1998M-E		Minutes	Procès Verbal De La Reunion Du Conseil D'Administration De Stella, L'Amie De Maimie; Tenue le 14 avril 1998
1998L-B		Letter	Letter from "Régie Régionale de la Santé et des Services Sociaux de Montréal-Centre" to Madame Karen Herland, a coordinator of Stella; Subject of letter: Programme de Prévention du VIH/SIDA et autres MTS—Prolongation 1998
1998M-F		Minutes	Procès Verbal De La Reunion Du Conseil D'Administration De Stella, L'Amie De Maimie; Tenue le 12 mai 1998
1998M-G		Minutes	Procès Verbal De La Reunion Du Conseil D'Administration De Stella, L'Amie De Maimie; Tenue le 23 juin 1998

Code	Date	Source Type	Description/Title
1998M-H		Minutes	Procès Verbal Assemblée Générale Spéciale De Stella, L'amie de Maimie; Mardi le 23 juin 1998
1998M-I		Minutes	Procès Verbal—Reunion Du Conseil D'Administration; Mardi le 12 août 1998 á 18h00
1998M-J		Minutes	Procès Verbal—Reunion Du Conseil D'Administration—Stella, L'amie de Maimie; jeudi le 17 septembre 1998 à 18h00
1998M-K		Minutes	Procès Verbal—Reunion Du Conseil D'Administration; Lundi le 7 décembre 1998, 18h00 à 21h30
1998R-B		Report	Empowerment at Stella; submitted by Karen Herland, a coordinator of Stella
1998R-C		Report	Rapport D'Étape—Project de Recherche-Évaluation; 1er juillet 1997 au 30 juin 1998
1998R-D		Report	Stella: HIV Prevention Activities: Final Report April 1, 1997—March 31, 1998; Régie régionale de la santé st des services sociaux—Montréal-Centre
1998R-E		Report	Stella, l'amie de Maimie; Rapport D'Activités—1er avril 1997 au 31 mars 1998
1998R-F		Annual Report	Stella—Annual Report; April 1997—March 1998
1998R-G		Report	Stella—Rapport D'Évaluation; Volet II: La Prise en Charge des Travailleuse du Sexe—Empowerment; 1er julliet au 31 mars 1998
1998R-H		Report	Le Projet Vulnérabilité de Stella; Rapport Intérimaire premiere analyses; May 1998
1998R-I		Report	Groupe de Travail Fédéral-Provincial-Territorial sur la Prostitution: Rapport et recommandations realtives à législation, aux politique et aux pratiques concernant les activités à la prostitution; Décembre 1998
1998R-J		Report	Annual Report 1997–1998
1998L-C		Letter	Letter from Karen Herland, a coordinator of Stella, to Mme Lamoureux; le 26 août 1997
1999R-A	1999	Annual Report	Stella—Rapport annuel 1998–1999 (Juin 1999)
1999M-A		Minutes	Procès Verbal—Reunion Du Conseil D'Administration—Stella, L'amie de Maimie; Dimanche le 17 février 1999, 11h00 à 15h00

Code	Date	Source Type	Description/Title
1999M-B		Minutes	Procès Verbal—Reunion Du Conseil D'Administration—Stella, L'amie de Maimie; Lundi le 8 mars 1999
1999M-C		Minutes	Procès Verbal Assemblée Générale Annuelle—Stella, L'amie de Maimie; Mercredi le 9 juin 1999 à 18h00
1999Z-A		Misc.	Règlements Géneraux—Stella—Juillet 1997 (Révisé juin 1999)
1999R-B		Financial Report	Stella, L'aime de Maimie—États financiers au 31 mars 1999
1999Z-B		Misc.	Rapport du Comité Montréalais sur la prostitution de rue et la prostitution juvénile—Juin 1999
2000R-A	2000	Financial Report	Stella, L'aime de Maimie—États financiers au 31 mars 2000
2000R-B		Annual Report	Stella, Vivre et Travailler en Sécurité et avec Dignité—Rapport annuel (Juin 2000)
2000M-A		Minutes	Réunion du conseil d'administration de Stella: le 20 juin 2000
2000M-B		Minutes	Procès Verbal—Reunion Du Conseil D'Administration—Stella, L'amie de Maimie; Mardi le 26 septembre 2000
2000M-C		Minutes	Recontre du Conseil d'administration de Stella, le avril 2000
2000M-D		Minutes	Minutes—Meeting of the Board of Administration—Stella, L'amie de Maimie; Wednesday, Nov. 1, 2000
2000M-E		Minutes	Projet de procès-verbal du la réunion du conseil d'administration de Stella du 13 décembre 2000
2000Z-A		Misc.	Stella—Politique d'emploi
2000Z-B		Misc.	Pamphlet—Séminaire VIH/sida, droit et politique "Criminalisation et travail du sexe: enjeux pour la lutte contre le VIH/sida"
2000Z-C		Misc.	Portrait du travail de proximité tel que pratiqué par les organismes communautaires membres de la table de concertation jeunesse-itinerance du centre-ville—par Marc St-Louis (Automne 2000)
2000M-F		Minutes	Projet de procès-verbal du la réunion du conseil d'administration de Stella ayant et lieu le 29 août 2000 au 2035, boul. St-Laurent, 3e étage
2000Z-D		Misc.	Stella et La COALITION pour les droits des travailleuses et travailleurs du sexe—Document

Code	Date	Source Type	Description/Title
			déposé dans le cadre des travaux du Comité du Bloc Québécois sur la prostitution (15 août 200)
2000L-A		Letter	Letter from Madeleine Lacombe to Madame Darlène palmer
2001R-A	2001	Financial Report	Stella, L'aime de Maimie—États financiers au 31 mars 2001
2001R-B		Annual Report	Stella, Vivre et Travailler en Sécurité et avec Dignité—Rapport annuel Août 2001
2001M-A		Minutes	Réunion du conseil d'administration de Stella— 2035, boulevard St-Laurent, 3e étage; Mardi, le 23 janvier 2001
2001M-B		Minutes	Procès Verbal—Reunion Du Conseil D'Administration—Stella, L'amie de Maimie; Mardi le 20 février 2001
2001M-C		Minutes	Procès Verbal—Reunion Du Conseil D'Administration—Stella, L'amie de Maimie; Lundi le 26 mars 2001
2001M-D		Minutes	Réunion du conseil d'administration de Stella— 2035, boulevard St-Laurent, 3ième étage; Mardi, le 15 mai 2001
2001M-E		Minutes	Conseil D'administration de Stella le juin 2001
2001M-F		Minutes	Stella, L'amie de Maimie; Procès verbal— Assemblée Générale Annuelle; Jeudi le 14 juin 2001
2001Z-A		Misc.	Bulletin d'information de l'IREF, no 35, hiver-printemps 2001; Stella—Vivre et travailler en sécurité et avec dignité
2001Z-B		Misc.	Proposition de plan d'action réalisé lors des journées d'orientation (2001)
2001Z-C		Misc.	Rapport final de la consultation auprès des membres d'Alerte Centre-Sud en regard de la prostitution de rue; Préparé par Maria Nengeh Mensah pour Alerte Centre-Sud (Avril 2001)
2001L-A		Letter	Letter from Nathalie Labrecque, Coordonnatrice de la correspondance et de la rédaction, to Claire Thiboutot, Directrice générale de Stella (le 11 décembre 2001)
2001P-A		Pamphlet	Liste des mauvais clients et calendrier de septembre 2001
2002Z-A	2002	Misc.	Stella, groupe de services et de défense des droits des travailleuses du sexe, et le débat sur la prostitution (13 septembre 2002)

Code	Date	Source Type	Description/Title
2002Z-B		Misc.	Document de réflection: Stella; Personne ne connaît mon nom; Légiférer l'identité de la prostituée de rue (Juillet 2002)
2002R-A		Annual Report	Stella—Rapport d'activités 2001–2002 (le 6 juin 2002)
2002Z-C		Misc.	Résponse au rapport du Comité du Bloc Québécois sur la prostitution de rue (Mars 2002)
2002Z-D		Misc.	Pour des stratégies collectives concernant la prostitution de rue dans quartier Centre-Sud; (Document de réflexion et d'action, présenté au Conseil d'administration d'Alerte Centre-sud)
2002R-B		Financial Report	Stella, L'aime de Maimie—États financiers au 31 mars 2002
2002P-A		Pamphlet	Liste des mauvais clients et calendrier de Décembre 2001 Janvier 2002
2002P-B		Pamphlet	Stella—Liste des mauvais clients et calendrier de Mars 2002
2002P-C		Pamphlet	Stella pour Travailler en Sécurité et avec Dignité; Calendrier de Mai 2002; Liste des mauvais clients et agresseurs
2002P-D		Pamphlet	Stella—Liste des mauvais clients et calendrier de Avril 2002
2002P-E		Pamphlet	Bulletin Stellaire pour Travailler en Sécurité et avec Dignité; Calendrier de Octobre 2002; Liste des mauvais clients et agresseurs
2002P-F		Pamphlet	Bulletin Stellaire pour Travailler en Sécurité et avec Dignité; Calendrier de Septembre 2002; Liste des mauvais clients et agresseurs
2002P-G		Pamphlet	Bulletin Stellaire pour Travailler en Sécurité et avec Dignité; Calendrier de Novembre 2002; Liste des mauvais clients et agresseurs
2002P-H		Pamphlet	Bulletin Stellaire pour Travailler en Sécurité et avec Dignité; Calendrier de décembre et janvier 2003; Liste des mauvais clients et agresseurs
2002M-A		Minutes	"Coalition Nationale Des Femmes Contre La Pauvreté Et La Violence"; Comptu rendu de la réunion du 29 janvier 2002
2002M-B		Minutes	Comité vilence; Comptu-rendu réunion du 9 novembre 2002
2002M-C		Minutes	Compte-rendu AGA 2002—Michile Bourqur
2003L-A	2003	Letter	Letter from Stella to Mr. Paul Martin, Prime Minister of Canada (December 17, 2003)

Code	Date	Source Type	Description/Title
2003Z-A		Misc.	Email to Stella; subject: FWD-Asian prostitutes rights movement urgently needs support (Sat, 7 Jun, 2003)
2003Z-B		Misc.	Internet article—"Prostitution—Travail du sexe"—http://www.cybersolidaires.org/actus/sexe.html
2003Z-C		Misc.	Transcript of the second hour of debate on motion M-192 which took place on Friday February 7, 2003. Themotion was tabled by Libby Davies, NDP.; The motion stated: A special committee of the House be appointed to review the solicitation laws in order to improve the safety workers and communities overall, and to recommend changes that will reduce the exploitation of violence against sex-trade workers."
2003R-A		Financial Report	Stella, L'aime de Maimie—États financiers; Exercice clos le 31 mars 2003
2003M-A		Minutes	Compte-rendu rencontre du comité consultatif Montréalais sur la prostitution juvénile et la prositution de rue; le 30 septembre 2003
2003Z-D		Misc.	Projet: Porte Sainte-Marie SAQ; Mémoire Présenté à l'office de consultation publique de Montréal par le groupe (conseil en développement de l'habitation)
2003Z-E		Misc.	Projet Pore Ste-Marie; Mémoire d'Alerte Cente-Sud; Présenté à l'Office de consultation publique de Montréal
2003M-B		Minutes	Compte rendu de la réunion du Comité Politique; Octobre 7, 2003
2003Z-F		Misc.	Dossier Prostitution de rue / Adulte Vers un plan d'action intégrée—2003–2006 (mardi 30 septembre 2003)
2003Z-G		Misc.	Document de travail—Projet-pilote: La Prostitution de rue—Intervention en situation de crise 2003
2003M-C		Minutes	Procès-verbal rencontre du comité Montréalais consulatif sur la prositution de rue et la prostitution juvénile; le 25 jullliet 2003
2003Z-H		Misc.	Orientation 2003–2006—Vers un plan d'action intégré—Dossier prostitution de rue à Montréal; Préparé par le comité technique et présenté au comité institutionnel; le lundi 26 mai 2003

Code	Date	Source Type	Description/Title
2003Z-I		Misc.	Plan d'action intégré Prostitution de rue à Montréal; Commentaires de l'Association Des Résidants et Résidantes des Fourbourgs de Montréal; Septembre 2003
2003M-D		Minutes	Comité Montréalais consultatif sur la prostitution de rue et la prostitution juvénile; Rencontre du vendredi 25 julliet 2003
2003Z-J		Misc.	Communiqué pour diffusion immédiate—Un partnariat pour mieux comprendre le phénomène de la prostitution et de la toxicomanie
2003M-E		Minutes	Comité Montréalais consultatif sur la prostitution de rue et la prostitution juvénile; Rencontre du mardi 30 septembre 2003
2004Z-A	2004	Misc.	La judiciarisation des populations itinérantes à Montréal de 1994 à 2004
2004R-A		Annual Report	Stella—Rapport annuel 2003–2004; Stella . . . Toujours en mouvement! (3 juin 2004)
2004Z-B		Misc.	Email from Nicole Nepton of cybersolidaires.org to Stella; subject: Operation droits devant: Discrimination dans la remise de contraventions
2004Z-C		Misc.	Été 2004: Un portait de la situation dans l'espace public (Opération Droits devants!)
2004L-A		Letter	Lettre au Devoir; Pourquoi décriminaliser le travail du sexe; Par Colette Parent, Chris Bruckert et Maria Nengeh Mensah
2004Z-D		Misc.	Email from Karine Guilbeault to Stella; subject: conditions de travail
2004M-A		Minutes	Procés verbal de la réunion du comité organisateur du project forum XXX; tenue à Stella; Lundi, 4 octobre 2004
2004M-B		Minutes	Procés verbal de la réunion du comité organisateur du project forum XXX; tenue à Stella; Jeudi, 9 septembre 2004
2004M-C		Minutes	Procés verbal de la réunion du comité organisateur du project forum XXX; tenue à Stella; Lundi, 7 juin 2004
2004M-D		Minutes	Procès Verbal De L'Assemblée Générale Annuelle des Membres de Stella, L'amie de Maimie; tenue le 3 juin 2004
2004M-E		Minutes	Comité politique mardi le 17 février 2004
2004M-F		Minutes	Comité politique 23 mars 2004

Code	Date	Source Type	Description/Title
2004Z-E		Misc.	Email from Barb MacQuarrie, a Community Development Coordinator for "Centre for research on Violence Agaisnt Women and Children," to Francine Tremblay
2004Z-F		Misc.	Email from Micheline Carrier, Éditrice de Sisyphe, to Madame Lynette Tremblay; subject: Lettre à Lynette Tremblay sur la prostitution
2004Z-G		Misc.	Règlements Géneraux—Stella—(Révisé 3 juin 2004)
2004Z-H		Financial Report	Stella, L'aime de Maimie—États financiers au 31 mars 2004
2004Z-I		Misc.	Note from "Service du dévelopement culturel et de la qulité du millieu de vie" to "Members du Comité consultatif sur la prostitution de rue et la prostitution juvénille"; object: Prochaine rencontre du Comité consultatif sur la prostitution de rue et la prostitution juvénile; le 8 mars 2004
2004Z-J		Misc.	Plan d'action Montréalais sur la prostitution de rue / adulte; 2004–2007 (11 mars 2004); Ville de Montréal—Agence de développement de réseaux de services de santé et de services sociaux de Montréal
2005Z-A		Misc.	eXXXoressions: Forum XXX Proceedings—eXXXpressions is a compilation of presentations, discussions, and perspectives from 250 sex workers from all over the world that converged in Montréal, Canada, on May 18–22, 2005, for the Forum XXX. The Forum XXX, organized by Stella, Montréal's peer-run sex worker organization, marked Stella's 10th anniversary and a chance to take collective stock of the sex worker rights movement. (2 cd format)
2005R-A		Annual Report	Stella—Rapport d'activités; 1ier Avril 2004–30 juin 2005 (le 21 septembre 2005)
2006Z-A		Misc.	Description de poste—Coordonnatrice à la mobilisation (20 avril 2006)
2006Z-B		Misc.	Description de poste—Directrice générale (20 avril 2006)
2006Z-C		Misc.	Description de poste—Coordonnatrice aux communications (20 avril 2006)
2006M-A		Minutes	Procès Verbal De L'Assemblée Générale Annuelle des Membres de Stella, L'amie de Maimie; tenue le 28 juin 2006

Code	Date	Source Type	Description/Title
2006Z-D		Misc.	Règlements Généraux—Stella—(Révisé 28 juin 2006)
2006Z-E		Misc.	Manuel des employées—Octobre 2006
2006Z-F		Misc.	Organigramme de Stella (13 février 2006)
2006R-A		Report	Stella—Rapport d'activitiés (2005–2006)
2006M-B		Minutes	Procès-verbal de la session d'orientation du conseil d'administration de Stella, L'amie de Maimie; Tenue à Montréal, le 21 septembre 2006, de 13h à 16h
2006M-C		Minutes	Procès Verbal De La Reunion Du Conseil D'Administration De Stella, L'Amie De Maimie; Tenue à Montréal, le 26 mai 2006, de 10h à 11h30
2006M-D		Minutes	Procès Verbal De La Reunion Du Conseil D'Administration De Stella, L'Amie De Maimie; Tenue à Montréal, le 27 octobre 2006
2006M-E		Minutes	Procès Verbal De La Reunion Du Conseil D'Administration De Stella, L'Amie De Maimie; Tenue à Montréal, le 10 novembre 2006, de 13h à 16h30
2006M-F		Minutes	Document préparatoire—Conseil d'administration (10 novembre 2006)
2006R-B		Financial Report	Stella, L'amie de Maimie—Rapport Financier Annuel au 31 mars 2006
2006Z-G		Misc.	Stella—Priorités d'action 2006/2007
2006R-C		Annual Report	Rapport d'activitiés et d'évaluation— ConStellation 10ième anniversaire
2006Z-H		Misc.	(Project proposal) Des ailes pour notre avenir / Wings for our future : Contribuer à la prévention de la tranmission du VIH et de l'hépatite C en milieu carcéral et à l'accroissement du réseau de soutien aux détenues et ex-détenues infectées par le VIH et/ou le VHC (8 mai 2006)
2006Z-I		Misc.	Proposée par Irène Demczuk et déposé en séance le 24 avril 2008—Proposition d'une méthode de règlement de différends Fondé sur la philosophie de gestion et les règles en vigueur à Stella
2006M-G		Minutes	Réducution des méfaits appliquée au travail du sexe; Comptu-rendu des réflexions de la 2iéme rencontre; Réunion tenue à Stella le mercredi 26 novembre 2006

Code	Date	Source Type	Description/Title
2006P-A		Pamphlet	Notice for "Marche des parapluies rouge contre la violenec e faites aux travailleuses et travailleurs du sexe" (le 17 décembre 2006 à 18h)
2006Z-J		Misc.	Thibodeau, Claire. (2006). "Lutte contre le VIH/SIDA: Les travailleuses du sexe sur la ligne de front!" *Le point de vie: Bulletin du comité des personnes atteintes du VIH du Quebec.*
2007Z-A		Misc.	Ordre du jour proposé—Assemblée Générale Annuelle des membres de Stella, L'amie de Maimie, 21 juin 2007
2007M-C		Minutes	Procès Verbal Du Conseil D'Administration De Stella, L'amie de Maimie; Réunion Séciale: restructuration de l'organisation; Tenue à Montréal, le 19 février 2007
2007Z-B		Misc.	Formulaire de damande de financement / projet spécifique—Initiative des partenariats de lutte contre l'itinèrance (IPLI)
2007M-D		Minutes	Procès Verbal De La Reunion Du Conseil D'Administration du 7 septembre 2007
2007M-E		Minutes	Rencontre du 1er novembre sur l'approche Réduction des méfaits
2007R-A		Annual Report	Rapport d'activitiés et d'évaluation—Le Forum XXX—Célébrer une décennie d'action, façonner notre avenir (mars 2007)
2007Z-C		Misc.	The Gazette newspaper article—"Marchers speak up for sex-trade workers" (Dec 2007)
2007Z-D		Misc.	La Presse newspaper article—"Une autre réalité: La présence de danseuses mineures est davantage contrôlée dans les bars" (31 juillet 2007)
2007Z-E		Misc.	The Globe newspaper article—"Legalize prostitution, for all our sakes: How do we stop the disappearance and killing of sex-trade workers? Asks law professor" (January 19, 2007)
2007R-B		Financial Report	Stella, L'aime de Maimie—États financiers au 31 mars 2007
2007R-C		Annual Report	Stella, L'aime de Maimie—Par et pour les travailleuses du sexe pour vivre et travailler en santé, en sécurité et avec dignité!—Rapport d'activités 2007–2008
2007M-F		Minutes	Procès Verbal Du Conseil D'Administration De Stella, L'amie de Maimie; Réunion Séciale:

Code	Date	Source Type	Description/Title
			restructuration de l'organisation; Tenue à Montréal, le 3 octobre 2007 17:30 à 19:30
2007M-G		Minutes	Comité D'Action—Le 3 octobre 2007—Chez Stella
2007Z-F		Misc.	"Quand rôde la prostition" par Hugo Meunier et Anabelle Nicoud (le dimanche 22 juillet 2007)—http://www.cyberpresse.ca/apps/pbcs.dll/article?AID=/200070722/CPACTUALITES/70718119/6686/CPACTUEL¶template=printart&print=1
2007R-D		Report	Realizing the human rights of sex workers in Canada: Report of strategy meeting Canadian HIV/AIDS Legal Network (May 2007)
PP-A		Misc.	Prostitution de chez les adultes—Un projet d'alternative à la judiciarisation; Comité consultatif permanent sur la prostitution de rue et la prostitution juvénile
PP-B		Report	Pour faire avancer l'action—Rapport sur le projet-pilote de non judiciarisation de la prostitution de recherche-terrain; Rapport prépare par Daniel Sansfaçon pour le Comité de la Ville Montréal sur la prostitution de mineurs (mai 2000)
PP-C		Misc.	Recherche Amandine Guilbert—13 juin 2008—travail en cours / Chronologie des évènements (dégrager les enjeux des différentes périodes)
PP-D		Misc.	Inivitation—Le Comité consultatif permanent sur la prostitution de rue et la prostitution juvénille de Montréal invite les résidents, les organismes et les commerçants des secteurs Saint-Jacques et Sainte-Marieà des assemblées publiques portant sur le projet-pilote favorisant la non-judiciarisation de la prostitution de rue. (mars 2000)
PP-E		Letter	Letter from Rosaire Théorêt, President de la Corporation de développement Berri-UQAM, to Monsieur Jean-Pierre Synnett, Commandant Chef du poste de quartier 21 (5 septembre 2000)
PP-F		Misc.	Document de travail pour le projet-pilote
WM-A		Report	Marche mondaiale des femmes . . . au Quebec!; Bilan 2001
WM-B		Report	Marche mondiale des femmes: Comité canadien de la Marche des femmes / Rapport (juin 2001)

Code	Date	Source Type	Description/Title
WM-C		Report	Fédération des femmes du Quebec / Rapport d'activités 2000/2001; présenté à l'assemblée générale des 1, 2, et 3 juin 2001
WM-D		Letter	Lettre aux partenaires de Stella; Réaction à l'initiative de recrutement de travailleuses du sexe par la CLES
WM-E		Minutes	The Canadian Sociology Association 43rd Annual Meeting / Sociological Perspectives—Thinking Beyond Borders: Global Ideas, Global Values; The University of British Columbia, June 3–6, 2008
WM-F		Misc.	Notice of event—FIRST, Decriminalize Sex Work / "Why Decriminalize Sex Work?" (Wed., June 11, 2008)
WM-G		Report	Projet de Plate-forme politique; Document de consultation rédigé par Gisèle Bourret (le 17 mai 2002)
WM-H		Report	Fédération des femmes du Quebec / Une démarche d'évalution et d'orientation qui s'impose!; Document préparatoire à l'assemblée générale des membres 2002 (mai 2002)
WM-I		Report	Fédération des femmes du Quebec / Rapport d'activités 1999/2000; présenté à l'assemblée générale des 26 et 27 mai 2000
WM-J		Report	Le respect des droits fondamentaux des travailleuse du sexe: Développer une position féministe / Document de réflexion; Comité sur la violence faite aux femmes; Coalition nationale des femmes contre la pauvreté et la violence (juin 1999)
WM-K		Report	Rapport du Comité sur la prostitution et le travail du sexe / Assemblée générale (juin 2001)
WM-L		Report	"Prostitution Ou Travail Du Sexe: Les Débats Sonts Ouverts!" par Francoise David (1er février 2002)
XX-A		Misc.	"Position of the Coalition to Decriminalize Adult Prostitution in Canada"
XX-B		Misc.	"Dispositions du Code criminel canadien relatives à la prostitution"—Code criminel, 1996, articles 210 à 213.
XX-C		Misc.	Revendications sur la violence faite aux femmes; Revendiction proposée: Que les femmes qui pratiquent une forme ou une autre

Code	Date	Source Type	Description/Title
			de travail du sexe ne soient plus criminalisées, judicarisées en raison de leurs pratique.

Bibliography

Adler, P., and P. Adler. 2003. *Constructions of Deviance: Social Power, Context and Interaction*. Fourth edition. Belmont, CA: Wadworth.

Albertini, C., and E. Blake. 2005. Interview with Catharine A. MacKinnon: "They Haven't Crushed Me Yet." http://sisyphe.org/article.php3?id_article=2001.

Agustin, L. M. 2002. "Challenging Place: Leaving Home for Sex." *Development* 45: 110–16.

———. 2007a. "The Myth of the Migrant." *Reason*, December 26. http://reason.com/archives/2007/12/26/the-myth-of-the-migrant.

———. 2007b. "Well-Meaning Interference." *The Philadelphia Inquirer*. http://www.philly.com/inquirer/currents/8268457.html.

Amit-Talai, V. 1996. "The Minority Circuit: Identity Politics and the Professionalization of Ethnic Activism." In *Re-Situating Identities: The Politics of Race, Ethnicity and Culture*, edited by Vered Amit-Talai and Caroline Knowles, 89–114. Peterborough, ON: Broadview Press.

Arenas, Ivan. 2015. "The Mobile Politics of Emotions and Social Movement in Oaxaca, Mexico." *Antipode* 47, no. 5: 1121–40.

Association des résidantes et résidants des Faubourgs de Montréal (ARRFM). 2005. Narco-Prostitution de Rue et Vie de Quartier. Hard copy available on request at Stella.

Banyard, K. 2016. *Pimp State: Sex, Money and the Future of Equality*. London: Faber and Faber.

Barry, K. 1979. *Female Sexual Slavery*. New York: New York University Press.

———. 1984. "The Opening Paper: International Politics of Female Sexual Slavery." In *International Feminism: Networking against Female Sexual Slavery*. Report of the Global Feminist Workshop to Organize Against Traffic in Women, Rotterdam, the Netherlands.

Bartley, P. 1998. "Preventing Prostitution: The Ladies' Association for the Care and Protection of Young Girls in Birmingham, 1887–1914." *Women's Historical Review* 7, no. 1.

Bauman, Z. 1999. "Urban Space Wars: On Destructive Order and Creative Chaos." *Citizenship Studies* 3, no. 2: 173–85.

———. 2004. *Identity*. Cambridge, UK: Polity.

Beer, S., and F. Tremblay. 2014. "Sex Workers' Rights Organizations and Government Funding in Canada." In *Negotiating Sex Work*, edited by Carisa R. Showden and Samantha Makic. Minneapolis: University of Minnesota Press.

Bélanger, A. 2005. "Montréal vernaculaire/Montréal spectaculaire: Dialectique de l'imaginaire urbain." *Sociologie et Sociétés*, 13–34. Les Presses de l'Université de Montréal.

Benford, R. D., and D. A. Snow. 2000. "Framing Processes and Social Movements: An Overview and Assesment." *Annual Review of Sociology* 26: 611–39.

Benoit, C., M. Jansson, M. Smith, and J. Flagg. 2017. "Prostitution Stigma and Its Effect on the Working Conditions, Personal Lives, and Health of Sex Workers." *The Journal of Sex Research* 55, nos. 4 –5: 457–71.

Berg, H. 2014. "Working for Love, Loving for Work: Discourses of Labor in Feminist Sex-Work Activism." *Feminist Studies* 40, no. 3: 693–721.

Berkowitz, E. 2015. *The Boundaries of Desire*. Berkeley, CA: Counterpoint Press.

Bernstein, E. 2017. "Carceral Politics as Gender Justice? The 'Traffic in Women' and Neoliberal Circuits of Crime, Sex and Rights." In *Sex War*, edited by David M. Halperin and Trevor Hoppe. Durham and London: Duke University Press.

Bilodeau, A., C. Lefebvre, and D. Allard. 2002. *Les priorités nationales de santé publié 1997 – 2002: Une évaluation de l'actualisation de leurs principes directeurs. Le cas des programmes de prévention du VIH/SIDA chez les hommes gais dans la région de Montréal-Centre*. Direction du développement et des programmes unité connaissance-surveillance.

Blake, R. 2014. *Religion in the British Navy 1815–1879: Piety and Professionalism*. Suffolk, UK: Boydell Press.

Blankenship, B. T.,J. K. Frederick, O. Savas, and A. J. Stewart. 2017. University of Michigan Samantha Montgomery Professional Employees Association. "Privilege and Marginality: How Group Identification and Personality Predict Right- and Left-Wing Political Activism." *Analyses of Social Issues and Public Policy* 17, no. 1: 161–83.

Bourdieu, P. 1999. "Understanding." In *The Weight of the World*, edited by Pierre Bourdieu, 607–26. Stanford, CA: Stanford University Press.

———. 2000. *Pascalian Meditations*. Cambridge, UK: Polity Press.

———. 2004. *Science of Science and Reflexivity*. Chicago: University of Chicago Press.

Brock, D. 1998. *Making Work, Making Trouble*. Toronto: University of Toronto Press.

———. 2003. "Moving Beyond Deviance: Power, Regulation, and Governmentality." In *Making Normal: Social Regulation in Canada*, edited by Deborah Brock, ix–xxxii. Toronto: Nelson.

Brigman, W. E. 1985. "Pornography as Group Libel: the Indianapolis Sex Discrimination Ordinance Indiana." *Law Review* 18, no. 2.

Brodeur, J. P. 2007. *La délinquance de l'ordre. Les classiques des sciences sociales*. http://classiques.uqac.ca/contemporains/brodeur_jean_paul/delinquance_de_ordre/delinquance_ordre.html.

Brown, R. 1986. *Social Psychology*, second edition. New York: The Free Press.

Bruckert, C. 2002. *Taking It Off, Putting It On*. Toronto: Women Press.

———. 2014. "Academic, Activist, Whore: Negotiating the Fractured Otherness Abyss." In *Demarginalizing Voices: Commitment, Emotion, and Action in Qualitative Research*, edited by Jennifer M. Kilty, Maritza Felices-Luna, and Sheryl C. Fabian. Vancouver: University of British Columbia Press.

Bruckert, C., and C. Parent, eds. 2018. *Getting Past "the Pimp": Management in the Sex Industry*. Toronto: University of Toronto Press.

Brym, R. 2012. *Sociology as a Life or Death Issue*. Toronto: Nelson College Indigenous.

Buechler, S. M. 2000. *Social Movements in Advanced Capitalism: The Political Economy and Cultural Construction of Social Activism*. New York: Oxford University Press.

Burchardt, M. 2014. "Bourgeois Abstinence: Sexuality, Individualism, and Performances of Class among Pentecostal Middle Class Youth in South Africa." *Research in the Social Scientific Study of Religion* 25. 126–59. 10.1163/9789004272385_009.

Burleigh, N. 2017. "Tech Bros Bought Sex Trafficking Victims by Using Amazon and Microsoft Work Emails." *Newsweek*. https://www.newsweek.com/metoo-microsoft-amazon-trafficking-prostitution-sex-silicon-valley-755611.

Butler, J. 2009. *Frames of War: When Is Life Grievable?* London: Verso.

Calhoun, C. A. 2004. "World of Emergencies: Fear, Intervention, and the Limits of Cosmopolitan Order." *The Canadian Review of Sociology and Anthropology* 41, no. 4: 373–95.

Cameron, S. 2004. "Space, Risk and Opportunity: The Evolution of Paid Sex Markets." *Urban Studies* 41, no. 9: 1643–57.

Carrier, M. 2005. "À même les fonds pour la lutte contre le sida 270 000$ au groupe Stella pour une rencontre de 4 jours sur le 'travail du sexe.'" *Sisyphe*. http://sisyphe.org/article.php3?id_article=1777.

Casavant, L., and D. Valiquet. 2014. Bill C-36: An Act to amend the Criminal Code in response to the Supreme Court of Canada decision in Attorney General of Canada v. Bedford and to make consequential amendments to other Acts. Legal and Social Affairs Division. Ottawa, Canada: Publication No. 41-2-C36-E.

Cauchy, C. 2005. "Montréal, capitale mondiale du XXX le temps d'un forum sur la prostitution." Le Devoir, Cahier A5 Montréal. 17 mai.

Cederblom, J., D. W. and Paulsen. 1996. *Critical Reasoning*. Fourth edition. Belmont: Wadsworth.

Centre d'étude sur le sida (CES). 1993a. *Exploration de la faisibilité d'une intervention en prévention du VIH/sida et autres MTS pour les femmes prostituées de Montréal-Centre.* Compte-rendu de la première réunion des intervenants. 29 septembre.

———. 1993b. *Pour une intervention en prévention du VIH/sida et autres MTS pour les femmes prostituées de Montréal-Centre.* Compte-rendu de la deuxième réunion des intervenants. 5 novembre.

———. 1993c. *Pour une intervention en prévention du VIH/sida et autres MTS pour les femmes prostituées de Montréal-Centre.* Compte-rendu de la troisième réunion des intervenants. 20 décembre.

———. 1994a. *Pour une intervention en prévention du VIH/sida et autres MTS pour les femmes prostituées de Montréal-Centre.* Compte-rendu de la quatrième réunion des intervenants. 27 janvier.

———. 1994b. *Pour une intervention en prévention du VIH/sida et autres MTS pour les femmes prostituées de Montréal-Centre.* Compte-rendu de la cinquième réunion des intervenants. 23 février.

———. 1994c. *Pour une intervention en prévention du VIH/sida et autres MTS pour les femmes prostituées de Montréal-Centre.* Compte-rendu de la sixième réunion des intervenants. 20 avril.

———. 1994d. *Pour une intervention en prévention du VIH/sida et autres MTS pour les femmes prostituées de Montréal-Centre.* Compte-rendu de la septième réunion des intervenants. 13 mai.

———. 1994e. Compte-rendu de la huitième réunion du comité aviseur Projet Stella. 15 juin.

———. 1994f. Compte-rendu de la neuvième réunion du comité aviseur Projet Stella. September 9.

Chapkis, W. 1997. *Live Sex Acts*. New York: Routledge.

Chaumont, J.-M., and A.-L. Wibrin. 2007. "Traite des Noirs, traite des Blanches: Même combat?" *Cahiers de Recherche Sociologique*, 121–33. Montréal: Liber.

Clamen, J. 2006. "Participant's eXXXpressions on 'Sex Work and Society': Diversity and Inclusion, Culture, Education, Mobilization and Organization." In *Stella eXXXpressions*, Forum XXX Proceedings, edited by Émilie Cantin, Jenn Clamen, Jocelyne Lamoureux, Maria Nengeh Mensah, Pascale Robitaille, Claire Thiboutot, Louise Toupin, and Francine Tremblay, 74–82. Montréal: Stella.

Clamen, J., and A.-L. Crago. 2013. "Ne dans le Redlight: The Sex Workers' Movement in Montreal." In *Selling Sex: Experience, Advocacy, and Research on Sex Work in Canada*, edited by Emily van der Meulen, Elya M. Durisin, and Victoria Love. Vancouver: University of British Columbia Press.

Coalition national contre la pauvreté et de la violence faite aux femmes (CNPV). 1999. http://www.relais-femmes.qc.ca/FADAFEM/html/module2/bio/groupe7.html.

Cohen, S. 1972. *Folk Devils and Moral Panics: The Creation of the Mods and Rockers*. London: Routledge.

Comité interquartiers sur la prostitution et les intervenant-es Minutes 2022 rue de la Vistation. 1995.

ConStellation. 1997. Automne édition 3, volume 1.

———. 1998. Décembre volume 4, no. 1.

———. 1999a. Volume 4, no. 2.

————. 1999b. Volume 4, no. 3.

————. 2000a. Spécial Politique, volume 5, no. 2.

————. 2000b. Spécial Striptease, volume 6, no. 1.

————. 2002. International.

————. 2005a. Spécial Prison, volume 9, no. 1.

————. 2005b. Hors Série Spécial Stella 10 ans.

Comité interquartiers sur la prostitution et les intervenant-es. 1995a.

Cohen, J. L. 1985. "Strategy or Identity: New Theoretical Paradigms and Contemporary Social Movements." *Social Research* 52, no. 4: 663–716.

Corbin, A. 1990. *Women for Hire*. London: Harvard University Press.

Cornish, F. 2006. "Empowerment to Participate: A Case Study of Participation by Indian Sex Workers in HIV Prevention." *Journal of Community & Applied Social Psychology* 16: 301–15.

Corporation de développement Berri-UQAM. 2000. https://archives.uqam.ca/upload/files/journal_uqam/1990-1991/journal_uqam_17_11_supp.pdf.

Côté, J. F. 2015. *George Herbert Mead's Concept of Society: A Critical Reconstruction*. Boulder, CO: Paradigm Publishers.

Cott, N. F. 1993. "Domesticity." In *Family Patterns Gender Relations*, edited by Bonnie Fox, 114–19. Toronto: Oxford University Press.

Criminal Code of Canada – House of Commons. 2006. https://laws-lois.justice.gc.ca/eng/acts/p-1/FullText.html.

Cronk, G. F. 1973. "Symbolic Interactionism: A 'Left-Meadian' Interpretation." *Social Theory and Practice* 2: 313–33.

Cunningham, S. 2016. "Reinforcing or Challenging Stigma? The Risks and Benefits of 'Dignity Talk' in Sex Work Discourse." *International Journal for the Semiotics Law* 29: 45–65.

Curtis, V., M. de Barra, and R. Aunger. 2011. "Disgust as an Adaptive System for Disease Avoidance Behaviour." *Philosophical Transactions of The Royal Society B Biological Sciences* 366(1563): 389–401.

Davies, L. 2002. *Time to Review Canada Solicitation Laws*. https://libbydavies.ca/parliament/speech/time-to-review-canadas-solicitation-laws/.

Della Porta, D., and M. Diani. 2006. *Social Movement*. Second edition. Oxford: Blackwell Publishing.

Demazière, D., and T. Pignoni. 1999. *Chômeur: Du silence à la révolte*. Paris: Hachette Littérature.

Deslauriers, J. P, and M. Kérisit. 1997. "Le devis de recherche qualitative." In *La recherche qualitative*, 85–169. Ottawa: Gaêtan Morin Éditeur.

Deutschmann, L. 2004. *Deviance and Social Control*. Third edition. Scarborough: Thomson.

DiNardo, K. 2007. http://www.kellydinardo.com/main/index.cfm?Category=Gilded_Lili&Section=Main.

Dodd, Z. 2016 "Recognition, Exploitation, or Both?: Roundtable on Peer Labour and Harm Reduction." In *Critical Approaches to Harm Reduction: Conflict, Institutionalisation, (De-)Politicization and Direct Action*, edited by Christopher Smith and Zack Marshall, 185–209. New York: Nova Science Publisher.

Doezema, J. 1998. "Forced to Choose: Beyond the Voluntary v. Forced Prostitution Debate." In *Global Sex Workers: Rights, Resistance, and Redefinition*, edited by K. Kempadoo and J. Doezema, 34–50. New York: Routledge.

Doyle, K., and D. Lacombe. 2003. "Moral Panic and Child Pornography: The Case of Robin Sharpe." In *Making Normal*, edited by Deborah Brock, 285–305. Scarborough: Thomson.

Drury, J., S. Reicher, and C. Stott. 2003. "Transforming the Boundaries of Collective Identity: From the 'Local' Anti-Road Campaign to 'Global' Resistance?" *Social Movement Studies* 2, no. 2: 191–212.

Dubet, F., and H. L. Thaler. 2004. "The Sociology of Collective Action Reconsidered." *Current Sociology* 52, no. 4: 557–73.

Dumont, M., and L. Toupin. 2003. *La pensée féministe au Québec*. Les Édition remue-ménage.

Dunezat, X. 1998. Des mouvements sociaux sexués. Numéro conjoint *Nouvelles questions féministes/Recherches féministes* : Université Laval, GREMF. (NQF, vol. 19, n°2-3-4 et RF, vol. 11, n° 2

Duperré, M. 2002. "Constitution des acteurs collectifs et dynamique de développement régional; Le cas d'une association régionale en santé et services sociaux." Unpublished dissertation.

Durisin, E. M., E. Meulen, and C. Bruckert, eds. 2018. *Red Light Labour*. Vancouver: University of British Columbia Press.

Duval, M., and A. Fontaine. 2000. "Lorsque des pratiques différentes se heurtent: Les relations entre les travailleurs de rue et les autres intervenants." *Revue Nouvelles Pratiques Sociales* 13, no. 1.

Dworkin, A. 1974. *Woman Hating*. New York: E. P. Dutton.

———. 1981. "Pornography: Men Possessing Women." http://www.nostatusquo.com/ACLU/dworkin/PornAList.html.

Engle Merry, S. 2016. *The Seductions of Quantification Measuring Human Rights, Gender Violence, and Sex Trafficking*. Chicago, London: Chicago University Press.

Eisinger, P. K. 1973. "The Conditions of Protest Behavior in American Cities." *The American Political Science Review* 67, no. 1: 11–28.

Etzioni, A. 1968. *The Active Society: A Theory of Societal and Political Processes*. New York: The Free Press.

Eyerman, R. 2005. "How Social Movements Move." In *Emotions and Social Movements*, edited by Helena Flam and Debra Kind, 42–56. London: Routledge

Farrell, J. 2017. "Vixens, Sirens and Whores: The Persistence of Stereotypes in Sexual Offence Law." *Trinity College Law Review* 20: 30–52.

Federal/Provincial-Territorial Working Group on Prostitution Report and Recommendations in Respect of Legislation, Policy and Practices concerning Prostitution-Related Activities. 1998. http://www.google.ca/search?sourceid=navclient&ie=UTF-8&rlz=1T4RNWN_enCA308CA313&q=federal%2fprovincial-territorial+working+goup+on+prostitution.

Fédération des femmes du Québec (FFQ). 2001. *Comité de réflexion sur la prostitution et le travail du sexe*. Un document préparatoire à la tournée provincial de l'automne.

Freeman, M. 1993. *Rewriting the Self: History, Memory, Narrative*. London: Routledge.

Forrester, V. 2000. *For Man Must Work or the End of Work*. National Film Board of Canada.

Fox, B. 1993. "The Rise and Fall of the Breadwinner-Homemaker Family." In *Family Patterns Gender Relations*, edited by Bonnie Fox, 147–57. Toronto: University Press.

Foucault, M. 1976. *Histoire de la sexualité*. Paris: Gallimard.

———. 1978. *The History of Sexuality*. New York: Pantheon Books.

Friedman, D., and D. McAdam. 1992. "Collective Identity and Activism: Networks, Choices and the Life of a Social Movement." In *Frontiers in Social Movement Theory*, edited by A. D. Morris and C. M. Mueller, 156–73. New Haven, CT: Yale University Press.

Gallie, D. 2014. *Economic Crisis, the Quality of Work, and Social Integration: Issues and Context*. Oxford Online.

Gardner, D. 2006. "Arguments. The Many Faces of Prostitution: Opposition to Legalized Prostitution Lies in Its Public Perception as a Drug Addict, Violent, Criminal Trade. But the Stereotype Is Not True." *Ottawa Citizen*, March 20.

Gaudreault-DesBiens, J. F. 2001. *Le sexe et le droit. Sur le féminisme juridique de Catherine MacKinnon*. Montréal: Liber.

Geadah, Y. 1999. La prostitution: rien d ' autre qu'un mal de société Le Devoir, Cahier A9 Montréal. 27 août 1999.

———. 2002. Il faut dire non à la libéralisation totale de la prostitution. Le Devoir, Cahier A Montréal. 3 juillet 2002.

———. 2003. *La prostitution: Un métier comme un autre?* Montréal: VLB.

———. 2006. *The Challenge of Change: A Study of Canada's Criminal Prostitution Laws*. Report of the Standing Committee on Justice and Human Rights. Report of the Subcommittee on Solicitation Laws. Testified on February 7, 2005, House of Commons.

Gendron, S. 1998. "La recherché participative: un cas d'illustration et quelques réflexions pour la santé publique." *Ruptures, revue transdiciplinaire en santé* 5, no. 2: 180–91.

Ghorashi, H. 2005. "When the Boundaries Are Blurred." *European Journal of Women's Studies* 12, no. 3: 363–75.

Gibbons, J., M. Barton, and E. Brault. 2008. "Evaluating Gentrification's Relation to Neighbourhood and City Health." *PLoS ONE*, November 19. https://journals.plos.org/plosone/article?id=10.1371/journal.pone0207432.

Giddens, A. 1991. Modernity and Self-Identity. Self and Society in the Late Modern Age. Stanford California: Stanford University Press.

Gilfoyle, P. 1999. "Prostitutes in History: From Parables of Pornography to Metaphors of Modernity." *The American Historical Review* 104, no. 1.

Gillies, K. 2006. "Initiating with Our Peers in Canada." In *Stella eXXXpressions*, Forum XXX Proceedings, edited by Émilie Cantin, Jenn Clamen, Jocelyne Lamoureux, Maria Nengeh Mensah, Pascale Robitaille, Claire Thiboutot, Louise Toupin, and Francine Tremblay, 70–74. Montréal: Stella.

Gobbon, J., M. Barton, E. and Brault. 2018. "Evaluating Gentrification's Relation to Neighborhood and City Health." https://journals.plos.org/plosone/article?id=10.1371/journal.pone.0207432.

Goffman, E. 1963. *Stigma: Notes on the Management of Spoiled Identity.* Englewood Cliffs, NJ: Prentice-Hall.

———. 1974. *Frame Analysis: An Essay on the Organization of Experience.* New York: Harper & Row.

———. 1986. *Frame Analysis: An Essay on the Organization of Experience.* New York: Harper and Row.

Goodwin, J., J. M. Jasper, and F. Poletta. 2001. "Why is Emotions Matter." In *Passionate Politics: Emotions and Social Movements*, edited by Jeff Goodwin, James M. Jasper, and Francesca Polletta, 1–24. Chicago: University of Chicago Press.

Gouvernement du Québec. 2002. *Avis du Conseil du statut de la femme. La prostitution: Profession ou exploitation? Une réflexion à poursuivre.*

Gouvernement du Québec Standing Committee on Justice and Human Rights. 2006.

Gouvernement du Québec. 2005. https://www.quebec.ca/en/.

Gutiérrez Garza, A. P. 2019. *Care for Sale.* New York: Oxford University Press.

Habermas, J. 1981. "New Social Movements." *Telos* 49: 33–37.

Hall, L. 2004. "Hauling Down the Double Standard: Feminism, Social Purity and Sexual Science in the Late Nineteenth-Century Britain." *Gender & History* 16, no. 1: 36–56.

Halperin, D. M. 2017. "The Introduction: The War on Sex." In *The War on Sex*, edited by David M. Halperin and Trevor Hoppe. London: Duke University Press.

Hankins, C. A., S. Gendron, M. A. Handley, C. Richard, M. T. Lai Tung, and O'Shaughnessy, M. 1994. "HIV Infection among Women in Prison: An Assessment of Risk Factors Using Nonnominal Methodology." *American Journal of Public Health* 84, no. 10 (October): 1637–40.

Hauck, P., and S. Peterke. 2010. "Organized Crime and Gang Violence in National and International Law." *International Review of the Red Cross* 92, no. 878.

Hawker, E. 1821. "Statement concerning Certain Immoral Practices Prevailing in the HM Navy." Access via Jstor.

Henry, M., and P. Farvid. 2017. "'Always hot, always live': Computer-Mediated Sex Work in the Era of 'Camming.'" *Women's Studies Journal* 31, no. 2 (December): 113–28.

Hervieux, C., and A. Voltan. 2018. "Framing Social Problems in Social Entrepreneurship." *Journal of Business Ethics* 151: 279–93.

Hewitt, J. P. 1989. *Dilemmas of the American Self.* Philadelphia: Temple University Press.

Hoffman, D. 1991. *The Seeds of the Sixties.* The Making of the Sixties Series. PBS Video.

Hoggan, J. 2016. *I'm Right and You're an Idiot. New Society. The Toxic State of Public Discourse and How to Clean it Up.* With Grania Litwin. Gabriola Island, BC: New Society Publisher.

Honneth, A. 1996. *The Struggle for Recognition: The Moral Grammar of Social Conflict.* Cambridge: Polity Press.

———. 2004. "Invisibility: On the Epistemology of 'Recognition.'" *La Revue Mauss*. RdM 1ᵉʳ s. no. 23: 136–50.

———. 2007. *Disrespect. The Normative Foundations of Critical Theory*. Cambridge, UK: Polity Press.

House of Commons. 2006. *The Challenge of Change: A Study of Canada's Criminal Prostitution Laws*. Report of the Standing Committee on Justice and Human Rights. Report of the Subcommittee on Solicitation Laws, House of Commons, December.

Howell, P. 2000. "Prostitution and Racialised Sexuality: The Regulation of Prostitution in Britain and the British Empire before the Contagious Diseases Acts." *Environment and Planning D: Society and Space* 18: 321–39.

Hubbard, P. 2004. "Cleansing the Metropolis: Sex Work and the Politics of Zero Tolerance." *Urban Studies* 41, no. 9: 1687–702.

Hubbard, P., and T. Sanders. 2003. "Making Space for Sex Work: Female Street Prostitution and the Production of Urban Space." *International Journal of Urban and Regional Research* 27, no. 1: 75–89.

Hurt, B. 2006. *Hip-Hop: Beyond Beats and Rhymes*. Byron Hurt, producer. Video.

Javelin, D. 2003. "The Role of Blame in Collective Action: Evidence from Russia." *American Political Science Review* 97, no. 1: 107–21.

Jenness, V. 1993. *Making It Work: The Prostitutes' Rights Movement in Perspective*. New York: Routledge.

———. 1995. "Social Movement Growth, Domain Expansion, Framing Processes: The Gay/Lesbian Movement and Violence against Gays and Lesbians as a Social Problem." *Social Problems* 42, no. 1: 145–70.

Joas, H. 1996. *The Creativity of Action*. Chicago: University of Chicago Press.

———. 1997. *Mead: A Contemporary Re-Examination of His Thought*. Cambridge, MA: The MIT Press.

Jochelson, R., and K. Kramar. 2011. *Sex and the Supreme Court: Obscenity and Indecency Law in Canada*. Halifax, Nova Scotia: Fernwood Publishing.

Johnson, G. F. 2015. "Governing Sex Work: An Agonistic Policy Community and Its Relational Dynamics." *Critical Policy Studies* 9, no. 3: 259–77.

Johnson, H. 1995. "A Methodology for Frame Analysis: From Discourse to Cognitive Schemata." In *Social Movement and Culture*, Volume 4, edited by Austin H. Johnson and Bert Klanderman, 217–46. Minneapolis: University of Minneapolis Press.

Jordan, B. 2004. *Sex, Money and Power*. Cambridge: Polity.

Jones, A. 2016. "'I get paid to have orgasms': Adult Webcam Models' Negation of Pleasure and Danger." *Signs: Journal of Women in Culture and Society* 42, no. 1: 227–56.

Jones, G. S. 1971. *Outcast London*. Oxford: Clarendon Press.

Jones, S., J. King, N. Edwards. 2018. "Human-Trafficking Prevention Is Not Sexy: Impact of the Rescue Industry on Thailand NGO Programs and the Need for a Human Rights Approach." *Journal of Human Trafficking* 4, no. 3: 231–55.

Jonsson, S. 2006. "The Invention of the Masses: The Crowd in French Culture from the Revolution to the Commune." In *Crowds*, edited by Jeffrey, T. Schnapp, and Matthew Tiews. Stanford, CA: Stanford University Press.

Kabeer, N. 2001. "Resources, Agency, Achievements: Reflections on the Measurement of Women's Empowerment. Discussing Women's Empowerment-Theory and Practice." *SIDA Studies* No. 3, Swedish International Development Cooperation Agency, Sweden.

———. 2005. "Gender Equality and Women's Empowerment: A Critical Analysis of the Third Millennium Development Goal." *Gender and Development* 13, no. 1 (March).

Kelling, G., and J. Q. Wilson. 1982. "Broken Windows: The Police and Neighborhood Safety." *Atlantic Monthly*, March.

Kempadoo, K. 1998. "Globalizing Sex Workers' Rights." In *Global Sex Workers: Rights, Resistance, and Redefinition*, edited by Kamala Kempadoo and Jo Doezema, 1–33. New York: Routledge.

Keire, M. L. 2001. "The Vice Trust: A Reinterpretation of the White Slavery Scare in the United States, 1907–1917." *Journal of Social History* 35, no. 1: 5–41.

King, D. S. 2006. "Activists and Emotional Reflexivity: Toward Touraine's Subject as Social Movement." *Sociology* 40, no. 5: 873–91.

Knowles, C. 1996. *Family Boundaries: The Construction of Dangerousness*. Peterborough, ON: Broadview.

Krüsi, A., T. Kerr, C. Taylor, T. Rhodes, and K. Shannon. 2016. "'They won't change it back in their head that we're trash': The Intersection of Sex Work-Related Stigma and Evolving Policing Strategies." *Sociology of Health & Illness* 38, no. 7: 1137–50.

Labonté, R. 1990. "Empowerment: Notes on Professional and Community Dimensions." *Canadian Review of Social Policy/Revue canadienne de politique sociale*, no. 26: 64–75.

Lacasse, D. 1994. *La prostitution féminine à Montréal 1945 – 1970*. Montréal: Boréal.

Laite, J. 2006. "Paying the Price Again: Prostitution Policy in Historical Perspective." *Policy Paper* 46 (October). http://www.historyandpolicy.org/policy-papers/papers/paying-the-price-again-prostitution-policy-in-historical-perspective.

L'Amicale du Nid. http://www.mouvementdunid.org/50-propositions-abolitionnistes.

Lam, E. 2018. "Behind the Rescue: How Anti-Trafficking Investigations and Policies Harm Migrant Sex Workers." *Butterfly Publication*, April.

Lam, E., and C. Gallant. 2018. "Migrant Sex Workers' Justice." In *Red Light Labour*, edited by Elya M. Durisin, Emily van der Meulen, and Chris Bruckert. Vancouver: University of British Columbia Press.

Lamoureux, H., R. Mayer, and J. Panet-Raymond. 1989. *Community Action*. Montréal: Black Rose Books.

Lamoureux, J. 2005. "Sex Workers Try to Democratically Broaden the Notion of the 'We Women' and Offer a Different Feminist Perspective." In *ConStellation* Spécial Tenth Anniversary Edition, 79–81. Montréal: Stella.

Lateiner, D., and D. Spatharas. 2017. *The Ancient Emotion of Disgust*. New York: Oxford University Press.

Lauzon, B. 2002. *Les Champs légitimes du droit criminal et à leur application aux manipulations génétiques transmissibles aux générations future 2002*. Cowansville, QC: Éditions Yvon Blais.

Lavenda, R. H., and E. A. Schultz. 2016. *Core Concepts in Cultural Anthropology*. Toronto: Oxford University Press.

Law Commission of Canada. 2003. "What Is a Crime? Challenges and Alternatives. Discussion paper." *Le Devoir*, Septembre 13.

Le *Devoir*. 2000. A4 centre sud violence Projet pilote.

Le *Devoir*. 2000. A5 6 août 2000 Projet pilot.

Legault-Roy, É. 2014. "Pernicieuse Décriminalisation." *Concertation Contre des luttes contre L'exploitation Sexuel*. http://www.lacles.org/lettre-pernicieuse-decriminalisation#more-2272.

Leigh, C. 2004. *Unrepentant Whore*. San Francisco: Last Gasp.

Le Pard, D. 2006. *The Challenge of Change: A Study of Canada's Criminal Prostitution Laws*. Report of the Standing Committee on Justice and Human Rights. Report of the Subcommittee on Solicitation Laws, House of Commons, December.

Lerum, K. 1998. "Twelve-Step Feminism Makes Sex Workers Sick: How the State and the Recovery Movement Turn Radical Women into 'Useless Citizens.'" *Sexuality & Culture* 2: 7–36.

Lévesque, A. 1995. *Résistance et trangression: Études en histoire des femmes au Québec*. Montreal: Les Éditions remue-ménage.

Lewis, H. 2016. *The Politics of Everybody Feminism, Queer Theory, and Marxism at the Intersection*. London: Zed Book.

Linteau, P.-A. 1998. "Le personnel politique de Montréal, 1880–1914: Évolution d'une élite municipale." *Revue d'histoire de l'Amérique Française* 52, no. 2 (automne).

Lombroso, C., and G. Ferrero. [1893] 2004. *Criminal Woman, the Prostitute, and the Normal Woman*. Durham, NC: Duke University Press.

The Love and Fidelity Network. 2017. *Building the Next Generation of Leaders for Marriage, Family, and Sexual Integrity*. http://loveandfidelity.org/.

Lowman, J. 1997. "Prostitution Law Reform in Canada." http://users.uniserve.com/~lowman/ProLaw/prolawcan.htm.

———. 2001. *Identifying Research Gaps in the Prostitution Literature*. Research and Statistics Division, Department of Justice, Canada.

———. 2005. *Submission to the Subcommittee on Solicitation Laws of the Standing Committee on Justice, Human Rights, Public Safety and Emergency Preparedness*. http://users.uniserve.com/~lowman/.

MacKinnon, C. A. 1987. *Feminism Unmodified*. Cambridge, MA: Harvard University Press.

———. 1989. *Toward a Feminist Theory of the State*. Cambridge, MA: Harvard University Press.

———. 2005. *Women's Lives—Men's Laws*. Cambridge: Harvard University Press.

———. 2011. "Trafficking, Prostitution, and Inequality." *Harvard Civil Rights-Civil Liberty Review* 46.

Maginn, P. J., and C. Steinmetz, eds. 2015. *(Sub)Urban Sexscapes Geographies and Regulation of the Sex Industry*. London: Routledge.

Majic, S. 2013. *Sex Work Politics from Protest to Service Provision*. Philadelphia: University of Pennsylvania Press.

Maheu, L. 1983. "Les mouvements de base et la lutte contre l'appropriation étatique du tissu social." *Sociologie et sociétés* 15, no. 1: 7–92.

———. 1991. "Les nouveaux mouvements sociaux entre les voies de l'identité et les enjeux du politique." In *La recomposition du politique*, edited by L. Maheu and A. Sales, 163–92. Montréal, Paris: Presse de l'université de Montréal.

Majic, S. 2014. *Sex Work Politics: From Protest to Service Provision*. Philadelphia: University of Pennsylvania Press.

Mallory, P., and P. Cormack. 2018. "The Two Durkheims: Founders and Classics in Canadian Introductory Sociology Textbooks." *Canadian Journal of Sociology/Cahiers Canadiens de Sociologie* 43, no. 1.

Maras, M. E. 2017. "Online Classified Advertisement Sites: Pimps and Facilitators of Prostitution and Sex Trafficking"? *Journal of Internet Law* 21, no. 5 (November): 17–21.

Marchand, M. H., J. Reid, and B. Berents. 1998. "Migration, (Im)mobility, and Modernity: Toward a Feminist Understanding of the 'Global' Prostitution Scene in Amsterdam." *Millennium: Journal of International Studies*. https://doi.org/10.1177/03058298980270040201.

Marche mondiale des femmes. 2001. "Histoire de la marche mondiale des femmes 2000." http://www.casac.ca/content/histoire-de-la-marche-mondiale-des-femmes-2000.

Martinovic, B., and M. Verkuyten. 2014. "The Political Downside of Dual Identity: Group Identifications and Religious Political Mobilization of Muslim Minorities." *British Journal of Social Psychology* 53: 711–30.

Mathieu, L. 2000. "The Emergence and Failure of Prostitutes' Social Movements." Paper presented at the 28th Joint Session of Workshops, European Consortium for Political Research, Copenhagen University, April 14–19. (Workshop 12: "Prostitution and Trafficking as Political Issues.") https://ecpr.eu/Filestore/PaperProposal/b0b079be-cfb2-4a9d-a2ee-c356ed682aa3.pdf.

———. 2001. *Mobilisations de prostituées*. Paris: Belin.

Maynard, R. 2018. "Do Black Sex Workers' Lives Matter?" In *Red Light Labour*, edited by Elya M. Durisin, Emily van der Meulen, and Chris Bruckert. Vancouver: University of British Columbia Press.

Mayrl, D., and Q. Sarak. 2016. "Defining the State from Within: Boundaries, Schemas, and Associational Policymaking." *Sociological Theory* 341: 1–26.

McAdam, D. 1994. "Culture and Social Movements." In *New Social Movements: From Ideology to Identity*, edited by Enrique Larana, Austin H. Johnson, and Joseph R. Gusfield, 36–57. Philadelphia: Temple University Press.

McCarthy J. D. 1994. "Activists, Authorities, and Media Framing of Drunk Driving." In *New Social Movements: From Ideology to Identity*, edited by Enrique Larana, Joseph R Gusfield, and Hank Johnson, 133–67. Philadelphia: Temple University Press.

McCarthy, J. D., and M. N. Zald. 1977. "Resource Mobilisation and Social Movements: A Partial Theory." *American Journal of Sociology* 82: 1212–41.

McDonald, K. 2002. "From Solidarity to Fluidity: Social Movements beyond Collective Identity—The Case of Globalization Conflicts." *Social Movement Studies* 1, no. 2: 109–28.

McDonald, L. 2005. "Florence Nightingale on Women, Medicine, Midwifery, and Prostitution." In *The Collected Works of Florence Nightingale*, volume 8: 411-515. Waterloo, Ontario: Wilfrid Laurier University Press.

McKewon, E. 2003. "The Historical Geography of Prostitution in Perth," *Western Australia Australian Geographer* 34, no. 3: 297–310.

McPhail, C. 2006. "The Crowd and Collective Behavior: Bringing Symbolic Interaction Back." *Symbolic Interaction* 29, no. 4: 433–64.

Mead, G. H. 1922. "A Behavioristic Account of the Significant Symbol." *The Journal of Philosophy* 19, no. 6: 157–63.

———. 1925. "The Genesis of the Self and Social Control." *International Journal of Ethics* 35: 251–77.

Melançon, J. 2018. *Idle No More: A Movement of Dissent Aboriginal Policy Studies* 7, no. 1, pp. 127–47.

Melucci, A. 1983. "Mouvements sociaux, mouvements post-politiques." *Revue Internationale d'actions communautaires*, no 10/50: 13–30.

———. 1988. "Getting Involved: Identity and Mobilization in Social Movements." *International Social Movement Research* 1: 329–48.

———. 1995. "The Process of Collective Identity." In *Social Movements and Culture*, Volume 4: *Social Movements, Protest and Contention*, edited by Austin H. Johnson and Bert Klandermans, 41–63. Minneapolis: University of Minnesota Press.

———. 1996. *Challenging Codes: Collective Action in the Communication Age*. Cambridge, UK: Cambridge University Press.

Mensah, M. N. 2006. "Introduction." In *Stella eXXXpressions*, Forum XXX Proceedings, edited by Émilie Cantin, Jenn Clamen, Jocelyne Lamoureux, Maria Nengeh Mensah, Pascale Robitaille, Claire Thiboutot, Louise Toupin, and Francine Tremblay, pp. 7–11. Montréal: Stella.

Michaud, L., R. Maynard, Z. Dodd, and N. Butler Burke. 2016. "Recognition, Exploitation, or Both?: A Roundtable on Peer Labour and Harm Reduction." In *Critical Approaches to Harm Reduction: Conflict, Institutionalisation, (De-)Politicization and Direct Action*, edited by Christopher Smith and Zack Marshall. New York: Nova Science Publisher.

Mills, C. W. 1940. "Situated Actions and Vocabularies of Motive." *American Sociological Review* 5, no. 6: 904–13.

Moore, T. 1994. *Dark Eros: The Imagination of Sadism*. Woodstock: Spring Publications.

Muszynski, A. 1999. "The Social Construction/Deconstruction of Sex, Gender, Race and Class." In *Social Issues and Contradictions in Canadian Society*, third edition, edited by B. Singh Bolaria, 95–132. Harcourt Brace Canada.

See Myles, B. 1999. La guerre à la prostitution se radicalise dans le Centre-Sud. Le Devoir, Cahier A9 Montréal. 27 août 1999.

Nightingale, F. 2005. "Florence Nightingale on Women, Medicine, Midwifery and Prostitution." In *Collected Works of Florence Nightingale*, Volume 8, edited by Lynn McDonald, 411–515. Waterloo, Ontario: Wilfrid Laurier University Press.

Nussbaum, M. 1995. "Objectification." *Philosophy and Public Affairs* 24, no. 4: 279–83.

———. 1998. "'Whether from Reason or Prejudice': Taking Money for Bodily Services." *The Journal of Legal Studies* 27, no. S2 (June): 693–723.

———. 2004. *Hiding from Humanity: Disgust, Shame, and the Law*. Princeton, NJ: Princeton University Press.

Oaten, M., R. J. Stevenson, and I. Trevor. 2011. "Disease Avoidance as a Functional Basis for Stigmatization." *Case Philosophical Transaction of the Royal Society B* 366: 3433–52. doi:10.1098/ rstb.2011.0095.

Oberschall, A. 1973. *Social Conflict and Social Movements*. Englewood Cliffs, NJ: Prentice-Hall.

O'Connor, M. 2017. "Choice, Agency, Consent, and Coercion: Complex Issues in the Lives of Prostituted and Trafficked Women." *Women's Studies International Forum* 62, May–June, pp. 8–16.

Ost, D. 2004. "Politics as the Mobilization of Anger: Emotions in Movements and in Power." *European Journal of Social Theory* 7, no. 2: 229–44.

Page, C. 2006. *The Roles of Public Opinion Research in Canadian Government*. Toronto: University of Toronto Press.

Parent, C. 2001. "Les identitées sexuelles et les travailleuses de l'industrie du sexe à l'aube du nouveau millénaire." *Sociologie et Sociétés* 33, no. 1: 159–78.

Parent, C., C. Bruckert, P. Corriveau, M. N. Mensah, and L. Toupin. 2013. *Sex Work Rethinking the Job, Respecting the Workers*. Vancouver: UBC Press.

Parazelli, M. 2000. "L'encombrement sociosymbolique des jeunes de la rue au centre-ville de Montréal. Le cas d'un quartier en revitalisation: Le Faubourg Saint-Laurent." In *Sites publics, lieux communs. Aperçus sur l'aménagement de places et de parcs au Québec*, edited by Claude Sorbets and Jean-Pierre Augustin, 169–99. Maison des Sciences de l'homme d'Aquitaine. Talence: France.

Perozzo, C., R. de la Sablonnière, E. Auger, and M. Caron-Diotte. 2016. "Social Identity Change in Response to Discrimination." *British Journal of Social Psychology* 55: 438–56.

Pertersen, A., and R. Willig. 2002. "An Interview with Axel Honneth: The Role of Sociology in the Theory of Recognition." *European Journal of Social Theory* 5, no. 2: 265–27.

Pheterson, G. 1996. *The Prostitution Prism*. Amsterdam: Amsterdam University Press.

Philips, T. 2002. "Imagined Communities and Self-Identity: An Exploratory Quantitative Analysis." *Sociology* 36, no. 3: 597–617.

Phoenix, J. 1999. *Making Sense of Prostitution*. Chippenham: Palgrave.

Phoenix, J., and S. Oerton. 2005. *Illicit and Illegal*. Devon: William Publishing.

P.I.a.M.P. Le projet Stella. 1994. "Une intervention destine aux femmes pratiquant la prostitution dans les rues de Montréal-Centre." Montréal 15 mai.

Pinzer, M. 1977. *The Maimie Papers. Letters from an Ex-Prostitute*. New York: The Feminist Press.

Pivar, D. J. 1973. *Purity Crusade: Sexual Morality and Social Control, 1868–1900*. Westport, CT: Greenwood Press.

Porter, M. 1995. "Call Yourself a Sociologist—And You've Never Been Arrested?!" *Canadian Review of Sociology and Anthropology* 32, no. 4: 415–37.

Poulin, R. 2003. "Le marché mondial du sexe au temps de la vénalité triomphante." *Tiers Monde* XLIV, no. 176: 735–69.

———. 2004. *La mondialisation des industries du sexe. Prostitution, pornographie, traite des femmes et des enfants*. Ottawa: Interligne.

———. 2005. "Abolir la prostitution? Entretien avec Richard Poulin. " *Solidarités*, no. 74 (Septembre 27): 6.

Poutanen, M.-A. 1998. "The Geography of Prostitution in an Early Nineteenth-Century Urban Centre. Montreal, 1810–1842." In *Power, Place and Identity: Historical Studies of Social and Legal Regulation in Quebec*, edited by Tamara Myers, Kate Boyer, Mary Anne Poutanen, and Steven Watt, 101–28. Montréal: Montréal History Group.

Projet d'intervention de milieu dans le Centre-Sud de Montréal Rapport d'activités et d'évaluation du projet juin. 2001.

Projet d'intervention de milieu dans le Centre-Sud de Montréal Notes de rencontre des directions d'organismes 13 décembre 2001 à Passages.

Prior, J. Gorman-Murray. 2015. "Housing Sex within the City: The Placement of Sex Services beyond Respectable Domesticity?" In *(Sub)Urban Sexscapes Geographies and Regulation of the Sex Industry*, edited by Paul J. Maginn and Christine Steinmetz, 101–16. London: Routledge.

Quartier Latin. 1919. Accessed from http://numerique.banq.qc.ca/patrimoine/details/52327/1865200.

Redoutey, E. 2005. "Trottoirs et territoires." In *La prostitution a Paris Paris, Editions de la Martiniere*, edited by Marie- Elizabeth Handaman and Janine Mossuz Lavau, 39–90.

Régie régionale de la santé et des services sociaux de Montréal-Centre. 1998.

Reicher, S. 2004. "The Context of Social Identity: Domination, Resistance, and Change." *Political Psychology* 25, no. 6: 921–45.

194 *Bibliography*

Rioux Soucy, L-M. 2005. "Libérez-nous des exploiteurs sexuels!" Le Devoir, Cahier A5 Montréal. 17 mai.

Rodgers, K. 2018. *Protest, Activism, & Social Movements*. Toronto: Oxford University Press.

Rose, N. 1998. *Inventing Ourselves*. Cambridge: Cambridge University Press.

Ross, B., and R. Sullivan. 2012. "Tracing Lines of the Horizontal Hostility: How Sex Workers and Gay Activists Battled for Space, Voice, and Belonging in Vancouver, 1975–1985." *Sexualities* 15, no. 5/6: 604–21.

Ryder, A. 2004. "The Changing Nature of Adult Entertainment Districts: Between a Rock and a Hard Place or Going from Strength to Strength?" *Urban Studies* 41, no. 9: 1659–86.

Sanders, T. 2004. "The Risks of Street Prostitution: Punters, Police and Protesters." *Urban Studies* 41, no. 9: 1703–17.

Sansfaçon, D. 1999.Ville de Montréal. Rapport du Comité Montréalais sur la prostitution de rue et la prostitution juvénile.

———. 2000. *Pour faire avancer l'action*. Rapport sur le projet-pilote de non judiciarisation de la prostitution de rue et propositions de recherche-terrain.

Scheff, T. J. 1990. *Microsociology: Discourse, Emotion and Social Structure*. London: University of Chicago Press.

———. 2000. "Shame and the Social Bond: A Sociological Theory." *Sociological Theory* 18, no. 1: 84–99.

Scheff, T. J. 1994. *Microsociology: Discourse, Emotion, and Social Structure*. Chicago: Chicago University Press.

Schmaus, W. 1994. *Durkheim's Philosophy of Science and the Sociology of Knowledge: Creating an Intellectual Niche*. Chicago: University of Chicago Press.

Sewell, W. H. A. 1992. "Theory of Structure: Duality, Agency, and Transformation." *American Journal of Sociology* 98, no. 1: 1–29

Shaver, F. M. 1996. "The Regulation of Prostitution: Setting the Morality Trap." In *Social Control in Canada*, edited by Bernard Schissel and Linda Mahood, 204–26. Oxford: Oxford University Press.

———. 2005. "A Sex Work Research: Methodological and Ethical Challenges." *The Journal of Interpersonal Violence* 20, no. 3: 296–319.

Sheldrick, B. M. 2004. *Perils and Possibilities: Social Activism and the Law*. Halifax: Fernwood Publishing.

Shragge, E. 2003. *Activism and Social Change: Lessons for Community and Local Organizing*. Peterborough, ON: Broadview Press.

Smith, E. M. 2017. "'It gets very intimate for me': Discursive Boundaries of Pleasure and Performance in Sex Work." *Sexualities* 20, no. 3: 344–63

Smith, J. 2014. *Tackling the Demand for Prostituted/Trafficked Women and Youth*. http://freethem.ca/wp-content/uploads/2014/02/The-Tipping-Point-MP-Joy-Smith-Full-Report-FEB-12-2014.pdf.

Soderlund, G. 2002. "Covering Urban Vice: The New York Times, 'White Slavery,' and the Construction of Journalistic Knowledge." *Critical Studies in Media Communication* 19, no. 4: 438–60.

Solé, J. 1993. *L'Âge d'or de la prostitution. De 1870 à nos jours*. Paris: Plon.

St-James, M. 1988. "The Reclamation of Whores." In *Good Girls/Bad Girls: Sex Trade Workers and Feminists Face to Face*, edited by Laurie Bell. Toronto: The Women's Press.

Staggenborg, S. 2008. *Social Movement*. New York: Oxford University Press.

Stella. 1995a. Lettres Patentes—Loi sur les compagnies, Partie III (L.R.Q., chap. C-38, a. 218); L'Inspecteur général des institutions financières, sous l'autorité de la partie III de la Loi sur les compagnies, accorde les présentes lettres patentes aux requérants ci-après désignés, les constituant en corporation sous la dénomination sociale: Stella, L'aime De Maimie; Délivrées À Québec Le 17 Novembre.

———. 1995b. MinutesStella: Compte-Rendu De La Réunion Du 15 mars 1995; tenue au CLSC Cenre-Ville de 17h00 à 18h30.

———. 1995c. Project Stella—Procès verbal de la réunion du comité consultative, 24 janvier.

———. 1995d. Stella—Compte Rendu De La Réunion Du 19 avril 1995; tenue chez Stella de 17h30 à 19h30.

————. 1995e. Stella—Compte Rendu De La Réunion Du 24 mai 1995; tenue a STELLA 1422 ST-Laurent #2.

————. 1996a. Annual Report of Activities, March.

————. 1996b. Centre d'étude sur le sida (CEI) Minutes Project Stella Minutes; Tuesday, October25, 1994 at CLSC Centre—3:00pm.

————. 1996v. Compte Rendu De La Réunion Du 15 janvier 1996; tenue au CLSC centre-ville.

————. 1996d. Compte rendu du comité des finances, 17 juillet.

————. 1996e. La Prostitution De Rue à Montréal—L'urgence d'une nouvelle approche.

————. 1996f. Procès-Verbal—Assemblé Général Annuell2—17 juin 1996, 18h00; CLSC Des Faubourg - 1250 Sanguinet, Mtl.

————. 1996g. Procès Verbal—Conseil d'administration de Stella; 16 septembre 1996; 18h15 à 20h10.

————. 1996h. Réunion du C.A.; tenue le 20 novembre.

————. 1996i. Réunion du C.A.; tenue le 18 décembre.

————. 1996j. Stella - Réunion du C.A.; tenue le 23 octobre.

————. 1996k. Table Interquartiers Sur La Prostitution; Montréal, le 1er février.

————. 1997a. April 1, 1996–March 31, 1997 Annual Report, June.

————. 1997b. L'histoire de Stella.

————. 1997c. Procès Verbal Réunion Conseil d'Administration Tenue le 16 septembre.

————. 1997d. PV June 18.

————. 1997e. Rapport d'évaluation Volet I: La participation de travailleuses et ex-travailleuses du sexe dans la structure de Stella et le soutien apporté à cette participation.

————. 1997f. Reduction of barriers to accessing health and social services. Trimester Report July 1997–September 1997.

————. 1997g. Stella Action Plan (draft).

————. 1998a. Annual Report, June.

————. 1998b. Empowerment at Stella.

————. 1998c. Procès Verbal Assemblée Générale Spéciale, tenue le 22 janvier.

————. 1998d. Procès Verbal Conseil d'administration, tenue le 6 février.

————. 1998e. Procès-Verbal Conseil D'Administration, tenue le 13 mars.

————. 1998f. Procès Verbal Conseil D'Administration, Tenue le 14 avril.

————. 1999a. Guide XXX. Montréal: Stella.

————. 1999b. Procès Verbal, Conseil D'Administration, dimanche le 17 février.

————. 1999c. Rapport Annuel, Juin.

————. 2000a. Annual Report, June.

————. 2000b. Procès Verbal Conseil D'Administration, tenue mardi le 26 septembre.

————. 2000c. Minutes Board of Administration, Wednesday, November 1.

————. 2000d. Procès-verbal du la réunion du conseil d'administration du 13 décembre.

————. 2002a. Rapport d'activité, Juin.

————. 2002b. "Stella, groupe de services et défense des droits des travailleuses du sexe, et le débat sur la prostitution." Unpublished letter to *Le Devoir*, September 13.

————. 2003a. Guide Striptease. Montréal: Stella.

————. 2003b. Projet d'intervention de milieu dans le Centre-Sud de Montréal. Rapport d'activité et d'évaluation du projet.

————. 2003c. Rapport annuel.

————. 2004a. *Dear John*. Montréal: Stella.

————. 2004b. Manuel de l'employée.

————. 2006a. *eXXXpressions*. Forum XXX Proceedings. Edited by Émilie Cantin, Jenn Clamen, Jocelyne Lamoureux, Maria Nengeh Mensah, Pascale Robitaille, Claire Thiboutot, Louise Toupin, and Francine Tremblay. Montréal: Stella.

————. 2006b. Travail du sexe: Tout ce que vous avez toujours voulu savoir mais n'avez jamais osé demander! Guide d'accompagnement à la formation.

————. 2007. Procès Verbal Conseil D'Administration; Réunion Spéciale: restructuration de l'organisation; Tenue à Montréal, le 19 février.

Stella Projet. 1994a. Compte-rendu de la rencontre au poste de police 33, 6 mai.

Stella Projet. 1994b. Compte-rendu de la rencontre avec le conseiller municipal du district St-Jacques, 9 mai.

Stella Projet. 1994c. Minutes, Tuesday, October 25.

Stella Projet. 1994d. Procès verbal de la réunion du comité consultatif, 29 novembre.

Stella Projet. 1994e. Procès verbal de la réunion du comité consultatif, 22 décembre.

Stokes, R., and J. P. Hewitt. 1976. "Aligning Actions." *American Sociological Review* 41, no. 5, 838–49.

Sumner, L. W. 2004. *The Hateful and the Obscene.* Toronto: University of Toronto Press.

Sutherland, K. 2004. "Work, Sex and Sex Work: Competing Feminist Discourses on the International Sex Trade." *Osgoode Hall Law Journal* 42, no. 1.

Swanson, J. 2016. "Sexual Liberation or Violence Against Women? The Debate on the Legalization of Prostitution and the Relationship to Human Trafficking." *New Criminal Law Review* 19, no. 4: 592–639.

Swendeman, D., A. Fehrenbacher, S. Ali, S. George, D. Mindry, M. Collins, and B. Dey. 2015. "'Whatever I have, I have made by coming into this profession': The Intersection of Resources, Agency, and Achievements in Pathways to Sex Work in Kolkata, India." *Archives of Sexual Behavior* 44, no 4: 1011–23.

Swiffen, A., and M. French. 2018. "Seropolitics and the Criminal Accusation of HIV Non-Disclosure in Canada." *New Criminal Law Review* 21, no. 4: 545–66.

Sztompka, P. 1994. "Social Movements as Forces of Change." In *The Sociology of Social Change*, 274–300. Oxford: Blackwell Publishers.

Tabet, P. 1987. "Du don au tarif. Les relations sexuelles impliquant une compensation." *Les Temps Modernes*, no. 490: 1–53.

Table Interquartiers sur la prostitution (TIQ). 1996a. (1)

Table Interquartiers sur la prostitution (TIQ). 1996b. (2)

Taylor, C. 1989. *Sources of the Self.* Cambridge, MA: Harvard University Press.

Taylor, C. 1994. "The Politics of Recognition." In *Multiculturalism*, edited by Amy Gutmann, 25–73. Princeton, NJ: Princeton University Press.

Thiboutot, C. 1994. "Le mouvements des prostituées: Bientôt vingt ans." *Perspective* (automne): 14–15.

———. 2006. "A Montréal Perspective." In *Stella eXXXpressions*, Forum XXX Proceedings, edited by Émilie Cantin, Jenn Clamen, Jocelyne Lamoureux, Maria Nengeh Mensah, Pascale Robitaille, Claire Thiboutot, Louise Toupin, and Francine Tremblay, 22–27. Montréal: Stella.

Tigchelaar, A. 2019. "Sex Worker Resistance in the Neoliberal Creative City: An Auto/Ethnography." *Anti-Trafficking Review*, no 12, Special Issue–Sex Work.

Tilly, C. 1999. *Durable Inequality.* Berkeley: University of California Press.

Tonkens, E. 2012. "Working with Arlie Hochschild: Connecting Feelings to Social Change." *Social Politics* 19, no. 2: 194–218.

Toupin, L. 2002a. "La question du 'traffic des femmes.' Points de repères dans la documentation des coalitions féministes internationals anti-trafic." Document de travail, Stella, Mars.

———. 2002b. "La scission politique du féminisme international sur la question du 'trafic des femmes': Vers la 'migration' d'un certain féminisme radical?" *Recherches Féministes* 15, no. 2: 9–40.

———. 2009. "La Légitimité incertaine des travailleuses du sexe dans le mouvement des femmes au Québec." *Globe. Revue internationale d'études québécoises* 12, no. 2: 109–27.

———. 2013. "Clandestine Migrations by Women and the Risk of Trafficking." In *Sex Work Rethinking the Job, Respecting the Workers*, edited by Colette Parent, Chris Bruckert, Patrice Corriveau, Maria Nengeh Mensah, and Louise Toupin; translated by Käthe Roth. Vancouver: University of British Columbia Press.

Touraine, A. 1985. "An Introduction to the Study of Social Movements." *Social Research* 52, no. 4: 749–87.

———. 1997. *Pourrons-Nous Vivre Ensemble?* Paris: Fayard.

———. 2000. *Can We Live Together?* Stanford: Stanford University Press.

"Trafficking in Persons Report." 2019. United States Department of State. https://www.state.gov/wp-content/uploads/2019/06/2019-Trafficking-in-Persons-Report.pdf.

Tremblay, F. 2001. "L'individu dans la modernité—Georges Herbert Mead, Charles Taylor et Alain Touraine." Unpublished master thesis Concordia University.

Vahabzadeh, P. 2003. *Articulated Experiences: Toward a Radical Phenomenology of Contemporary Social Movements*. New York: State University of New York Press.

Valverde, M. 1991. *The Age of Light, Soap, and Water*. Toronto: McClelland and Stewart.

van Der Poel, S. 1995. "Solidarity as Boomerang. The Fiasco of the Prostitutes' Rights Movement in the Netherlands." *Crime, Law & Social Change* 23: 41–65.

Verhulst, J., and S. Walgrave. 2009. "The First Time is the Hardest? A Cross-National and Cross-Issue Comparison of First-Time Protest." *Political Behavior* 31, no. 3: 455–84.

Voir, 2000 23–29 novembre

Walker, J., and C. Palacios. 2016. "A Pedagogy of Emotion in Teaching about Social Movement Learning." *Teaching in Higher Education* 21, no. 2: 175–90.

Walkowitz, J. 1980. *Prostitution and Victorian Society*. Cambridge: Cambridge University Press.

Walkowitz, J., and D. Walkowitz. 1973. "'We are not Beasts of the Field': Prostitution and the Poor in Plymouth and Southhampton under the Contagious Diseases Acts." *Feminist Studies*, no. 3–4 (Winter/Spring): 73–106.

Wallerstein, N. 1988. "Empowerment Education: Freire's Idea Adapted to Health Education." *Health Education and Behavior* 15: 379–94.

———. 1992. "Powerlessness, Empowerment, and Health: Implications for Health Promotion Programs." *Behavior Change* 6, no. 3 (January/February).

Waring, M. 1996. *Politics: Local and Global*. A National Film Board Production (NFB). Video.

Warner, S. 1978. "Toward a Redefinition of Action Theory: Paying the Cognitive Element Its Due." *American Journal of Sociology* 83, no. 6: 1317–48.

Weber, M. 1946. *From Max Weber: Essays in Sociology*. Edited by Hans Gerth and C. Wright Mills. New York: Oxford University Press.

Weitzer, R. 1991. "Prostitutes' Rights in the United States. The Failure of a Movement." *Sociological Quarterly* 32: 23–41.

———. 2018. "Resistance to Sex Work Stigma." *Sexualities* 21, nos. 5–6: 717–29.

Wilkerson, W. S. 2012. "What is Sexual Orientation?" In *The Philosophy of Sex: Contemporary Readings*, edited by Nicolas Power, Raja Halwani, and Alain Soble, 195–214. Lanham, MD: Rowman & Littlefield.

Wilson, A. 2002. *Fix: A Tale of an Addicted City*. Directed by Nettie Wilde. NFB.

Winters, L. 2016. "Everything About Them, Without Them." In *Critical Approaches to Harm Reduction: Conflict, Institutionalisation, (De-)Politicization and Direct Action*, edited by Christopher Smith and Zack Marshall, 137–69. New York: Nova Science Publisher.

World March. 2001. "Marche mondiale des femmes . . . au Québec!" Assessment May. https://www.dssu.qc.ca/wp-content/uploads/Histoire_de_la_Marche_mondiale_des_femmes.pdf.

Young, J. 2007. "Slipping Away—Moral Panics Each Side of the 'Golden Age.'" In *Crime, Social Control and Human Rights*, edited by David Downes et al., 53–65. London: Willan Publishing.

Index

Call Off Your Old Tired Ethics
(COYOTE), x, 39, 153, 154, 155, 162
Canadian Alliance for Sex Work Law
Reform, 100, 116, 122, 127, 130;
recommendations and, 100, 130
Canadian Charter of Human Rights and
Freedoms, 118
Canadian Social Purity Movement, 32
Canadian Standing Committee on Justice
and Human Rights, 3, 80, 190
Cannon, Judge, 28, 33, 36n14;
recommendations and, 28
Casgrain, Thérèse, 60
Centre d'action communautaire auprès des
toxicomanes utilisateurs de seringues
(CACTUS), 37, 42, 43, 45, 47, 58,
70n22, 72, 79
Centre Québécois de coordination sur le
sida (CQCA), 41, 42, 53
charity number, 46, 55, 59, 59–60;
marginalized population and, 60
Chaumont, Jean-Michel, 92
child prostitution, 85
Clamen, Jenn, 99, 115–144
CLÉS. *See* Concertation des luttes contre
l'exploitation sexuelle
clients, 1, 2, 12, 25, 31, 32, 33, 162
CLAA. *See* Criminal Law Amendment Act
CLFM. *See* Conseil local des femmes de
Montréal
CNPV. *See* National Coalition against
Poverty and Violence against Women
COCQ-sida. *See* Coalition des organismes
communautaires québécois de lutte
contre le sida
COYOTE. *See* Call Off Your Old Tired
Ethics
Coalition des organismes communautaires
québécois de lutte contre le sida
(COCQ), 41
Coalition for the Rights of Sex Workers,
49, 57, 58, 63
collective action, xi, 41, 65, 69n16, 84,
108, 110, 111, 120; frame and, 8, 21,
44, 65, 69n16
collective consciousness, 108
collective identity, 50, 58, 82, 102, 104
collective representation, 89, 145, 146
Comité des Seize, 28, 31

Comité d'action femmes et sécurité
urbaine, 53
Committee on Justice and Human Rights, 3
commission: Coderre and, 31; hygiene, 33
Concerned Residents of the West End. *See*
CROWE
Concertation des luttes contre l'exploitation
sexuelle (CLÉS), 104
Conseil local des femmes de Montréal
(CLFM), 29
Concerned Residents of the West End, 37
conservative, 3, 106, 126, 127, 145, 146
Contagious Diseases Acts, 16, 17, 18,
22n15
Coormaraswany, Radhiha, 161
Corbin, Alain, 15, 18, 86, 147
criminal code, 30, 38, 118, 161
criminal justice system, 26
Criminal Law Amendment Act, 86
CQCS. *See* Centre Québécois de
coordination sur le sida
criminal laws, 38, 43, 86, 118, 127, 130,
131, 150
criminality, 4, 53, 65, 128
criminalization, xi, 18, 19, 22n7, 26, 38,
42–44, 52, 60, 79–80, 87, 115; client
and, 155, 161
Concerned Residents of the West End
(CROWE), 37
cultural capital, 6, 107, 112
cultural revolution, 94
culture, 5–13, 22n7, 23n19, 23n21, 26, 61,
64, 66; frame and, 66; symbol and, 5–6,
11, 111
cyber-pornography, 94

David, Françoise, 62, 76, 142
Davies, Libby, 2, 3
Debnath, Rama, 101, 112
De Rode Draad, 40
decriminalization, 159, 161; Alliance, The
and, 38, 39; Association Québécoise
des travailleuses et travailleurs du sexe
and (AQTTS), 43; Forum XXX and,
100, 101, 104, 113; National Coalition
against Poverty and Violence against
Women (CNPV) and, 62; mobilization
and, 115–122, 127, 129–131, 142; pilot
project and, 75, 87; Stella and, 49;

About the Author

Francine Tremblay has a B.A. specialization in Psychology (1978–1984), a B.A. in Applied Social Science (1994–2001) and an M.A. in Sociology (1999–2001), from Concordia University, and a Ph.D. from l'UQÀM (2012). She has been teaching at Concordia University since 2002, and taught at Carleton University (Ottawa) from 2005 to 2010. The courses and her research focus on social issues, such as inequality, social construction of deviance, sexuality, and social movement. As a retired sex worker (1969–1988), and a member of Stella since 1999, Francine remains a dedicated scholar and activist.

www.ingramcontent.com/pod-product-compliance
Lightning Source LLC
Chambersburg PA
CBHW022312280326
41932CB00010B/1075